COMPUTING MADE SIMPLE

These books explain the basics of software packages and computer topics in a clear and simple manner, providing just enough information to get started. For users who want an insight into software packages and computers without being overwhelmed by technical terminology they are ideal.

ALL YOU NEED TO GET STARTED

- Easy to Follow
- Task Based
- Jargon Free
- Easy Steps
- Practical
- Excellent Value

BESTSELLER
Works for Windows 3.1 (Version 3)
P. K. McBride
0 7506 2065 X   1994

Lotus 1-2-3 (2.4 DOS Version)
Ian Robertson
0 7506 2066 8   1994

WordPerfect (DOS 6.0)
Stephen Copestake
0 7506 2068 4   1994

BESTSELLER
MS DOS (Up To Version 6.22)
Ian Sinclair
0 7506 2069 2   1994

BESTSELLER
Excel For Windows 3.1 (Version 5)
Stephen Morris
0 7506 2070 6   1994

BESTSELLER
Word For Windows 3.1 (Version 6)
Keith Brindley
0 7506 2071 4   1994

BESTSELLER
Windows 3.1
P. K. McBride
0 7506 2072 2   1994

BESTSELLER
Windows 95
P. K. McBride
0 7506 2306 3   1995

Lotus 1-2-3 for Windows 3.1 (Version 5)
Stephen Morris
0 7506 2307 1   1995

BESTSELLER
Access For Windows 3.1 (Version 2)
Moira Stephen
0 7506 2309 8   1995

BESTSELLER
Internet for Windows 3.1
P. K. McBride
0 7506 2311 X   1995

Pageplus for Windows 3.1 (Version 3)
Ian Sinclair
0 7506 2312 8   1995

Hard Drives
Ian Sinclair
0 7506 2313 6   1995

BESTSELLER
Multimedia for Windows 3.1
Simon Collin
0 7506 2314 4   1995

Powerpoint for Windows 3.1 (Version 4.0)
Moira Stephen
0 7506 2420 5   1995

Office 95
P. K. McBride
0 7506 2625 9   1995

Word Pro for Windows 3.1 (Version 4.0)
Moira Stephen
0 7506 2626 7   1995

BESTSELLER
Word for Windows 95 (Version 7)
Keith Brindley
0 7506 2815 4   1996

BESTSELLER
Excel for Windows 95 (Version 7)
Stephen Morris
0 7506 2816 2   1996

Powerpoint for Windows 95 (Version 7)
Moira Stephen
0 7506 2817 0   1996

BESTSELLER
Access for Windows 95 (Version 7)
Moira Stephen
0 7506 2818 9   1996

BESTSELLER
Internet for Windows 95
P. K. McBride
0 7506 2835 9   1996

Internet Resources
P. K. McBride
0 7506 2836 7   1996

Microsoft Networking
P. K. McBride
0 7506 2837 5   1996

Designing Internet Home Pages
Lilian Hobbs
0 7506 2941 X   1996

BESTSELLER
Works for Windows 95 (Version 4.0)
P. K. McBride
0 7506 3396 4   1996

NEW
Windows NT (Version 4.0)
Lilian Hobbs
0 7506 3511 8   1997

NEW
Compuserve
Keith Brindley
0 7506 3512 6   1997

NEW
Microsoft Internet Explorer
Sam Kennington
0 7506 3513 4   1997

NEW
Netscape Navigator
Sam Kennington
0 7506 3514 2   1997

NEW
Searching The Internet
Sam Kennington
0 7506 3794 3   1997

NEW
The Internet for Windows 3.1 (Second Edition)
P. K. McBride
0 7506 3795 1   1997

NEW
The Internet for Windows 95 (Second Edition)
P. K. McBride
0 7506 3846 X   1997

NEW
Office 97 for Windows
P. K. McBride
0 7506 3798 6   1997

NEW
Powerpoint 97 For Windows
Moira Stephen
0 7506 3799 4   1997

NEW
Access 97 For Windows
Moira Stephen
0 7506 3800 1   1997

NEW
Word 97 For Windows
Keith Brindley
0 7506 3801 X   1997

NEW
Excel 97 For Windows
Stephen Morris
0 7506 3802 8   1997

COBOL
Made Simple

Conor Sexton

**MADE SIMPLE
BOOKS**

Made Simple
An imprint of Butterworth-Heinemann
Linacre House, Jordan Hill, Oxford OX2 8DP
A division of Reed Educational and Professional Publishing Ltd

ℛ   A member of the Reed Elsevier plc group

OXFORD   BOSTON   JOHANNESBURG
MELBOURNE   NEW DELHI   SINGAPORE

First published 1998
© Conor Sexton 1998

TRADEMARKS/REGISTERED TRADEMARKS
Computer hardware and software brand names mentioned in this book are protected
by their respective trademarks and are acknowledged.

British Library Cataloguing in Publication Data
A catalogue record for this book is available from the British Library

ISBN 0 7506 3834 6

Typeset by P.K.McBride, Southampton

Archtype, Bash Casual, Cotswold and Gravity fonts from Advanced Graphics Ltd
Icons designed by Sarah Ward © 1994
Printed and bound in Great Britain by Scotprint, Musselburgh, Scotland

Contents

Dedication

For Lisa and Lorcan

Preface

When Butterworth-Heinemann asked me, in mid-1997, to do a COBOL book, I experienced a distinctly late-1970s sense of *deja vu*. Since the early 1980s, I had specialised in UNIX, C, C++ and, latterly, system programming for Windows and OS/2. I had spent my first five years in software doing commercial applications programming using COBOL but had since become more used to such things as compilers and communication state machines written in C or C++.

I had always liked COBOL, for some reason. Maybe it's because, compared to C and, particularly, C++, COBOL is *easy*: most of the time, it does the 'reasonable thing' for you, even if you make a mistake or fail to make complete specifications. In short, the defaults are user-friendly. I also enjoyed the clean, unsubtle precision of building, say, a report program, in COBOL. And how much easier it is in COBOL than in C to create a file and search its index with a key!

The main reason for this book is the resurgence in the currency of the COBOL language because of the twin pressures of the Year 2000 problem and imminent European Economic and Monetary Union (EMU). A whole generation of retired and semi-retired COBOL programmers is coming out of the shadows to take on the challenge. In response to nearly unlimited demand, younger folk are also being crash-trained in this most venerable of programming languages. It seemed like a good idea, in addressing this market, to write a small, 'tight', book covering the essence of COBOL using modern programming idioms, and giving a synopsis of the Year 2000 problem along with the solutions which can be applied to it. Most of the (few) existing COBOL textbooks are of the Swedish-forest, 1,000-page variety. Under today's pressures, many people will be more attracted to a 200-page coverage of the essentials.

COBOL is frequently derided as verbose, clumsy, old-fashioned and so on, and so on but, when you face facts, there's probably more COBOL in the world than there is written in all the other high-level programming languages combined. The only competition, in terms of code volume, is the C/C++ combination used in very different technical software applications. For commercial applications, COBOL has won hands-down. The sheer volume of existing COBOL code and its ease of use are factors that ensure the language will be used forever, near enough.

This book contains seven chapters, with exercises. (You'll find answers to the exercises on the World-Wide Web, in the Butterworth-Heinemann *Made Simple* pages at **www.bh.com**.) The first chapter is a fast tour of some of the main points of COBOL. It is aimed at enabling you, in the shortest time possible, to become a functioning COBOL programmer. COBOL is a very large language, so to try and give any kind of complete overview in Chapter 1 is impossible. Instead, you're quickly taken to the position of being able to write limited, but useful, programs. Early on, I realised that I had to settle on one COBOL compiler and environment for this book. Any other approach, and we'd be headed for the 1,000 pages I've just criticised. I chose the Micro Focus Personal COBOL system because it is inexpensive, widely-used, works on any PC and conforms with the 1985 ANSI-standard COBOL specification. If you work in a different environment, you should have little difficulty adapting.

Chapter 2 covers the PICTURE clause – how you describe data in COBOL programs. Chapter 3 is about moving data around, doing sums, dealing with text and putting things in tables. Chapter 4 looks at using COBOL's control structures as an aid to writing good, structured, programs in the modern idiom. Chapters 5 and 6 deal with the core of COBOL, file I/O using sequential, indexed and relative files. Chapter 7 is all about Year 2000. Here I try hard to describe in few words the heart of the problem and how you might solve it in your organisation. Too many words, with too much sensationalism, have been written about this essentially simple subject.

This aspiration is in keeping with my aim for the book as a whole: to give a modern, level-headed, accurate, short, jargon-free and sometimes humorous coverage of a subject that is very useful to know and really not very difficult. I hope you like it.

Conor Sexton,
Dublin, January, 1998.

1 A quick start with COBOL

Background and standards

COBOL is the archetypal third-generation business programming language. Even its name — COmmon Business Oriented Language — gives the game away. COBOL is to business software development what C is to technical programming. C is internationally standardised — a given standard C program will run unchanged on almost all computer systems — and is effectively the common-denominator language for system (non-business) programming. COBOL, likewise, has been standardised. With a number of limitations, COBOL programs are fairly easily portable between computers, and the language is the accepted medium for business software development.

I've referred to COBOL as a *third-generation language* (3GL). In the jargon, the sequences of ones and zeros that were used in the 1950s to program the first computers were collectively called *machine code*, and this was the first-generation language. The *assembly* languages, which use symbolic instructions such as

    AR 1,2

to add the numbers stored in two registers are second-generation languages. COBOL is more English-like and demonstrates its third-generation credentials by using an instruction like

    ADD A TO B.

to add two numbers. With a so-called *fourth-generation language* (4GL), higher-level instructions such as

    SELECT FROM CUSTOMER WHERE BAL < 1000

are possible. The 4GL approach is powerful but has two disadvantages that increase the appeal of 3GL. First, a command like the SELECT is far removed from the ones and zeros that a computer understands. There may therefore be a significant performance penalty associated with executing it. Second, 4GLs are usually promoted by individual vendors, which means that a program written in a given 4GL is unlikely to be portable among different kinds of computer. 3GLs such as COBOL and (rather more so) C offer the best compromise between performance and portability and are therefore predominant.

COBOL shows its power in the language constructs it provides for operations such as *file*-handling, decimal money calculations, sorting records in a file and report-writing, to name but a few. Although you could do all these things in C, the C language is not optimised for them in the way COBOL is. Implementing an *indexed* file is straightforward in COBOL but is difficult, and requires a high level of expertise, in C. Here are some other reasons why COBOL is the world's most prevalent programming language:

- COBOL is relatively easy to write. For many people the COBOL syntax `ADD A TO B.` is more attractive than the equivalent `B += A;` found in the C language.

- COBOL was designed in the late 1950s by a committee that had the support of all the major computer system vendors including, crucially, IBM. IBM provided COBOL compilers and an execution environment for COBOL programs on all models of the emergent System/360 mainframes of the period. This support for COBOL has persisted to the present day. COBOL has also been internationally standardised, a fact which in turn increases support for the language.

- Because it has been standardised. COBOL is fairly portable: programs written in it work on computers of all kinds. For example, all the programs in this book have been written using a PC version of COBOL. They would require very little change to be transferred (*ported*) to an IBM mainframe system.

- COBOL supports databases. Major system vendors, and particularly IBM, provide 'hooks' in their versions of COBOL that allow programmers to access and update easily the databases on which modern businesses depend so heavily.

- COBOL is everywhere. Untold billions of lines of COBOL code run on millions of computers. The simple fact that there's more COBOL code in the world than code written in any other language ensures that the COBOL will exist into the indefinite future.

- COBOL is in demand. Because of its ubiquity but particularly because of the Year-2000 (Y2K) problem (summarised in Chapter 7), there is an increasing requirement for capable COBOL programmers. The immediacy of the Y2K crisis means that grizzled, middle-aged programmers are being offered serious money to return and fix the problems that they themselves largely created in the 1960s and 1970s. There's irony for you.

Some of COBOL's perceived limitations can be summarised thus: it tends to be verbose; it provides limited support for mathematical calculations; COBOL programs by and large are not interactive or screen-oriented; data definitions are visible throughout the program and cannot be limited in *scope*; *procedures* (subprograms) cannot call themselves.

COBOL, originating with the first meeting of the Conference on Data Systems Languages (CODASYL) in May 1959, is among the most venerable of the third-generation, high-level languages. It cedes this honour to Fortran (Formula Translation, a language oriented towards scientific and mathematical applications), which was developed earlier in the 1950s by a committee including IBM and a number of user groups. The CODASYL meeting was called by the US Department of Defense with the aim of devising a common, high-level, language for business programming which would not be proprietary to any vendor.

The first COBOL language specification and compilers appeared in 1960. The language has repeatedly (1968, 1974 and 1985) been standardised. American National Standards Institute (ANSI) standards were approved in each of these years; COBOL-85, as ANSI 85 COBOL is usually known, additionally went on to become an ISO (International Standards Organisation) standard in 1989.

COBOL development systems, including compilers, have been made available on pretty much every kind of computer from the mainframe (COBOL's spiritual home, really), down through minis like the Digital VAX series, to PCs running MS-DOS or the later Windows or OS/2 operating systems. Because of the standardisation I've mentioned above, there's a good chance that your COBOL source code (the English-like code you write) will be transferable with little or no change to another system supporting a COBOL-85-conforming compiler.

For the example programs in this book, I've used the popular Micro Focus Personal COBOL for DOS compiler, version 2.0.02. (From now on, I refer to this as just Personal COBOL). As well as reflecting the COBOL-85 standard, this compiler is inexpensive (about UK£50, US$90) and runs on any IBM-compatible PC that supports MS-DOS. To stay within the scope made possible by a book of this size – 200 pages or thereabouts – the programs presented are character-mode only. I don't try, for example, to put a Graphical User Interface (GUI) front-end on COBOL programs. I only give a very limited presentation (in Chapter 3) of the Screens subsystem of Personal COBOL itself. What you'll learn from this book is mainstream COBOL, oriented towards file- and character-handling. These are the jobs the language was originally designed to do and what it's best at.

This book is based on COBOL-85 but, given the size of this *Made Simple* book, the COBOL language as specified by that standard is neither completely nor rigorously covered. You can get a heavy-duty textbook (usually about 1,000 pages!), or the ANSI Standard document, if you're interested in rigour and completeness. The focus of this book is to get you up to speed with a functioning and common subset of COBOL in the shortest possible time. With that in mind, here we go!

Take note

COBOL is an acronym. As such, it should be represented in capitals – not, as is often the case, as 'Cobol'. Throughout this book, you'll see COBOL written in upper-case only.

The do-nothing program

The fully-formed do-nothing COBOL program is this:

```
***********************************************************************
*                                                                     *
*                          MINIMAL.CBL                                *
*    This program demonstrates the minimum standard COBOL program     *
*                                                                     *
***********************************************************************
 IDENTIFICATION DIVISION.
 PROGRAM-ID. MINIMAL.

 ENVIRONMENT DIVISION.

 DATA DIVISION.

 PROCEDURE DIVISION.
 PROG-END.
     STOP RUN.
```

This isn't really the shortest possible COBOL program. You can see that the program is made up of four *division*s (never mind for the moment what they are). The COBOL-85 standard only specifies the IDENTIFICATION division as necessary. Personal COBOL can handle an empty program – one with no divisions or other code at all. Other compilers have different minimum requirements. MINIMAL.CBL is the smallest COBOL program that will satisfy most, if not all, of the compilers and that's why I've shown it here as your first example.

What does MINIMAL.CBL do when you execute it? Nothing, but it's nonetheless a complete COBOL program. Its main value to you right now is that it contains the four divisions found in every serious COBOL program. The PROGRAM-ID clause is required to specify the program's name which, in the program, must not contain the .CBL suffix. STOP RUN tells the COBOL run-time system to do exactly that (stop!) when the program's execution has finished.

Notice that I've written the whole program in upper-case characters, except for those within the comment block (the asterisk box at the top of the program). In fact, modern COBOL compilers, including Personal COBOL, allow you to use either upper- or lower-case characters anywhere in your program code. The reason I don't use lower-case is that capitals are more portable: COBOL programs written in upper-case will be transferable without change to environments which require upper-case. For this reason, I use the upper-case convention throughout this book.

If you choose to use lower-case in your programs, note that case alone is not sufficient to distinguish two text items. For example, the compiler will treat the text items WS-ABC and ws-abc as duplicates.

The first asterisk in each of the comment-block lines is in column 7, not, as you might think, in column 1. All the other lines of code start in column 8, with the exception of STOP RUN, which starts in column 12. I explain the reasons for these conventions in the section *Structure of a COBOL program*, below.

Here's a program that does something as opposed to nothing. It's called HELLO.CBL and it's my COBOL version of the somewhat-hackneyed conventional opening program:

```
*******************************************************************
*                                                                 *
*                         HELLO.CBL                               *
*             This program does the Hello World thing             *
*                                                                 *
*******************************************************************
 IDENTIFICATION DIVISION.
 PROGRAM-ID. HELLO.

 ENVIRONMENT DIVISION.

 DATA DIVISION.

 PROCEDURE DIVISION.
 PROGRAM-START.
     DISPLAY "Hello World".

 PROGRAM-END.
     STOP RUN.
```

As you'd expect, HELLO.CBL, displays on the screen the message Hello World. The display from Personal COBOL appearing like this:

```
Personal COBOL version 2.0 from Micro Focus
PCOBRUN V2.0.02  Copyright (C) 1983-1993 Micro Focus Ltd.
Hello World
```

The program has the four divisions, although only two, the IDENTIFICATION and the PROCEDURE divisions, contain anything.

The IDENTIFICATION division identifies the program by name and can also include the author's name and the date the program was written. The ENVIRONMENT division would (if it weren't empty!) contain information about the sort of computer on which HELLO.CBL is to run. It is also used to specify any data files used by the program.

The DATA division is used to specify the data used by the program. This includes file layouts and the definitions of any temporary data items (also called *variables*) – changeable storage areas in the computer's memory – to be used by the program. The names given to data items are sometimes called *identifiers*.

The place where any such variables would be used is the PROCEDURE division. Here, you write all your COBOL sections, paragraphs and sentences: the actual logic of your program. The PROCEDURE division is the only part of HELLO.CBL that needs any explaining. It contains two paragraphs, called PROGRAM-START and PROGRAM-END. The first name prefixes the program's only real statement, which is:

```
    DISPLAY "Hello World".
```

The DISPLAY causes the message enclosed in the double quotes (but not the double quotes themselves) to be displayed on your computer's *standard output* – by default the screen. By the way, statements such as the above are often said in COBOL to contain *verbs*, in this case DISPLAY. Notice also that the statement is terminated by the full-stop. In fact, a COBOL sentence is defined as a statement terminated by a full-stop. It's possible to write a multi-statement sentence which is only ended by a full-stop after its final constituent statement.

The run-time system executes the paragraphs of HELLO.CBL in sequence unless otherwise directed, so PROGRAM-END follows the display operation. This contains the STOP RUN directive and program execution accordingly halts. Notice that the paragraph names must be all one string: PROGRAM-END is a valid paragraph name; PROGRAM START is not. The hyphen is specially allowed in COBOL to promote readability in cases such as this.

Building and running a program

There are many different COBOL compilers and run-time systems, available on all sorts of computers. For this book I have used Personal COBOL, a popular and inexpensive implementation of COBOL-85. To follow the build sequence described below, you must have a copy of Personal COBOL on your PC. If you use a different COBOL product, refer to its documentation for guidance on building a program. To order a copy of Personal COBOL in the UK or the US, call:

 UK: Micro Focus Limited (01635) 32646
 US: Micro Focus Inc. (650) 938 3700

Personal COBOL is delivered on two 3.5 inch diskettes and installation is simple – *follow the instructions in your supplier's documentation.*

If you read the Personal COBOL documentation, you'll notice that the product offers extensive options and a lengthy set of instructions for building COBOL programs. Here I give what I believe to be the shortest possible sequence for building and executing a Personal COBOL program such as HELLO.CBL.

1   **Run the command** PCOBOL HELLO at the DOS command-line. The default filename extension for Personal COBOL and many other COBOL environments is .CBL. PCOBOL expects this extension, so you can omit explicitly typing it. After entering this command, you'll see the first Personal COBOL window (Figure 1.1).

2   **Press [Return].** The text of the program appears in the edit window. If HELLO.CBL is empty, the edit window is also empty and you will need to press the spacebar to start entering text. (You can, if you prefer, use your favourite text editor, instead of the Personal COBOL editor, to create HELLO.CBL). The Personal COBOL window containing the code looks like Figure 1.2.

3   **Press [F2] twice** and **[Return]** once to *check* (compile) the program.

4   **Quit the Personal COBOL environment** by pressing [Esc] once and answering 'Y' when asked whether or not you want to exit.

5   **Run the compiled program** by entering at the DOS command-line: PCOBRUN HELLO. The program executes, with visible results.

Figure 1.1
The Personal COBOL
start-up screen, running
at the MS-DOS prompt
in Windows 95.

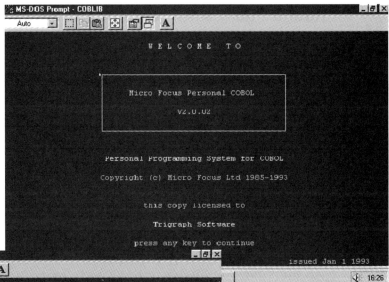

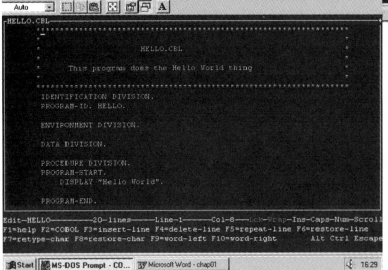

Figure 1.2
Using the Personal
COBOL editor to create
the source code.

Take note

You can only learn programming – in COBOL or any language – by doing
it, not by reading about doing it. At this point, spend all the time that's
necessary to successfully enter, build and execute HELLO.CBL.

Structure of a COBOL program

There are three aspects to the structure of COBOL programs:

- The layout expressed in terms of DIVISIONs, SECTIONs, paragraphs and sentences.

- Columnar spacing rules according to which you must write your COBOL programs; for example, the asterisk denoting a comment must be in column 7.

- The modularity of your code: whether or not it is well-structured and executed in a disciplined way.

This section deals with the first two items. The last, which could be described as considerations of *structured programming*, is referred to at a number of points later on, and particularly in Chapter 4.

Program layout

Let's look at another program, this time SKELETON.CBL:

```
***********************************************************************
*                                                                     *
*                          SKELETON.CBL                               *
*                                                                     *
*  This program demonstrates the skeleton COBOL program syntax        *
*                                                                     *
***********************************************************************
 IDENTIFICATION DIVISION.
 PROGRAM-ID. SKELETON.

 ENVIRONMENT DIVISION.
 CONFIGURATION SECTION.
 INPUT-OUTPUT SECTION.
 FILE-CONTROL.

 DATA DIVISION.
 FILE SECTION.
 WORKING-STORAGE SECTION.
 REPORT SECTION.

 PROCEDURE DIVISION.
 PROGRAM-START.

 PROGRAM-END.
    STOP RUN.
```

Once again, the program, when built and executed, does nothing. Its purpose is to present a reasonable skeleton COBOL program, showing all of the DIVISIONs and most of the SECTIONs that you will ever use as a COBOL programmer, as well as their order with respect to each other. The program is not exhaustive: to show every SECTION would be meaningless at this point. Anyway, nobody (not even highly-experienced COBOL programmers) ever remembers all the SECTIONs and the order in which they appear. Every COBOL compiler environment provides a language reference document containing a detailed specification of this syntax, and you will find yourself referring to it often.

Nonetheless, SKELETON.CBL is a reasonable template which you might use as a basis for writing your programs. I've already described the purpose of the DIVISIONs. Within the ENVIRONMENT division, the CONFIGURATION section contains system-dependent inform-ation, while the INPUT-OUTPUT section is used to specify the names and types of data files used by the program.

The DATA division actually can have six subordinate SECTIONs, of which I have only included three in SKELETON.CBL. (The others are for handling communications, screen definitions and inter-program linkage). Within the FILE section, you describe in detail the layout of your program's data files and their constituent *records*.

The WORKING-STORAGE section is where you define variables that you will need as part of your program's logic. Note that there's no hyphen between STORAGE and SECTION. Putting one there will give you an astonishing number of compiler errors; this is a place that experienced COBOL programmers often check first when they get 250 diagnostic messages on compiling their program!

The REPORT section is where you define the formats of reports to be produced by your program.

The PROCEDURE division, as with the earlier program HELLO.CBL, has two paragraphs. As an aid to modularity, this division can also contain SECTIONs. I'll show you in Chapter 4 how to use SECTIONs within the PROCEDURE division.

Columnar spacing

Up to the late 1970s, COBOL programs were usually written and then transferred to 80-column punched cards ('IBM cards'), with the text encoded by means of different combinations of holes being punched in each column. So, one encoding of holes might represent the letter 'K', another the hyphen, and so on. The program was then fed into the computer via a card-reader, a machine designed to read cards punched with holes. Older programmers – and your present author is, unfortunately, one of them! – remember the nightmare of the dropped 'card deck' and the inconvenience caused by one mis-punched column. It was only when the forests started to run out of timber that the world moved to terminals and electronic input of COBOL programs.

The legacy of the 80-column card is still with us and is reflected in the different columnar *areas* found in all COBOL programs. There are five of these areas:

- Columns 1 – 6: reserved for the optional line-sequence number.

- Column 7: optionally contains the comment '*' or the '-' string-continuation character.

- Columns 8 – 11 (Area A): all DIVISION, SECTION and paragraph headers, as well as all file-descriptions, must begin in this area.

- Columns 12 – 72 (Area B): all executable COBOL sentences must begin in this area; they can be continued over several lines but must remain within Area B.

- Columns 73 – 80 (Identification Area): anything can be placed in this area, which is often used by the compiler for its own purposes.

SKELETON.CBL is given on the next page, with its columnar areas indicated.

Notice that there are no line-sequence numbers – we could use a compiler option to activate them – and that the only line that must start in Area B and not Area A is STOP RUN, the program's last line.

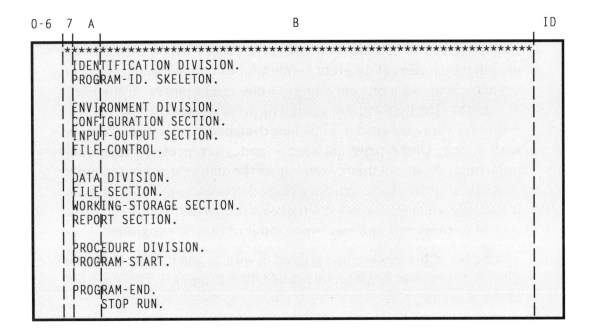

```
0-6  7  A                                B                              ID
    |  |  |                                                               |
    |******************************************************************|
    | IDENTIFICATION DIVISION.                                          |
    | PROGRAM-ID. SKELETON.                                             |
    | |  |                                                              |
    | ENVIRONMENT DIVISION.                                             |
    | CONFIGURATION SECTION.                                            |
    | INPUT-OUTPUT SECTION.                                             |
    | FILE-CONTROL.                                                     |
    | |  |                                                              |
    | DATA DIVISION.                                                    |
    | FILE SECTION.                                                     |
    | WORKING-STORAGE SECTION.                                          |
    | REPORT SECTION.                                                   |
    | |  |                                                              |
    | PROCEDURE DIVISION.                                               |
    | PROGRAM-START.                                                    |
    | |  |                                                              |
    | PROGRAM-END.                                                      |
    | |    STOP RUN.                                                    |
    | |  |                                                              |
```

Take note

Now you know enough about the layout of all COBOL programs that you'll soon be able to write useful ones. In case this Area A/Area B stuff seems a bit arcane, be disabused of the notion now. It isn't. You've no idea how useful your new knowledge will prove to be when you're confronted with compilation errors complaining about your columns being wrong.

Simple Input/Output

Programs (COBOL or otherwise) only start being useful when they can perform input and output (I/O) operations. There are several kinds of I/O: keyboard input and screen output; reading from and writing to disk files; and sending data to a printer or a communications device. For now, I'm only going to deal with keyboard/screen I/O.

To take input from the keyboard and to display it on the screen, you'll need to know how to define COBOL variables and how to use the ACCEPT and DISPLAY verbs. To break the ice, here's a program, MINIO.CBL, which reads from the keyboard and displays on the screen your name and age:

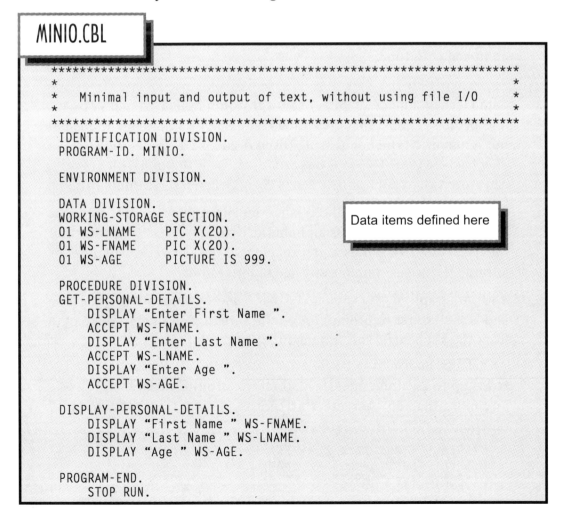

```
MINIO.CBL

***********************************************************************
*                                                                     *
*    Minimal input and output of text, without using file I/O         *
*                                                                     *
***********************************************************************
 IDENTIFICATION DIVISION.
 PROGRAM-ID. MINIO.

 ENVIRONMENT DIVISION.

 DATA DIVISION.
 WORKING-STORAGE SECTION.                    ┌─────────────────────────┐
 01 WS-LNAME     PIC X(20).                  │ Data items defined here  │
 01 WS-FNAME     PIC X(20).                  └─────────────────────────┘
 01 WS-AGE       PICTURE IS 999.

 PROCEDURE DIVISION.
 GET-PERSONAL-DETAILS.
     DISPLAY "Enter First Name ".
     ACCEPT WS-FNAME.
     DISPLAY "Enter Last Name ".
     ACCEPT WS-LNAME.
     DISPLAY "Enter Age ".
     ACCEPT WS-AGE.

 DISPLAY-PERSONAL-DETAILS.
     DISPLAY "First Name " WS-FNAME.
     DISPLAY "Last Name " WS-LNAME.
     DISPLAY "Age " WS-AGE.

 PROGRAM-END.
     STOP RUN.
```

For the first time, you're seeing a non-empty WORKING-STORAGE section. It contains the definitions of three data items.

The first two are respectively for storing in memory a last (family) name and a first (given) name. Each of these is defined as having a maximum length of 20 *alphanumeric* (letters or numbers allowed) characters. The 01 *level-number* specifies that they are *elementary data items* (also called *simple variables*).

Similarly, the data item WS-AGE is a simple variable, but this variable is of purely numeric *type*. In COBOL, data type is also (and more usually) referred to as *data class*. WS-AGE can have a value in the range zero to 999. This is the number nine hundred and ninety-nine (the numeric quantity one less than one thousand!) and is *not* to be confused with the 999 in PIC 999.

PIC is short for PICTURE. PICTURE is COBOL's way of specifying the data class of a piece of data, or how it would appear visually (hence 'picture'). PIC 999 specifies not a value one less than one thousand but a numeric type comprising three digits. PIC 999 is the same in effect as PICTURE IS 999. The variable WS-AGE, defined with PIC 999, can store values such as 023, 574, 876 and, of course, the numeric 999.

Where 9 used in a PICTURE clause means numeric data, X means alphanumeric and A means alphabetic. Hence, PIC X(20) means that the associated variable can store a maximum of twenty numbers or letters; PIC A(20) implies storage of letters only.

The paragraph GET-PERSONAL-DETAILS uses a sequence of DISPLAYs and ACCEPTs first to prompt for on the screen, and then to read, data from the keyboard. The statement:

```
ACCEPT WS-FNAME.
```

reads up to 20 alphanumeric characters into the variable WS-FNAME. Any more than 20 characters are not read from the *standard input* (keyboard). The three statements:

```
DISPLAY "First Name " WS-FNAME.
DISPLAY "Last Name " WS-LNAME.
DISPLAY "Age " WS-AGE.
```

display on the screen the text in quotes, followed by the memory contents represented by the three data items WS-FNAME, WS-FLNAME and WS-AGE. The full interaction when I ran the program was this (my input shown in boldface):

```
Personal COBOL version 2.0 from Micro Focus
PCOBRUN V2.0.02  Copyright (C) 1983-1993 Micro Focus Ltd.
Enter First Name
Conor
Enter Last Name
Sexton
Enter Age
29
First Name Conor
Last Name Sexton
Age 029
```

That's it. Now you can do simple *console I/O*. The simple techniques shown in MINIO.CBL can be adapted to produce surprisingly sophisticated results. You'll see more of ACCEPT and DISPLAY in Chapter 3.

The one remaining weapon that you need in your armoury of minimal COBOL programming competence is simple file I/O, and that's the subject of the next section.

Your first real COBOL program

COBOL is about file processing. Files are repositories of data and are usually made up of records. There are different kinds of files, varying in complexity from simple *sequential* files, through *indexed-sequential* and *relative*, to complex database systems. This book deals with sequential, indexed and relative files; in this section, you'll see your first implementation in COBOL of a very simple sequential file. You'll also write data to and read data from that file.

I have written two programs to implement the sequential file. The first, called FOUTPUT.CBL, creates a file on your system's disk and writes data, in records, to it. The second, called FINPUT.CBL, reads the same file and displays the data contained in its records – the same data accepted by FOUTPUT.CBL. The first program is shown opposite.

Don't panic. It's actually a simple program. In a short, *Made Simple*, book like this, the only way to cover the required programming techniques is first to show the program in its entirety and then explain the salient features of it. Here's the explanation.

The file ADDRFILE.DAT is specified by the FILE-CONTROL clause in the INPUT-OUTPUT section of the ENVIRONMENT division:

```
INPUT-OUTPUT SECTION.
FILE-CONTROL.
    SELECT ADDRFILE ASSIGN TO "ADDRFILE.DAT"
        ORGANIZATION IS SEQUENTIAL
        ACCESS MODE IS SEQUENTIAL.
```

The SELECT statement specifies the file's name as it will appear when created in the current DOS directory. The current directory is the one you were in when you started the Personal COBOL environment with the PCOBOL command. The file's name in that directory is ADDRFILE.DAT. The name that FOUTPUT.CBL uses internally for the file, and which corresponds to ADDRFILE.DAT, is ADDRFILE. There is no significance in the correspondence of names: ADDRFILE.DAT could be represented within the program by an arbitrary name such as ZQNT14, instead of ADDRFILE. The SELECT statement also specifies that the file is organised as sequential (every record follows the last in the order written) and is accessed (read) accordingly.

FOUTPUT.CBL

```cobol
********************************************************************
*                                                                  *
*   This program demonstrates how to write to a sequential file    *
*                                                                  *
********************************************************************
 IDENTIFICATION DIVISION.
 PROGRAM-ID. FOUTPUT.

 ENVIRONMENT DIVISION.
 INPUT-OUTPUT SECTION.
 FILE-CONTROL.
     SELECT ADDRFILE ASSIGN TO "ADDRFILE.DAT"
         ORGANIZATION IS SEQUENTIAL
         ACCESS MODE IS SEQUENTIAL.

 DATA DIVISION.
 FILE SECTION.
 FD ADDRFILE
     LABEL RECORDS ARE STANDARD
     RECORD CONTAINS 53 CHARACTERS.
 01 ADDRFILE-RECORD.
     02 ADDRFILE-NAME    PIC X(20).
     02 ADDRFILE-ADDR    PIC X(30).
     02 ADDRFILE-AGE     PIC 999.

 PROCEDURE DIVISION.
 OPEN-FILE.
     OPEN OUTPUT ADDRFILE.

 WRITE-RECORDS.
     MOVE "Boris Yeltsin" TO ADDRFILE-NAME.
     MOVE "Kremlin, Moscow" TO ADDRFILE-ADDR.
     MOVE 66 TO ADDRFILE-AGE.
     WRITE ADDRFILE-RECORD.
     MOVE "Bill Clinton" TO ADDRFILE-NAME.
     MOVE "White House, Washington" TO ADDRFILE-ADDR.
     MOVE 52 TO ADDRFILE-AGE.
     WRITE ADDRFILE-RECORD.
     MOVE "Tony Blair" TO ADDRFILE-NAME.
     MOVE "10, Downing Street" TO ADDRFILE-ADDR.
     MOVE 44 TO ADDRFILE-AGE.
     WRITE ADDRFILE-RECORD.
     MOVE "Jacques Chirac" TO ADDRFILE-NAME.
     MOVE "Elysee Palace, Paris" TO ADDRFILE-ADDR.
     MOVE 65 TO ADDRFILE-AGE.
     WRITE ADDRFILE-RECORD.

 CLOSE-AND-STOP.
     CLOSE ADDRFILE.
     STOP RUN.
```

Defines the name and nature of the disk file.

Defines the structure of the records.

Opens the file on disk for writing data to it.

Data for the first record.

Record written to disk.

Disk file closed safely.

In the FILE section of the DATA division, you can see the *file definition*, or FD:

```
FD  ADDRFILE
    LABEL RECORDS ARE STANDARD
    RECORD CONTAINS 53 CHARACTERS.
01  ADDRFILE-RECORD.
    02 ADDRFILE-NAME    PIC X(20).
    02 ADDRFILE-ADDR    PIC X(30).
    02 ADDRFILE-AGE     PIC 999.
```

This defines the record layout of the file ADDRFILE.DAT as represented by ADDRFILE. As you can see, each record within the file is 53 characters – letters, digits, punctuation and other symbols – long. The definition of the file record has the name ADDRFILE-RECORD. This is a good name, in that it is intuitive, but, like the file name ADDRFILE, it's arbitrary and could be any valid name of up to 30 characters in length. The use of ADDRFILE in all the names specified in the record is not necessary; it's just conventional good practice.

The clause LABEL RECORDS ARE STANDARD is one of the places where COBOL shows its age. It's a throwback to processing files directly on tape devices. On tape, files could be either labelled or not. If labelled, you would use the LABEL RECORDS clause as above. If not, you'd put in LABEL RECORDS ARE OMITTED. With today's disk devices, there's actually no need for the LABEL RECORDS clause at all. Personal COBOL makes it optional, but it's a good idea to retain it for compatibility with older COBOL environments

The record name, ADDRFILE-RECORD, is (and must be) specified as a *level 01 variable*. As such, it is the name of a *group data item* or *structure* and, when used, implicitly includes all data items 'within' it: variables of level 02, level 03 and so on. If the level 01 variable does have subordinate variables, then it must not itself have any associated PIC (PICTURE) clause. In this case, the name is simply terminated with a full-stop.

The constituent *data fields* of the record ADDRFILE-RECORD are all 02 level data items. They don't have to be level 02; they could be level 05 or 07, at your discretion. The highest level number that you can use in a record is 49.

The variable `ADDRFILE-NAME` specifies a name field of up to 20 alphanumeric characters; the address field is of up to 30 alphanumerics; while the age field allows numeric values in the range zero to 999.

Each data item description – at level `01`, `02` and so on – is, and must be, ended with a full-stop. In the `FD` clause, a full-stop is only valid at the end of the last (`RECORD CONTAINS`) line.

After this series of explanations, the rest of the program is easy. In the first paragraph of the `PROCEDURE` division, `OPEN-FILE`, the file `ADDRFILE` (representing the file-on-disk `ADDRFILE.DAT`) is opened for output (writing to). Then, in the paragraph `WRITE-RECORDS`, a series of names, addresses and ages is moved to the data fields of the record `ADDRFILE-RECORD`. One record is written at a time: you can see that, in the case of Mr. Yeltsin, his name is moved, then his address and finally his age. When the record has been 'filled', the `WRITE` verb is used to write the record to the file on disk. Then Mr. Clinton's details are moved and written to file, and so on. When we've finished writing records to the file, we close the file and `STOP RUN`.

That's it. Enter, compile and execute this program and you'll find on disk in your current directory the file `ADDRFILE.DAT` containing (in readable, plain-text form) the names, addresses and ages of the four politicians. To temper your undoubted euphoria at this achievement, however, you should be aware of a few points. This is about the simplest possible file-processing program for writing to a file. It uses the minimum COBOL syntax to get the minimum result. There will be more on files in later chapters, and there's still more that it's beyond the scope of this book to cover. Similarly, I've used the `MOVE` and `WRITE` verbs simply in an intuitive way without comment. Again, the uses you see in `FOUTPUT.CBL` are straightforward and there's a lot more to `MOVE` and `WRITE` that I have not mentioned.

This book is about giving you the essential subset of COBOL that will allow you to become a functioning COBOL programmer in the shortest possible time. It's in this context that you should view `FOUTPUT.CBL`, and the program that's coming next, `FINPUT.CBL`.

Reading and displaying ADDRFILE.DAT

Now that you've written the data to file, the obvious reverse operation
is to open the same file for input, read the contents and display them
on the screen. That's what the program FINPUT.CBL, following, does.

FINPUT.CBL

```
**********************************************************************
*                                                                    *
*   This program demonstrates how to read from and display the       *
*   contents of a sequential file                                    *
*                                                                    *
**********************************************************************
    IDENTIFICATION DIVISION.
    PROGRAM-ID. FINPUT.

    ENVIRONMENT DIVISION.

    INPUT-OUTPUT SECTION.
    FILE-CONTROL.
        SELECT ADDRFILE ASSIGN TO "ADDRFILE.DAT"
            ORGANIZATION IS SEQUENTIAL
            ACCESS MODE IS SEQUENTIAL.

    DATA DIVISION.
    FILE SECTION.
    FD ADDRFILE
        LABEL RECORDS ARE STANDARD
        RECORD CONTAINS 53 CHARACTERS.
    01 ADDRFILE-RECORD.
        02 ADDRFILE-NAME PIC X(20).
        02 ADDRFILE-ADDR PIC X(30).
        02 ADDRFILE-AGE PIC 999.

    PROCEDURE DIVISION.
    OPEN-FILE.
        OPEN INPUT ADDRFILE.

    READ-RECORDS.
        READ ADDRFILE AT END GO TO CLOSE-AND-STOP.
        DISPLAY "Name: " ADDRFILE-NAME.
        DISPLAY "Address: " ADDRFILE-ADDR.
        DISPLAY "Age: " ADDRFILE-AGE.
        GO TO READ-RECORDS.

    CLOSE-AND-STOP.
        CLOSE ADDRFILE.
        STOP RUN.
```

> The file name and definition and the syntax used up to the PROCEDURE division header is the same, except for the name in the PROGRAM-ID clause.

Apart from the fact that `FINPUT.CBL` reads the file instead of writing to it, this program is identical to `FOUTPUT.CBL`. In the first paragraph of the `PROCEDURE` division, `OPEN-FILE`, the file `ADDRFILE.DAT`, represented by the variable `ADDRFILE`, is opened for input (reading). The 'business end' of this program then follows:

```
READ-RECORDS.
     READ ADDRFILE AT END GO TO CLOSE-AND-STOP.
     DISPLAY "Name: " ADDRFILE-NAME.
     DISPLAY "Address: " ADDRFILE-ADDR.
     DISPLAY "Age: " ADDRFILE-AGE.
     GO TO READ-RECORDS.
```

This is the first case of a COBOL *loop* – the code *iterates* through all the records of the file, reading them and displaying their contents. We read the file and at the end, go to the paragraph `CLOSE-AND-STOP`, where the file is closed and `STOP RUN` ends program execution. For each record in the file, the name, address and age field contents are displayed on screen. I've used a `GO TO` statement to return and read each next record. This technique is the easiest if not necessarily the best; I'll present alternatives later, in particular in Chapter 4.

When you enter and execute `FINPUT.CBL`, you should see this display:

```
Name: Boris Yeltsin
Address: Kremlin, Moscow
Age: 066
Name: Bill Clinton
Address: White House, Washington
Age: 052
Name: Tony Blair
Address: 10, Downing Street
Age: 044
Name: Jacques Chirac
Address: Elysee Palace, Paris
Age: 065
```

Take note

In COBOL, you read *files* and write *records*. In FOUTPUT.CBL, you repeatedly WRITE ADDRFILE-RECORD. In FINPUT.CBL, you repeatedly READ ADDRFILE ... If you try to do it the other way round, you'll get compile-time errors.

Things you will need to know

We're going at warp speed through the essential constructs of the COBOL language. So far, I've simply not dealt with a number important aspects of COBOL. The focus is on rushing you along the short path to minimal competency in COBOL programming. Then, you will be more ready to face the other 97% of the language. Constructs and techniques you will have to understand include those that follow.

Data representation

This is the subject of Chapter 2, which covers the `PICTURE` clause, and the available COBOL data types in rather more detail than the quick glance we gave `PIC` in this chapter. You'll learn more about how COBOL handles numbers and text, naming conventions for data items, how to use working storage and complex data structures such as *array*s (which, in COBOL, are also called *table*s).

Data manipulation

In Chapter 3, you'll see more about data I/O using `ACCEPT` and `DISPLAY`, as well as some of the details of the syntax of the `MOVE` verb. `MOVE` is the most heavily used COBOL verb and it's vital to understand its behaviour. Also, we'll cover COBOL arithmetic, as well as using arrays and sorting and searching.

Program structure and control flow

In the program `FINPUT.CBL` in the last section, I use a `GO TO` statement to return and read another file record. This was the original way in COBOL to construct a loop, but it's a technique now frowned upon somewhat by the *cognoscenti*. It's better to structure your programs using `SECTION`s and the `PERFORM` verb. Chapter 4 deals with this.

Sequential files

For many COBOL applications, you only need sequential files of the type exemplified by `ADDRFILE.DAT` in this chapter. For large files where it's necessary to search for particular records, sequential organisation isn't good enough but sequential files are used in many *batch-processing* jobs. Consider as an example a program to generate, one after another, a million electricity bills. Ploughing through a sequential file is how you'd probably do it. Chapter 5 goes into much more detail on the definition of sequential files, as well as techniques for using them, including such things as sorting records, matching files, printing and the classical sequential file-update application.

Indexed and non-sequential files

Indexed and relative files are used for those application where speed is required in searching for individual records. Chapter 6 explains these file organisation schemes and the various modes in which they are used.

Programming date applications

And so to the flavour (panic?) of the month, dates, old COBOL code (about 90 billion lines of it!) and the Year 2000 (Y2K) problem. In Chapter 7, I dish out a lot of (actually important) trivia about dates, techniques for programming them and ways of fixing and avoiding Y2K bugs. Part of this chapter also summarises the business consequences and likely practical effects of *legacy code* (code dating from the 1960s and 1970s) which encounter the Y2K bug.

If you understand and apply all of this stuff, you'll be a pretty competent and well-grounded COBOL programmer. That's the objective of this book and, if 200-odd pages can achieve that objective, it's a good result. But there are some things that are simply beyond the scope of a book of this size. Examples: graphical and form display; communications; using the Report Writer; and files with variable-length records. Feel good about it, though: these are rather specialised areas and, if you're working in a commercial COBOL environment, there will be documentation that covers them. The mainstream knowledge you'll get from the remaining chapters of this book will carry you though most of the COBOL programming challenges you are likely to encounter.

Exercises

1   What's wrong with this program?

```
IDENTIFICATION DIVISION.
PROGRAM-ID. SKELETON.

ENVIRONMENT DIVISION.
CONFIGURATION SECTION.
INPUT-OUTPUT SECTION.
FILE-CONTROL.

DATA DIVISION.
FILE SECTION.
WORKING-STORAGE-SECTION.
REPORT SECTION.

PROCEDURE DIVISION.
PROGRAM-START.

PROGRAM-END.
   STOP RUN.
```

2   Write a WORKING-STORAGE variable definition such that the data item defined can accommodate three exclusively alphabetic characters in memory.

3   If the variable A has the value 5 and the variable B has the value 6 then, after execution of the COBOL statement:

```
ADD A TO B GIVING C.
```

C contains the value 11. With this knowledge, see if you can write a COBOL program that ACCEPTs two numbers, DISPLAYs them, adds them and DISPLAYs the result of the addition.

Take note

The answers to these exercises can be found in the Made Simple pages of the Butterworth-Heinemann Web site at:

http://www.bh.com

2 Handling data

The COBOL Alphabet

This chapter is concerned with the details of data representation in COBOL: the classes (types) of data that you can use; the syntax that you have to use to define data items (variables) of those types; and the set of characters – the *alphabet*, to use COBOL-speak – that you're allowed employ in writing these definitions and the rest of your program.

There's a great deal of information in all of this, and most textbooks and manuals, in covering it, tend to 'sprawl' a bit: the material on the COBOL alphabet, PICTUREs, level numbers and group data definitions is all over the place. This chapter is my attempt to get it all together, concisely, in a very few pages. Here goes.

The COBOL alphabet is the *character set* (to borrow a phrase used by other languages) available to you. There are 77 individual letters, numbers, punctuation and special characters available. They are:

Characters	Use
0-9	Numeric
A-Z	Alphabetic
a-z	alphabetic
().";,	Delimiters and decimal point
+-*/	Arithmetic, hyphen, comment
<>=	Relational operators (comparisons)
$	Currency symbol
	Single blank space

Using this alphabet, you can write variable names such as ADDRFILE-NAME, where the hyphen is treated by the COBOL compiler as just a hyphen. The arithmetic operation A - B is possible also; because there's a space on either side of the hyphen, the hyphen is treated by the compiler as the subtraction operator. In column 7, the asterisk, *, denotes a comment line following; used elsewhere, it's the arithmetic multiplication operator or (perhaps) exponentiation, **. Lower-case alphabetics were introduced by COBOL-85, in addition to upper-case, which have been there since the inception of the COBOL language. I restrict usage in this book to upper-case for portability reasons.

Using the alphabet: cConstants

Constants (usually called *literal*s in COBOL) are the opposite of variables: they are quantities that, once defined, cannot be changed by the program. There are three kinds of constants: numeric, alphanumeric and figurative.

Numeric constants are numbers, written directly as such in the program and not bounded by any delimiter characters: `1411` and `1.73205` are numeric constants, and can also be called numeric literals.

Alphanumeric literals are strings of text, which may contain alphabetic, numeric, blank, punctuation and special characters from the alphabet in any combination. Alphanumeric literals must be delimited by either single or double quotes to identify them to the compiler, e.g.

```
WORKING-STORAGE SECTION.
01 WS-NAME1      PIC X(30) VALUE IS 'Signor Antonio'.
01 WS-NAME2      PIC X(30) VALUE IS "Signor Bassanio".
```

Note the initialisation of data items using the `VALUE IS` clause. When `WS-NAME1` is defined, it takes on the value of the string literal 'Signor Antonio', while `WS-NAME2` is initialised to "Signor Bassanio". You can use either single or double quotes as delimiters, but you mustn't mix them: 'Signor Antonio" is invalid. Note that the variables above are initialised to the literal text minus the delimiters: `WS-NAME2` has the value `Signor Bassanio`, not "Signor Bassanio". The COBOL-85 standard specifies that string literals can be of up to 160 characters in length.

The third kind of constant is the *figurative constant*. These are COBOL reserved words that stand for often-used constants, and make COBOL code more readable. Here's the full list of figurative constants:

Figurative Constant	Meaning
ZERO, ZEROS, ZEROES	Value of all zeroes (numeric or alphanumeric)
SPACE, SPACES	Value of blanks in alphabetic or alphanumeric items
LOW-VALUE, LOW-VALUES	Lowest collating-sequence value
HIGH-VALUE, HIGH-VALUES	Highest collating-sequence value
QUOTE, QUOTES	Double-quotes
ALL	Repetition of a literal

Reasonable uses of figurative constants are:

```
MOVE SPACES TO OUTPUT-PRINT-LINE.
MOVE ZEROS TO RUNNING-TOTAL.
MOVE ALL 0 to RUNNING-TOTAL.
```

HIGH-VALUES and LOW-VALUES are usually used to represent some impossibly high or low value that will signify the end of a file or some process. An alternative is to use ZEROS or, say, 999999 but, as you'll see in Chapter 7, from the perspective of avoiding problems with dates, this may not be a good idea. As an example of their use, you could MOVE HIGH-VALUES or LOW-VALUES to a record in a file to signify that it had been (logically) deleted.

Using the alphabet: column 7

An asterisk is found in column 7, it means that the rest of that line is treated by the compiler as a comment line – all text on that line is ignored and serves only for documentary purposes.

If a slash, /, is found in column 7, the compiler treats that line as a comment-line also but additionally causes that line to be the start of a page if a program listing is sent to the printer.

You can use a hyphen in column 7 to define a data item and initialise it with a very long string literal. See what happens when the length of an alphanumeric literal takes it beyond the bounds (Column 72).

```
**********************************************************************
*                          LONGLIT.CBL                              *
*  Demonstrates definition and use of a long string literal         *
*                                                                   *
**********************************************************************
IDENTIFICATION DIVISION.
PROGRAM-ID. LONGLIT.
DATA DIVISION.
WORKING-STORAGE SECTION.
01 WS-LONG-LITERAL PIC X(200) VALUE IS "Signor Antonio, many a time".

PROCEDURE DIVISION.
DISPLAY-LONG-LITERAL.
    DISPLAY "Long Literal: " WS-LONG-LITERAL.

PROGRAM-END.
    STOP RUN.
```

In this case, the literal ends in column 74. The compiler issues a warning and truncates the literal at column 72. The program's output is this:

```
Personal COBOL version 2.0 from Micro Focus
PCOBRUN V2.0.02  Copyright (C) 1983-1993 Micro Focus
Ltd.
Long Literal: Signor Antonio, many a ti
```

To allow alphanumeric literals extend beyond the ends of lines, we must use the hyphen continuation character in column 7:

```
WORKING-STORAGE SECTION.
01 WS-LONG-LITERAL PIC X(200) VALUE IS "Signor Antonio, many a ti
-          "me and oft on the Rialto, you have rated me for my mone
-          "ys and my usances. Still have I borne it with a patient
-          "shrug, for suffering is the badge of all our tribe.".
```

Now, when you run the program, the output looks like this:

```
Personal COBOL version 2.0 from Micro Focus
PCOBRUN V2.0.02  Copyright (C) 1983-1993 Micro Focus Ltd.
Long Literal: Signor Antonio, many a time and oft on the Rialto, you
have rated me for my moneys and my usances. Still have I borne it with
a patient shrug, for suffering is the badge of all our tribe.
```

The 1974 COBOL (COBOL-74) standard allows 120-character literals; COBOL-85 increases the limit to 160. The initialising string above is over 180 characters, but Personal COBOL nonetheless allows it.

Using the alphabet: operators

Arithmetic operators available in COBOL are:

unary + and -	as in -5 and +8
+ (addition)	- (subtraction)
* (multiplication)	/ (division)
** (exponentiation)	

These operators can only be used with the COMPUTE verb, which I explain in Chapter 3.

Relational operators are used in comparisons. In COBOL, you can check for the truth or falsehood of the condition A < B, which is '*A less than B*'. The operator < is a relational operator.

The full set of COBOL relational operators is:

< (less than)   = (equal to)   > (greater than)

<= (less than or equal to)   >= (greater than or equal to)

Data item naming rules

Data items we have already seen, for example `ADDRFILE-FNAME`, are data names constructed at the discretion of the programmer. You can invent any names you want, provided they're legal in the eyes of the COBOL compiler. Most organisations engaged in software development also adopt naming *conventions* for their COBOL programs. Good conventions are desirable (I recommend some in Chapter 4); rules are necessary. `ADDRFILE-FNAME` is both legal and an example of a reasonable naming convention (file name, hyphen, data item name). While all the data item names you'll see in this book will be conventionally reasonable and intuitive, here, I'm more concerned with the naming rules, which are:

● Each data name (including paragraph names) can be of up to 30 characters and must contain at least one alphabetic character.

● Allowable characters for data names are alphabetic characters (both upper- and lower-case, but I'm using only capitals), digits and the hyphen.

● A data name must not begin or end with a hyphen and must not have embedded blanks.

● A data name must not be a reserved word. There are about 300 reserved words in COBOL-85; they include `DISPLAY`, `MOVE` and `PROCEDURE`.

The PICTURE Clause

The `PICTURE` clause is COBOL's way of specifying the data class (type) and capacity of a data item (variable) during its definition. A data item represents a value stored in the computer's memory which can be changed by the program of which the data item is part. As I point out in Chapter 1, the full syntax is to use `PICTURE IS`:

```
01 WS-FNAME             PICTURE IS A(20).
```

but this is the same in effect as the much more commonly-used `PIC`:

```
01 WS-FNAME             PIC A(20).
```

In a manner unlike the internal numeric representations found in other languages such as Fortran and C, COBOL's numeric definitions accord with how the number appears:

```
01 WS-INCOME            PIC 9(7).
```

specifies a whole number which can have any value from zero up to one short of ten million. This visual (picture!) representation may not be suitable for the computer's internal arithmetic calculations and, for efficiency, you may choose to store such a number differently. You'll see the techniques for doing this in this chapter and the next, but `PIC 9(7)` is fine for most purposes.

The full set of field definition characters that you can use in `PIC` clauses is this:

Character	Meaning	Editing char	Meaning
9	Numeric field	$	Dollar sign
A	Alphabetic field	Z	Zero suppression
X	Alphanumeric data	-	Minus sign
S	Arithmetic sign	+	Plus sign
V	Assumed decimal point	,	Comma
P	Position of decimal point	.	Decimal point
		DB	Debit
		CR	Credit
		B	Blank insertion
		0	Zero insertion
		/	Slash insertion

You'll find most, if not all, of these demonstrated in the example programs in this book. These PICTURE symbols are used to define five types of data (data classes):

Data Class	Symbols Used
Numeric	9 S V P
Alphanumeric	A
Alphabetic	X (and group items)
Numeric Edited	Numeric and all Editing symbols
Alphanumeric Edited	Alphanumeric and B 0 /

You've already seen some of the numeric, alphanumeric and alphabetic PIC symbols in use. The example program below shows more. The *editing* symbols are new; they are used for formatting and beautifying the appearance of data when the data is being output to a screen, printer or other display device. I cover data editing later in this chapter.

The maximum allowable size of a numeric data item specified using PIC is 18 digits: PIC 9(18) is equivalent to PIC 999999999999999999, in the same way as PIC XXXXXX is equivalent to PIC X(6), PIC AAA is the same in effect as PIC A(3), and PIC 9 is equivalent to PIC 9(1). If numeric data being assigned to a data item is longer than the PICTURE specification of that data, the data is truncated to the left. If alphabetic or alphanumeric data being assigned to a data item is longer than the PICTURE specification of that data, then the data is truncated to the right.

Note also that a PIC clause, like a statement and a sentence, can be split over several lines, provided all of it remains within Area B.

Here's a program, EASYIO.CBL, that demonstrates use of many of the non-editing PIC symbols. Its job is familiar: accept input from the keyboard and display that input on the screen. No disk files are involved.

```
***********************************************************
*                                                         *
*    This program performs simple text I/O without using files  *
*                                                         *
***********************************************************
 IDENTIFICATION DIVISION.
 PROGRAM-ID. EASYIO.

 DATA DIVISION.
 WORKING-STORAGE SECTION.
 01 WS-PERSONAL-DETAILS.
      02 WS-LNAME    PIC A(15).
      02 WS-FNAME    PIC A(15).
      02 WS-ADDR1    PIC X(20).
      02 WS-ADDR2    PIC X(20).
      02 WS-ADDR3    PIC X(20).
      02 WS-AGE      PIC 9999.
      02 WS-HEIGHT   PIC 9V99.
      02 WS-GENDER   PIC A.

 PROCEDURE DIVISION.
 GET-PERSONAL-DETAILS.
      DISPLAY "Enter First Name ".
      ACCEPT WS-FNAME.
      DISPLAY "Enter Last Name ".
      ACCEPT WS-LNAME.
      DISPLAY "Enter Address Line 1 ".
      ACCEPT WS-ADDR1.
      DISPLAY "Enter Address Line 2 ".
      ACCEPT WS-ADDR2.
      DISPLAY "Enter Address Line 3 ".
      ACCEPT WS-ADDR3.
      DISPLAY "Enter Age ".
      ACCEPT WS-AGE.
      DISPLAY "Enter Height in Metres ".
      ACCEPT WS-HEIGHT.
      DISPLAY "Enter Gender ".
      ACCEPT WS-GENDER.

 DISPLAY-PERSONAL-DETAILS.
      DISPLAY "First Name " WS-FNAME.
      DISPLAY "Last Name " WS-LNAME.
      DISPLAY "Address 1 " WS-ADDR1.
      DISPLAY "Address 2 " WS-ADDR2.
      DISPLAY "Address 3 " WS-ADDR3.
      DISPLAY "Age " WS-AGE.
      DISPLAY "Height " WS-HEIGHT.
      DISPLAY "Gender " WS-GENDER.

 PROGRAM-END.
      STOP RUN.
```

> ACCEPT/DISPLAY sequence for interactive data I/O

```
Personal COBOL version 2.0 from Micro Focus
PCOBRUN V2.0.02  Copyright (C) 1983-1993 Micro Focus Ltd.
Enter First Name
Conor
Enter Last Name
Sexton
Enter Address Line 1
Halley Court
Enter Address Line 2
Jordan Hill
Enter Address Line 3
Oxford OX2 8DP
Enter Age
29
Enter Height in Metres
1.82
Enter Gender
m
First Name Conor
Last Name Sexton
Address 1 Halley Court
Address 2 Jordan Hill
Address 3 Oxford OX2 8DP
Age 0029
Height 182
Gender m
```

EASYIO.CBL I/O sequence, user input in **boldface**.

The result is fairly predictable, with two exceptions: my age (ahem…) is displayed as 0029 and there's no decimal point in my height data. We can improve the format of the output with the Editing PICTURE symbols, which I will explain later in this chapter.

PIC symbols 9, A and X specify numeric, purely alphabetic and alphanumeric (alphabetic, punctuation, special and numeric) data. PIC A is often unused: people tend to use PIC X for all non-numeric definitions. V represents the *assumed decimal point* – not an actual decimal point, but an indicator to the compiler that fractional arithmetic should be conducted on the data, e.g. WEEKLY-PAY:

```
01 WEEKLY-PAY PIC 999V99.
```

can hold (possibly non-whole-number) values in the range 000.00 to 999.99. If you're initialising a data item with an assumed decimal point, you do it in the way that might be expected:

```
01 WEEKLY-PAY PIC 999V99 VALUE 257.48.
```

and the number is stored as a fractional quantity a bit larger than 257.

Level numbers and group items

Up to now, we've used elementary data items defined in the WORKING-STORAGE section, or very simple group items either there or as part of file definitions in the FILE section of the DATA division. I've confined use of level numbers to 01 and 02. This section is about building more-complex group data items using more level numbers.

Level 77

One or two small matters to dispose of first: to begin with, level number 77. You'll see this everywhere in existing COBOL code. It was introduced by COBOL-74 as an alternative to level 01, to be used only when defining elementary data items in the WORKING-STORAGE section. As you've already seen in this book, you can define a level 01 item to be a group name or a record name:

```
01 ADDRFILE-RECORD.
    02 ADDRFILE-NAME   PIC X(20).
    02 ADDRFILE-ADDR   PIC X(30).
    02 ADDRFILE-AGE    PIC 999.
```

You can also define an elementary data item at level 01:

```
01 WEEKLY-PAY PIC 999V99 VALUE 257.48.
```

You could change the latter definition to:

```
77 WEEKLY-PAY PIC 999V99 VALUE 257.48.
```

but only if the definition is in the WORKING-STORAGE section. When it was introduced, some compilers optimised their translation of level 77s – the compilers could assume they were elementary items – with some performance benefits. Level 77 is still supported but is not part of the COBOL-85 standard. You should know how to use it in maintaining existing programs, but you shouldn't introduce it into new software – it may not be supported indefinitely.

Level 88

Less common and less important than level 77, level 88 still deserves a mention as COBOL's implementation of the *range-check*. This is an elegant test carried out on a data item to see which of several pre-determined values it contains. For example, we could have a variable for which the only reasonable values were RED, GREEN and BLUE; anything else is invalid. Instead of testing explicitly for each, we use a range check.

Here's an example that you'll encounter in the Exercises of Chapter 3. A user is presented with a screen display. Input keystrokes in the range zero to 3 are the only valid inputs. How do we check this? You could use a sequence of IF statements (see Chapter 4) to check the data item against each of the values. But, instead, we use an 88 level:

```
WORKING-STORAGE SECTION.
01  MENU-SELECT              PIC 9 VALUE 0.
    88 MENU-SELECT-OK        VALUE 0 THRU 3.
```

This specifies that MENU-SELECT can only hold a value in the range 0 to 3. Anything else is an error. MENU-SELECT is defined as PIC 9, but the 88 level MENU-SELECT-OK does not (and must not) have a PICTURE clause. At level 88, you can only specify a range of valid values for a data item. Now, using the IF verb for the first time (you'll see it in full in Chapter 4, but its use is intuitive here) we can check the contents:

```
IF MENU-SELECT-OK
    GO TO DISPLAY-OK.
* Otherwise out of range
```

Multi-level Group Items

PICTURE levels that you use in defining group items can be in the range 01 to 49. Group items must be formed as a hierarchy with levels in descending numeric order:

```
01 WS-PERSONAL-DETAILS.
    02 WS-NAME.
        03 WS-LNAME          PIC A(15).
        03 WS-FNAME          PIC A(15).
```

The level 01 data item must start in Area A (between columns 8 and 11, inclusive of both). Levels 02 and lower must start (and continue and be finished!) in Area B. A group data item such as the 01 and 02 items above must not have associated PICTURE clauses. The data item name must instead end with a full-stop. The numbers must be in descending order but not necessarily in sequential descending order. Level 01 must be level 01, but otherwise you could use 03 WS-NAME and 08 for WS-LNAME and WS-FNAME. To be *both* subordinate data items of WS-NAME, WS-LNAME and WS-FNAME must have the *same* level number, which is greater than that of WS-NAME and less than 50.

Every group item is of alphanumeric (X) data class (type), even if it contains subordinate numeric data items. This fact can lead to some interesting side-effects as you'll see later in this section.

The group item WS-PERSONAL-DETAILS is defined in the WORKING-STORAGE section. It's common to prefix data items defined in this section with WS-, so you could guess where WS-PERSONAL-DATES is defined even if you didn't know. You can assign items directly – for example, using MOVE or ACCEPT – to WS-PERSONAL-DETAILS or its subordinate data items. If you MOVE something to WS-PERSONAL-DETAILS, you'll find, on DISPLAYing the two subordinate data items, that their contents are part or all of the data that you MOVEd. In summary, the group item name is shorthand for all the subordinate items of the group.

In certain cases, you won't want to name elementary data items within the group at all. Consider this example:

```
01 WS-PERSONAL-DETAILS.
   02 WS-NAME.
      03 WS-FNAME      PIC A(15).
      03 WS-BLANK1     PIC A VALUE IS SPACE.
      03 WS-MINIT      PIC AA.
      03 WS-BLANK2     PIC A VALUE IS SPACE.
      03 WS-LNAME      PIC A(15).
```

It's intended that there be a single blank space between the three names. However, the space fields are constant – they aren't going to be changed – and you don't need to refer directly to them. Consequently, you don't really need to name them uniquely. You can instead use the reserved word FILLER to avoid naming these fields.

```
01 WS-PERSONAL-DETAILS.
   02 WS-NAME.
      03 WS-FNAME      PIC A(15).
      03 FILLER        PIC A VALUE IS SPACE.
      03 WS-MINIT      PIC AA.
      03 FILLER        PIC A VALUE IS SPACE.
      03 WS-LNAME      PIC A(15).
```

```
╔══════════════╗
║ ITEMIO.CBL   ║
╚══════════════╝

      *****************************************************************
      *                                                              *
      *   This program performs simple text I/O using group items    *
      *                                                              *
      *****************************************************************
       IDENTIFICATION DIVISION.
       PROGRAM-ID. ITEMIO.

       DATA DIVISION.
       WORKING-STORAGE SECTION.
       01 WS-PERSONAL-DETAILS.
           02 WS-NAME.
               03 WS-FNAME    PIC A(15).
               03 FILLER      PIC A VALUE IS 'X'.
               03 WS-MINIT    PIC AA.
               03 FILLER      PIC A VALUE IS 'X'.
               03 WS-LNAME    PIC A(15).
           02 WS-ADDR.
               03 WS-ADDR1    PIC X(20).
               03 WS-ADDR2    PIC X(20).
               03 WS-ADDR3    PIC X(20).
           02 WS-AGE          PIC 999.

       PROCEDURE DIVISION.
       GET-PERSONAL-DETAILS.
           DISPLAY "Enter First Name ".
           ACCEPT WS-FNAME.
           DISPLAY "Enter Middle Initial ".
           ACCEPT WS-MINIT.
           DISPLAY "Enter Last Name ".
           ACCEPT WS-LNAME.
           DISPLAY "Enter Address Line 1 ".
           ACCEPT WS-ADDR1.
           DISPLAY "Enter Address Line 2 ".
           ACCEPT WS-ADDR2.
           DISPLAY "Enter Address Line 3 ".
           ACCEPT WS-ADDR3.
           DISPLAY "Enter Age ".
           ACCEPT WS-AGE.

       DISPLAY-PERSONAL-DETAILS.
           DISPLAY "Name " WS-NAME.
           DISPLAY "Address " WS-ADDR.
           DISPLAY "Age " WS-AGE.
           DISPLAY "The Whole Thing " WS-PERSONAL-DETAILS.

       PROGRAM-END.
           STOP RUN.
```

> The group data item WS-PERSONAL-DETAILS contains two subordinate group data items, WS-NAME and WS-ADDR. These in turn contain a number of elementary data items, using FILLER twice and three different PICTURE symbols.

> The group data items are initialised by using ACCEPT statements with the elementary fields as *operands*.

> Displays the contents just entered by the user, but uses the group data items as the operands of its DISPLAY statements to do so.

Here's the text of my interaction with the program when I ran it (my input in boldface):

```
Personal COBOL version 2.0 from Micro Focus
PCOBRUN V2.0.02  Copyright (C) 1983-1993 Micro Focus Ltd.
Enter First Name
Conor
Enter Middle Initial
B
Enter Last Name
Sexton
Enter Address Line 1
Halley Court
Enter Address Line 2
Jordan Hill
Enter Address Line 3
Oxford OX2 8DP
Enter Age
29
Name Conor          XB XSexton
Address Halley Court        Jordan Hill         Oxford OX2 8DP
Age 029
The Whole Thing Conor        XB XSexton       Halley Court        Jord
an Hill          Oxford OX2 8DP       029
```

There are three DISPLAYed outputs:

        Name Conor   XB XSexton

which is the result of the statement:

        DISPLAY "Name " WS-NAME.

Note that I've made 'X' the filler character, so that it'll be obvious on output. The second output is the address, output all as one group data item WS-ADDR. The third is the whole thing, generated by using DISPLAY with the 01-level group data item WS-PERSONAL-DETAILS.

Not very difficult, is it? The essence of the thing is that an elementary data item can either be referred to directly by its name or indirectly by its group identifier (or by the group identifier of that group identifier, and so on). In this way, we get the flexibility to access and change small individual data items and the 'macro effect' of being able to assign to a large group item, thereby initialising all its elementary data items.

Recall that the data class of any group data item is alphanumeric, regardless of the classes of its elementary data items. Now look at an interesting conflict that arises when we make an assignment to the group data item. First, we initialise WS-PERSONAL-DETAILS:

```
    MOVE SPACES TO WS-PERSONAL-DETAILS.
```

Next, because I just grown one year older (happens too often these days...), we add one to my age:

```
    ADD 1 TO WS-AGE.
```

Because of the first statement above, WS-AGE will have been initialised with blanks: three of them to be exact. Then we add 1 to a quantity of three blanks. What happens? Here's what Personal COBOL says:

```
    ITEMIO Segment RT : Error 163 at COBOL PC 0125
    Description : Illegal Character in Numeric Field
```

The meaning is fairly obvious: it's an illegal arithmetic operation involving both numbers (1) and characters (blanks). In this situation, different COBOL compilers give different results, because the meaning of the mixed-type addition is not defined.

The moral of the story is that you should perform arithmetic only on operands that you *know* contain valid numeric data – *don't* use an uninitialised data item and hope for the best.

Here's another manifestation of the fact that group items have alphanumeric data class:

```
    01 WS-GROUP VALUE "ABC1234".
       02 WS-ALPHA    PIC XXX.
       02 WS-NUMERIC  PIC 9999.
```

After this initialisation, WS-ALPHA and WS-NUMERIC have the values "ABC" and 1234 respectively.

Further PICTURE Definitions

This section summarises the behaviour of the remaining qualifications you can insert in `PICTURE` clauses.

Signed numeric fields

A number in COBOL – represented, say, by `PIC 9(4)V99` – is by default always positive: you can't use it to store a negative quantity like your bank overdraft. To make the number *signed* – capable of going negative – you must prefix the numeric type with an `S`:

```
01 WS-OVERDRAFT    PIC S9(4)V99.
```

The S must be the first character in the `PICTURE` specification.

The assumed decimal point

I've already explained some of the basic behaviour of a `PIC` specification containing a V symbol. Here are a few more details. Where a data item is defined containing an assumed decimal point, it is treated in any subsequent arithmetic operations as a fractional quantity. On the following page is a program, `FRACTION.CBL`, that displays interesting aspects of the operation of the assumed decimal point:

The program displays the values of the two initialised data items `WS-WHOLE` and `WS-FRACTION`. It then introduces the `DIVIDE` verb (I explain this more fully in Chapter 3) to highlight the difference in behaviour of the fractional as opposed to the whole number.

`WS-WHOLE` is initialised to `2357`, which is right-justified with the positions to the left of the number being padded with zeros. If you try to use a decimal point in the number initialising `WS-WHOLE`, you'll get a compilation error. In the case of `WS-FRACTION`, the decimal point in the initialising value aligns with the V picture-symbol, with the result being displayed accordingly, left- and right-padded with a zero.

When `WS-WHOLE` is divided by 4, the result is the whole number `589`, about a quarter of `2,357`. When `WS-FRACTION` is divided by 4, the precise result is slightly less than 6 but is displayed as the whole number 5, because the fractional part is truncated. I show in the next section how to display a decimal point and the numbers to its right.

```
******************************************************************
*                                                                *
*   Demonstrates behaviour of the assumed decimal point          *
*                                                                *
******************************************************************
 IDENTIFICATION DIVISION.
 PROGRAM-ID. FRACTION.

 DATA DIVISION.
 WORKING-STORAGE SECTION.
 01 WS-WHOLE      PIC 999999 VALUE 2357.
 01 WS-FRACTION   PIC 999V999 VALUE 23.57.
 01 WS-ANSWER     PIC 9(4).

 PROCEDURE DIVISION.
 DISPLAY-FRACTION.
     DISPLAY "Initial value of whole " WS-WHOLE.
     DISPLAY "Initial value of fraction " WS-FRACTION.
     DIVIDE WS-FRACTION BY 4 GIVING WS-ANSWER.
     DISPLAY "Divided fraction " WS-ANSWER.
     DIVIDE WS-WHOLE BY 4 GIVING WS-ANSWER.
     DISPLAY "Divided whole " WS-ANSWER.
     MOVE 1234.5678 TO WS-WHOLE.
     DISPLAY "Reassigned value of whole " WS-WHOLE.
     MOVE 1234.5678 TO WS-FRACTION.
     DISPLAY "Reassigned value of fraction " WS-FRACTION.

 PROGRAM-END.
     STOP RUN.
```

> When 1234.5678 is assigned to WS-WHOLE, it's truncated at the decimal point...

> ... assigned to WS-FRACTION, the truncation is of the leading 1 and the trailing 8.

The output results of `FRACTION.CBL` are these:

```
Personal COBOL version 2.0 from Micro Focus
PCOBRUN V2.0.02  Copyright (C) 1983-1993 Micro Focus Ltd.
Initial value of whole 002357
Initial value of fraction 023570
Divided fraction 0005
Divided whole 0589
Reassigned value of whole 001234
Reassigned value of fraction 234567
```

This is a reasonably complete presentation of how the assumed decimal point works. When using fractional numbers (and whole numbers also!) in COBOL, you need to keep in mind their size as specified by their PICTURE clause and how truncation will occur if an assigned number is too large to fit that PIC specification. If you don't do this, you'll get some surprising and unpleasant errors.

USAGE

This subclause of PIC is used to specify how numbers are internally (in the computer's memory) represented by a COBOL program. You could, for example, define a data item as:

```
01 WS-STANDARD-NO  PIC 999 USAGE IS DISPLAY.
```

This is the default and is the same in effect as:

```
01 WS-STANDARD-NO  PIC 999.
```

The words USAGE IS are themselves optional; the following definitions are synonymous with the above two:

```
01 WS-STANDARD-NO  PIC 999 USAGE DISPLAY.
01 WS-STANDARD-NO  PIC 999 DISPLAY.
```

DISPLAY usage is the default. The other possibilities are:

```
BINARY                COMPUTATIONAL
COMP                  INDEX
PACKED-DECIMAL
```

Using any of these in place of the default DISPLAY allows you to specify that a data item is to be stored in the form required by the computer for internal numeric operations. If you do arithmetic with DISPLAY items, they must be converted by the compiler to an internal form before the sums can be done. Using BINARY, COMP or PACKED-DECIMAL, you eliminate the conversion step.

How do these specifications work? It takes one character position (eight *bits*, a series of 1s and 0s in the computer's memory) to store a number when you specify PIC 9. But it only takes the computer four bits to store a numeric value such as 5 (0101 in *binary*). That means that, in *computational* representation, the computer can internally use one character to store a much larger number than is possible with PIC 9. This saves space and increases number-crunching efficiency.

The downsides of this are that, before displaying such a computational quantity, you must first convert it to DISPLAY form by moving it to a DISPLAY data item; also, computational data is not necessarily portable between one COBOL environment and the next. You're best advised to use DISPLAY numeric data items only, unless performance, data size and computational efficiency are very important in your application.

Other qualifications

There are several other possible ways in which you can qualify your PICTURE definitions:

- SIGN, SYNC and JUST.
- BLANK WHEN ZERO.
- REDEFINES.

The SIGN option specifies how internal positive/negative signing is handled. The sign can be embedded in the data – taking no extra space – or separate; it can additionally be leading or trailing. Possibilities are:

```
01 WS-NO1 PIC S9(5) SIGN LEADING SEPARATE.
01 WS-NO2 PIC S9(5) SIGN TRAILING.
```

If the SIGN clause is omitted, the sign is not stored separately, but as part of the number itself. This form occupies less space and is more efficient in arithmetic than with separate storage but may be less portable between COBOL environments. Nevertheless, use of the SIGN clause is not very common.

SYNC and JUST are used to specify more closely the nature of numeric and alphanumeric storage. For example, you could specify:

```
01 WS-COMP    PIC 9(6) COMP SYNC RIGHT.
```

to mean computational (as defined above) storage, synchronised on a right-hand *word boundary*. On a given computer, this may make numeric calculations very efficient, but it's not very portable between systems. You should use these specifications with care. One of the more common uses of COMPUTATIONAL numeric data items is as table subscripts, of which more in this and the next two chapters. Using JUST (or JUSTIFIED) RIGHT overrides left-justification, which is the default when a data item is moved to an alphanumeric field.

BLANK WHEN ZERO is used with edit output fields, which I describe in the next section.

REDEFINES is for the redefinition of a group data item – looking at it in a different way – while RENAMES (Level 66) allows you to rename a given data item. I cover these in Chapters 3 (both) and Chapter 5 (REDEFINES in the context of printer output).

Data editing

Editing is the term used in COBOL for formatting output sent to a display or print device. There are two kinds of editing: numeric and alphanumeric, of which numeric is predominant.

Up to now, you've seen screen display (printing is in Chapter 5) but there has been no way, for example, to suppress leading zeros in a numeric field or to make a decimal point appear in the right place on output. Refining your program's output is what this section is about. You may recall from the beginning of this chapter the full set of field definition characters, or PICTURE symbols. Here are the ones that you can use to format (edit) your program's output:

Editing Character	Meaning
$	Dollar sign
Z	Zero suppression
-	Minus sign
+	Plus sign
,	Comma
.	Decimal point
DB	Debit
CR	Credit
B	Blank insertion
0	Zero insertion
/	Slash insertion

Editing symbols

Suppose you're displaying or printing a money amount that needs a leading (US dollar) currency symbol. How do you make it 'float' so that it appears in the correct place with respect to the number to its right? How do you display a minus or debit (DB) sign for a negative numeric or money quantity? How do you suppress leading zeros on a numeric field? How do you display decimal points and commas within numbers? The best way to answer these questions is to demonstrate a program that exercises the necessary output editing options. Here it is; it's called EDITIO.CBL:

EDITIO1.CBL

```
*********************************************************************
*                                                                   *
*   This program performs input and output of text and numerics     *
*   and uses a number of output edit formats                        *
*                                                                   *
*********************************************************************
    IDENTIFICATION DIVISION.
    PROGRAM-ID. EDITIO1.

    DATA DIVISION.
    WORKING-STORAGE SECTION.
    01 WS-PERSONAL-DETAILS.
        02 WS-NAME.
            03 WS-LNAME         PIC A(15).
            03 WS-FNAME         PIC A(15).
        02 WS-ADDR.
            03 WS-ADDR1         PIC X(20).
            03 WS-ADDR2         PIC X(20).
            03 WS-ADDR3         PIC X(20).
        02 WS-AGE               PIC 9999.
        02 WS-INCOME            PIC 9(7).
        02 WS-EXPEND            PIC 9(7).
        02 WS-HEIGHT            PIC 9V99.
        02 WS-GENDER            PIC A.

    01 WS-DISPLAY-HEIGHT        PIC 9.99.
    77 WS-DISPLAY-AGE           PIC ZZZ9.
    01 WS-DISPLAY-INCOME        PIC $(6)9.
    01 WS-DISPLAY-EXPEND        PIC $(6)9.
    01 WS-DISPLAY-BALANCE       PIC $,$$$,$$9-.

    PROCEDURE DIVISION.
    GET-PERSONAL-DETAILS.
        DISPLAY "Enter First Name ".
        ACCEPT WS-FNAME.
        DISPLAY "Enter Last Name ".
        ACCEPT WS-LNAME.
        DISPLAY "Enter Address Line 1 ".
        ACCEPT WS-ADDR1.
        DISPLAY "Enter Address Line 2 ".
        ACCEPT WS-ADDR2.
        DISPLAY "Enter Address Line 3 ".
        ACCEPT WS-ADDR3.
        DISPLAY "Enter Age ".
        ACCEPT WS-AGE.
        DISPLAY "Enter Income ".
        ACCEPT WS-INCOME.
```

This is the longest program so far, but it's also quite straightforward and you should be now be able to follow most aspects of it.

```
        DISPLAY "Enter Expenditure ".
        ACCEPT WS-EXPEND.
        DISPLAY "Enter Height in Metres ".
        ACCEPT WS-HEIGHT.
        DISPLAY "Enter Gender ".
        ACCEPT WS-GENDER.

        DISPLAY-PERSONAL-DETAILS.
        DISPLAY "First Name " WS-FNAME.
        DISPLAY "Last Name " WS-LNAME.
        DISPLAY "Address " WS-ADDR.
        MOVE WS-AGE TO WS-DISPLAY-AGE.
        DISPLAY "Age " WS-DISPLAY-AGE.
        MOVE WS-INCOME TO WS-DISPLAY-INCOME.
        DISPLAY "Income " WS-DISPLAY-INCOME.
        MOVE WS-EXPEND TO WS-DISPLAY-EXPEND.
        DISPLAY "Expenditure " WS-DISPLAY-EXPEND.
        SUBTRACT WS-EXPEND FROM WS-INCOME
              GIVING WS-DISPLAY-BALANCE.
        DISPLAY "Balance " WS-DISPLAY-BALANCE.
        MOVE WS-HEIGHT TO WS-DISPLAY-HEIGHT.
        DISPLAY "Height " WS-DISPLAY-HEIGHT.
        DISPLAY "Gender " WS-GENDER.

    PROGRAM-END.
        STOP RUN.
```

> Assignment to edit field causes money amount to be shown with '$' symbol.

Items which are new are the SUBTRACT verb (another look-ahead to COBOL arithmetic in Chapter 3) and the edit fields in the WORKING-STORAGE section. (Notice also the 77 level data item, which I include just to show that it's legal). Let's consider the edit fields:

```
01 WS-DISPLAY-HEIGHT        PIC 9.99.
77 WS-DISPLAY-AGE           PIC ZZZ9.
01 WS-DISPLAY-INCOME        PIC $(6)9.
01 WS-DISPLAY-EXPEND        PIC $(6)9.
01 WS-DISPLAY-BALANCE       PIC $,$$$,$$9-.
```

Suppose a number with an assumed decimal point is moved to WS-DISPLAY-HEIGHT. WS-DISPLAY-HEIGHT is an edit data item because of the presence of an edit character in its PICTURE specification. When that data item is displayed, the output has an actual decimal point (the full-stop editing character) in the place required by the V in the PIC definition of the number moved to WS-DISPLAY-HEIGHT.

If an age variable holding, say, 029 is moved to WS-DISPLAY-AGE and that variable is displayed, the zero is suppressed on output because of the presence of the Z editing characters in WS-DISPLAY-AGE. ZZZ9 means the 029 is displayed as just 29. 005 would display as 5 and zero as 0. If a simple zero is the display and you want that instead to be blank, you can use the BLANK WHEN ZERO clause:

```
77 WS-DISPLAY-AGE  PIC ZZZ9 BLANK WHEN ZERO.
```

For currency, the $ symbol 'floats' so that just one of them appears immediately to the left of the numeric amount. 1975.27 (stored in a data item with an assumed decimal point) assigned to WS-DISPLAY-BALANCE is displayed as $1,975.27. Note that WS-DISPLAY-BALANCE also contains the comma edit character, which makes commas appear in the 'thousand' positions of output numbers as required.

Here's the output that the program generated when I ran it:

```
Personal COBOL version 2.0 from Micro Focus
PCOBRUN V2.0.02  Copyright (C) 1983-1993 Micro Focus Ltd.
Enter First Name
Conor
Enter Last Name
Sexton
Enter Address Line 1
Halley Court
Enter Address Line 2
Jordan Hill
Enter Address Line 3
Oxford OX2 8DP
Enter Age
29
Enter Income
50000
Enter Expenditure
60000
Enter Height in Metres
1.82
Enter Gender
m
First Name Conor
Last Name Sexton
Address Halley Court       Jordan Hill        Oxford OX2 8DP
Age    29
Income  $50000
Expenditure  $60000
Balance   $10,000-
Height 1.82
Gender m
```

50

From this, you can see that I'm in hock to the bank; I owe them the sum of $10,000, as shown by the trailing-minus editing symbol. This program does not cover all possible edit characters, but it does cover a sample representative of ordinary usage. The operation of the other edit characters is according to the same pattern. One of the major applications of data editing in COBOL programs is in generating and printing output reports. You'll see more of this in Chapter 5.

Alphanumeric editing

If you define a data item `ALPHA-EDIT`:

```
01  ALPHA-EDIT    PIC XX/BXX00.
```
and if you move a value to it:

```
MOVE "CS14" TO ALPHA-EDIT.
```
the content of `ALPHA-EDIT` will be this:

```
CS/_1400
```
where the underscore represents a blank space on output. This is an example of use of the B and 0 editing characters shown earlier. If you move a date string to an alphanumeric edited field:

```
01  OUTPUT-DATE        PIC XX/XX/XX.
    .
    .
MOVE "270274" TO OUTPUT-DATE.
```
the contents of `OUTPUT-DATE` when you display them are 27/02/74.

Tables

In this section, I introduce tables as a final aspect of PICTURE syntax. I explain in more detail in Chapters 3 and 4 how you can use tables in your COBOL programs. A *table* in COBOL is what is known in other languages as an *array*: a complex data item in which fields repeat. For example, you could have a table of 50 elements, where each element was a numeric elementary data item with a PICTURE specification of 999. You would then access (get at in memory) any given element of the table using *subscripts* or *indexes*.

Applications of tables in commercial COBOL programs are many. Consider a bank's requirement for storing deposit interest rates applicable to different amounts of money in a savings account. £1,000 might attract interest of 3%, £10,000 4%, £100,000 5.5%, and so on. To hold this data, we need a table of whole numbers for the money and a table of fractional numbers for the interest rates. In fact, one table holding both is the best solution:

```
01 INT-RATE-TABLE.
    02 INT-RATE-DATA OCCURS 50 TIMES.
        03 INT-PRINCIPAL    PIC 9(7).
        03 INT-RATE         PIC 99V999.
```

This group data item stores 50 elements for money (principal) amounts and 50 elements for interest-rates. It's the equivalent of making 100 separate PIC definitions, so it's a definite gain if you find yourself needing to define many variables of the same data class. You can initialise the whole table:

```
MOVE SPACES TO INT-RATE-TABLE.
```

or just one element of it:

```
MOVE SPACES TO INT-RATE-TABLE(14).
```

The latter assignment blanks-out table-element 14 (counting starts at 1 in COBOL) including both the subordinate data items. Alternatively, you can initialise an instance of INT-RATE:

```
MOVE 5.5 to INT-RATE(3).
```

You might ask, in the example above, why are three levels needed? The answer is that COBOL-74 doesn't allow OCCURS clauses in 01-level specifications and prohibits the simpler form:

```
01 INT-RATE-TABLE OCCURS 50 TIMES.
    02 INT-PRINCIPAL      PIC 9(7).
    02 INT-RATE           PIC 99V999.
```

This form is allowed by many COBOL-85-conforming compilers (including Personal COBOL) but still raises an ambiguity: what do you mean when you refer to INT-RATE-TABLE: the whole table, or just one element of the fifty? Personal COBOL assumes just one element. Because of this ambiguity, and the COBOL-74 restriction, it's best to use the three-level table specification that I showed first.

You can use data items, not just constants, as subscripts. You can define tables in either the WORKING-STORAGE section or in file definitions. No more than seven subscripts are allowable: you can't have tables of more than seven dimensions. I give more rules for tables in Chapter 3.

One final aspect of tables definition: instead of using subscripts in the way I've shown, you have the option of defining and using an *index*:

```
01 INT-RATE-TABLE
    02 INT-RATE-DATA OCCURS 50 TIMES
       INDEXED BY RATE-INDEX.
        03 INT-PRINCIPAL       PIC 9(7).
        03 INT-RATE            PIC 99V999.
```

You don't assign to RATE-INDEX in the normal way (using MOVE). Instead, you use the SET verb:

```
SET RATE-INDEX TO 11.
MOVE 6.5 TO INT-RATE(RATE-INDEX).
```

You are not allowed perform arithmetic of any kind on index variables; to increment RATE-INDEX by 1, you use the following syntax:

```
SET RATE-INDEX UP BY 1.
```

Exercises

1   Write down a PICTURE specification that will store any fractional numeric value, to two decimal places, positive or negative, in the range minus ten million to ten million.

2   What's wrong with the following data-item definitions?

```
01 CURRENCY              PIC X(10) VALUE "DOLLARS".
01 -NEGATIVE-NO          PIC SV99.
01 BANK-BALANCE-AFTER-CURRENCY-CONVERSION
                         PIC S9(6)V99.
```

3   Write a program that defines in WORKING-STORAGE a plausible insurance-policy group data item, initialises it by ACCEPTing data from the standard input and displays the data, suitably edited for output, on the screen.

3 Manipulating data

ACCEPT and DISPLAY

This chapter is about how you move, copy, do arithmetic with and otherwise manipulate data in your COBOL programs. Like the coverage of PICTUREs in Chapter 2, what you get here is a summary. Complete explanation of all aspects of the MOVE command, for example, could take the space available for this whole chapter. Instead, in this chapter, I summarise the main points of MOVE (and Screen I/O, arithmetic commands, string handling and record copying, to name but a few).

First up are the screen I/O commands, in a little more detail than I've shown so far. It seems reasonable to cover these first – getting data into and out of the program – and then to deal in the next section with moving that data around when it's in the program.

COBOL-85 doesn't support *graphical user interface* (GUI) I/O of the type popularised by the Microsoft Windows operating environments. Some COBOL products do provide GUI support but the purpose of this *Made Simple* book is to cover mainstream COBOL, so I don't deal with those products.

COBOL-85 environments such as Personal COBOL support simple character keyboard/screen I/O. You've seen some examples of this in earlier chapters. Although it's not part of the COBOL-85 Standard, Personal COBOL also provides simple *full-screen* I/O which is better suited to commercial applications. In this section, I introduce both these forms of character I/O.

The COBOL verbs for keyboard input and screen output are ACCEPT and DISPLAY. These are quite simple in the range of their syntax and options, unlike many COBOL verbs. ACCEPT is intended to allow programs to receive interactive input from sources other than files. The two main forms of ACCEPT are these:

```
ACCEPT identifier [mnemonic-name].
ACCEPT identifier FROM {DATE, DAY, DAY-OF-WEEK, TIME}.
```

In these general formats (and for any that I include from now on), square brackets mean that something is optional, while curly braces mean that you have to select one item from a set of options within.

The first case is what you've already become used to: taking input from the standard input (keyboard) and placing that input in an area of the computer's memory named by an identifier, which is a COBOL data-item. So, in previous programs, we did this sort of thing:

```
ACCEPT WS-FNAME.
```

and your first name ended up in the memory represented by the data item WS-FNAME. The optional *mnemonic-name* is a name that you specify (in the SPECIAL-NAMES section of the ENVIRONMENT division) to represent, usually, a peripheral device such as a printer or teletype. I explain the mnemonic name a little more later in this section, but I'm not going to worry about it very much and you shouldn't either.

The second of the general forms of ACCEPT allows you to retrieve from the system one of the date, day (day number since the start of the year), time or the (numeric) day of the week. This is useful and I give a program a little later that shows all the possibilities.

The general form of DISPLAY is this:

```
DISPLAY identifier [UPON mnemonic-name] [WITH NO ADVANCING].
```

When I use underlining in these general forms, it means that the underlined words in an optional group must be used where the option is taken. So, in this case, you could write:

```
DISPLAY "Enter first name: " WS-FNAME NO ADVANCING.
```

NO ADVANCING means that the screen cursor does not advance to the next line on the display before waiting for input from you. The mnemonic-name could be used as with ACCEPT to represent an output device. The next program, SIMPLEIO.CBL, exercises some of these possibilities.

This program is similar to several that I present in Chapters 1 and 2. The two major changes are the uses of the NO ADVANCING subclause of DISPLAY and the introduction of the SPECIAL-NAMES clause. NO ADVANCING makes for cleaner-appearing screen I/O: the DISPLAYed prompt and your input can be on the same line.

```
*************************************************************
*                                                          *
*      This program performs simple input and output of text  *
*      using ACCEPT and DISPLAY.                           *
*                                                          *
*************************************************************
 IDENTIFICATION DIVISION.
 PROGRAM-ID. SIMPLEIO.

 ENVIRONMENT DIVISION.
 CONFIGURATION SECTION.
 SPECIAL-NAMES.
     CURRENCY SIGN IS "£".
 DATA DIVISION.
 WORKING-STORAGE SECTION.
 01 WS-PERSONAL-DETAILS.
     02 WS-LNAME          PIC X(15).
     02 WS-FNAME          PIC X(15).
     02 WS-ADDR.
         03 WS-ADDR1      PIC A(20).
         03 WS-ADDR2      PIC A(20).
         03 WS-ADDR3      PIC A(20).
     02 WS-INCOME         PIC 9(6)V99.

 01 WS-DISPLAY-INCOME     PIC £££,££9.99.

 PROCEDURE DIVISION.
 GET-PERSONAL-DETAILS.
     DISPLAY "Enter First Name " WITH NO ADVANCING.
     ACCEPT WS-FNAME.
     DISPLAY "Enter Last Name " WITH NO ADVANCING.
     ACCEPT WS-LNAME.
     DISPLAY "Enter Address Line 1 " WITH NO ADVANCING.
     ACCEPT WS-ADDR1.
     DISPLAY "Enter Address Line 2 " WITH NO ADVANCING.
     ACCEPT WS-ADDR2.
     DISPLAY "Enter Address Line 3 " NO ADVANCING.
     ACCEPT WS-ADDR3.
     DISPLAY "Enter Income " WITH NO ADVANCING.
     ACCEPT WS-INCOME.

 DISPLAY-PERSONAL-DETAILS.
     DISPLAY "First Name " WS-FNAME.
     DISPLAY "Last Name " WS-LNAME.
     DISPLAY "Address " WS-ADDR.
     MOVE WS-INCOME TO WS-DISPLAY-INCOME.
     DISPLAY "Income " WS-DISPLAY-INCOME.

 PROGRAM-END.
     STOP RUN.
```

NO ADVANCING sets the input is on the same lines as the successive prompts.

The **WITH** of the **NO ADVANCING** subclause is a *noise-word*: it's there for readability only and you may omit it.

58

Here's the sequence as it appeared when I ran the program:

```
Personal COBOL version 2.0 from Micro Focus
PCOBRUN V2.0.02  Copyright (C) 1983-1993 Micro Focus Ltd.
Enter First Name Conor
Enter Last Name Sexton
Enter Address Line 1 Halley Court
Enter Address Line 2 Jordan Hill
Enter Address Line 3 Oxford OX2 8DP
Enter Income 50000
First Name Conor
Last Name Sexton
Address Halley Court          Jordan Hill          Oxford OX2 8DP
Income £50,000.00
```

In previous examples, I used the US dollar symbol as the currency sign. In the UK (or Egypt, Ireland or Cyprust!), you'd prefer a pound-sign. Unfortunately, there's confusion here. To North Americans, the phrase *pound-sign* means the character '#' which, to inhabitants of the Old World is *hash*. Here, in the currency context, *pound-sign* means '£'. We can change from the default dollar-sign by specifying a new currency sign in the SPECIAL-NAMES clause:

```
SPECIAL-NAMES.
      CURRENCY SIGN IS "£".
```

Having done this, you can use the floating pound-sign in output edit fields as I did in Chapter 2 with the '$' symbol.

SPECIAL-NAMES is for definitions that you may use to customise your COBOL environment. Valid entries for Personal COBOL are:

```
SPECIAL-NAMES.
      CONSOLE IS CRT
      NUMERIC SIGN IS TRAILING.
```

after which you could write:

```
DISPLAY WS-FNAME UPON CRT.
```

COBOL-85 allows the entry:

```
SPECIAL-NAMES.
      DECIMAL POINT IS COMMA.
```

after which, in an edit field, the positions of the comma and the thousand-indicator can be transposed:

```
01 WS-MILLIONS     PIC Z.ZZZ.ZZ9,99.
```

as they would be on continental Europe.

Getting dates and times

As I've already pointed out, COBOL-85 allows you to get the system's date, time and other data. The program `DATEIO.CBL` shows these operations:

DATEIO.CBL

```
***********************************************************************
*                                                                     *
*   This program performs input and output of system date and         *
*   time using ACCEPT and DISPLAY.                                    *
*                                                                     *
***********************************************************************
    IDENTIFICATION DIVISION.
    PROGRAM-ID. DATEIO.

    DATA DIVISION.
    WORKING-STORAGE SECTION.
    01 WS-DATE.
        02 WS-DATE-YY    PIC 99.
        02 WS-DATE-MM    PIC 99.
        02 WS-DATE-DD    PIC 99.

    01 WS-DAY.
        02 WS-DAY-YY     PIC 99.
        02 WS-DAY-DDD    PIC 999.

    01 WS-TIME.
        02 WS-TIME-HH    PIC 99.
        02 WS-TIME-MM    PIC 99.
        02 WS-TIME-SS    PIC 99.
        02 WS-TIME-DD    PIC 99.

    01 WS-DAY-OF-WEEK    PIC 9.

    PROCEDURE DIVISION.
    GET-DATA.
        ACCEPT WS-DATE FROM DATE.
        ACCEPT WS-DAY FROM DAY.
        ACCEPT WS-TIME FROM TIME.
        ACCEPT WS-DAY-OF-WEEK FROM DAY-OF-WEEK.
        DISPLAY "System date " WS-DATE.
        DISPLAY "System day " WS-DAY.
        DISPLAY "System time " WS-TIME.
        DISPLAY "System day of week " WS-DAY-OF-WEEK.

    PROGRAM-END.
        STOP RUN.
```

You can ACCEPT data from the reserved words DATE, TIME, DAY or DAY-OF-WEEK as shown. The COBOL system gives you these as, effectively, built-in data items. These built-in data items have the same PICTUREs as I've used in the program. Note that WS-DATE assumes a two-digit year. Do you see a problem here? Have a look at Chapter 7. The output of DATEIO.CBL when I ran it was this:

```
Personal COBOL version 2.0 from Micro Focus
PCOBRUN V2.0.02  Copyright (C) 1983-1993 Micro Focus Ltd.
System date 971208
System day 97342
System time 15232960
System day of week 1
```

You can see from this that the format of the built-in DATE data item is *yymmdd*; DAY holds the year (97) and the day-number (342, or December 8); and the time is 29.6 seconds after 23 minutes past three in the afternoon. The day-of-the-week is 1 (Monday).

You'll find yourself, as a COBOL programmer, using these built-in date-day facilities all the time. If you're not careful, though, you can fall into the Year 2000 (Y2K) trap. This manifests itself in the form, for example, of the two-digit year ACCEPTed from the DATE variable. Again, for more on this, see Chapter 7.

Screen I/O

Getting and displaying data using sequences of ACCEPT and DISPLAY verbs as in the examples up to now is fine, but it's not suitable for many real-life purposes. For example, how would you check that, if the value of input field 2 were such-and-such, the contents of field 5 should not exceed something else? For this, we need full-screen I/O: the ability to accept a full screen at a time.

COBOL-85 doesn't specify screen I/O; it's left to individual COBOL environments to specify their own implementations. This means that there is no standard for screen I/O and programs that use it may not be portable between systems. In practice, however, there is a lot in common between screen I/O implementations and the next example should run on any. The size of the Personal COBOL screen I/O subsystem precludes any detailed consideration of it here. The program that follows, SCRNI01.CBL, is just to give you a flavour:

SCRNI01.CBL

```
**********************************************************************
*                                                                    *
*   Screen input and output using ACCEPT and DISPLAY.                *
*                                                                    *
**********************************************************************
       IDENTIFICATION DIVISION.
       PROGRAM-ID. SCRNI01.

       ENVIRONMENT DIVISION.
       CONFIGURATION SECTION.

       DATA DIVISION.
       WORKING-STORAGE SECTION.
       01   YOUR-ID       PIC X(10).
       01   YOUR-PASSWORD  PIC X(10).

       SCREEN SECTION.
       01 SCREEN-DISPLAY.
          02 BLANK SCREEN.
          02 LINE 10 COL 10   VALUE "Your login ID: ".
          02 LINE 10 COL 25   PIC X(10) USING YOUR-ID.
          02 LINE 12 COL 10   VALUE "Your password: ".
          02 LINE 12 COL 25   PIC X(10) USING YOUR-PASSWORD NO-ECHO.
```

NO-ECHO is just a hint of the power of this Screens system: to keep the password secret, it is not 'echoed' (displayed) on the screen as you type it

62

```
PROCEDURE DIVISION.
DISPLAY-ACCEPT.
    DISPLAY SCREEN-DISPLAY.
    ACCEPT SCREEN-DISPLAY.

DISPLAY-OK.
    DISPLAY "OK, " LINE 20 COL 15.
    DISPLAY YOUR-ID LINE 20 COL 20.
    DISPLAY "your password is: " LINE 20 COL 30.
    DISPLAY YOUR-PASSWORD LINE 20 COL 48.
    STOP RUN.
```

Notice that there's a SCREEN section following WORKING-STORAGE. This section defines, using a group data item, the layout of the form that SCRNI01.CBL displays when it runs. For example, the line:

    02 LINE 12 COL 25 PIC X(10) USING YOUR-PASSWORD NO-ECHO.

causes your input at line 12, column 25 of the screen to be accepted and stored in an area of memory represented by the data item YOUR-PASSWORD.

After you've run the program and made entries to the two data fields, the DOS screen looks like this:

63

MOVE

MOVE is the most heavily-used of all COBOL verbs. Its effect is to copy the contents of one data item to the memory represented by a second, overwriting its existing contents. The validity of the data transfer is governed by the classes of the 'sending' and 'receiving' data items.

MOVE is very simple in principle, with only one general form:

```
MOVE {CORRESPONDING, CORR} identifier1 TO identifier2.
```

Programmers often don't fully understand the operation of the MOVE command and its side-effects. If you know the rules, which are simple, you'll find that your life as a COBOL programmer is somewhat easier.

COBOL (unlike, say, C or Pascal) isn't a strongly-typed language: it's usually easy to mix and copy items of different data classes. For example, there's nothing wrong with moving a whole number (PIC 9) to an alphanumeric field (PIC X); the COBOL system will implement the move with a suitable (and usually desired) conversion.

COBOL-85 imposes only one major restriction in the data classes you can use in a MOVE statement: you cannot MOVE an alphanumeric-edited data item to a numeric data item. Depending on how your compiler implements the COBOL standard, however, there may be some further restrictions. For example, in addition to implementing the rules of COBOL-85, Personal COBOL doesn't let you move a numeric quantity to an alphabetic field. I wrote the next program, MOVEX.CBL, to check the behaviour of the Personal COBOL compiler.

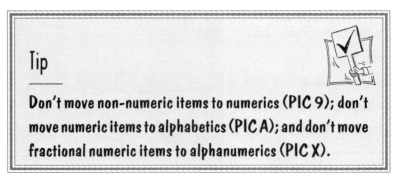

Tip

Don't move non-numeric items to numerics (PIC 9); don't move numeric items to alphabetics (PIC A); and don't move fractional numeric items to alphanumerics (PIC X).

If your code has survived all that, there's still the possibility either that the source data item (the one being MOVEd) is smaller than the destination data item (the one being MOVEd to), or vice-versa.

```
      IDENTIFICATION DIVISION.
      PROGRAM-ID. MOVEX.

      DATA DIVISION.
      WORKING-STORAGE SECTION.
      01 WS-DAY-X      PIC X(10).
      01 WS-DAY-A      PIC A(10).
      01 WS-DATE-EDIT  PIC XX/XX/XX.
      01 WS-DAYNO      PIC 9(10).

      PROCEDURE DIVISION.
      CLASS-TEST.
  *       Alphanumeric edited to numeric, COBOL-85 illegal
  *       MOVE WS-DATE-EDIT TO WS-DAYNO.
  *       Alphabetic to numeric, illegal
  *       MOVE WS-DAY-A TO WS-DAYNO.
  *       Alphanumeric to numeric, (surprisingly) legal
          MOVE WS-DAY-X TO WS-DAYNO.
  *       Numeric integer to alphabetic, illegal
  *       MOVE 5 TO WS-DAY-A.
  *       Fractional numeric to alphabetic, illegal
  *       MOVE 1.732 TO WS-DAY-A.
  *       Fractional numeric to alphanumeric, illegal
  *       MOVE 1.732 TO WS-DAY-X.

      PROGRAM-END.
          STOP RUN.
```

> The first MOVE statement is the only one that's strictly illegal according to the COBOL-85 specification. However, Personal COBOL rejects all but one of the other five MOVEs.

The following rules apply:

- If the destination data item is alphabetic or alphanumeric and is smaller than the source data item, the destination data item is left-adjusted and truncated from the right.

- If the destination data item is alphabetic or alphanumeric and is larger than the source data item, the destination data item is left-adjusted and padded with blanks on the right.

- If the destination data item is numeric and is smaller than the source data item, the destination data item is right-adjusted and truncated from the left.

- If the destination data item is numeric and is larger than the source data item, the destination data item is right-adjusted and padded with zeros on the left.

As I point out in Chapter 2, `JUST RIGHT` can be used to override the default left-alignment of data `MOVE`d to an alphanumeric data item.

```
01  SOURCE-ITEM        PIC XXX VALUE "AAA".
01  DEST-ITEM          PIC X(7) JUST RIGHT.
         .
         MOVE SOURCE-ITEM TO DEST-ITEM.
*   DEST-ITEM contents: ____AAA
```

In general a group data item (a `01`-level identifier with one or more subordinate data items) is of alphanumeric data class. Where one group data item is moved to another, the receiving structure will be left aligned, but the alignment of data within the constituent elementary data items may not be correct. The program `MOVEGRP.CBL` shows this:

MOVEGRP.CBL

```
******************************************************************
*                                                                *
* This program shows the consequences of an unaligned group MOVE *
*                                                                *
******************************************************************
      IDENTIFICATION DIVISION.
      PROGRAM-ID. MOVEGRP.

      DATA DIVISION.
      WORKING-STORAGE SECTION.
      01 WS-GROUP-1.
         02 WS-ITEM-1-1   PIC X(15).
         02 WS-ITEM-2-1   PIC 9(6).

      01 WS-GROUP-2.
         02 WS-ITEM-1-2   PIC 9(6).
         02 WS-ITEM-2-2   PIC X(15).

      PROCEDURE DIVISION.
      GROUP-INIT.
         MOVE 123456 TO WS-ITEM-1-2.
         MOVE "ABCDEFGHIJKLMNO" TO WS-ITEM-2-2.
         DISPLAY "Group item 2 " WS-GROUP-2.
         MOVE WS-GROUP-2 TO WS-GROUP-1.
         DISPLAY "Group item 1 " WS-GROUP-1.
         DISPLAY "Alphanumeric " WS-ITEM-1-1.
         DISPLAY "Numeric " WS-ITEM-2-1.

      PROGRAM-END.
         STOP RUN.
```

Group assignment causes numeric data item in **WS-GROUP-1** to be filled with letters.

66

The output clearly shows what happens with this:

```
Personal COBOL version 2.0 from Micro Focus
PCOBRUN V2.0.02  Copyright (C) 1983-1993 Micro Focus Ltd.
Group item 2 123456ABCDEFGHIJKLMNO
Group item 1 123456ABCDEFGHIJKLMNO
Alphanumeric 123456ABCDEFGHI
Numeric JKLMNO
```

The two group data items are quite different in the alignments of their elementary data items. In the end, because of the group-level MOVE, the numeric field WS-ITEM-2-1 comes to (wrongly) contain the text JKLMNO. When moving group data items, you should either move the subordinate elementary data items individually or, if you must MOVE at the 01 level, make sure that the layouts and lengths of the source and destination items are identical.

MOVE CORRESPONDING

The second form of the MOVE command is MOVE CORRESPONDING. Rather than give lengthy examples of this, I summarise its effect.

If two group data items G1 and G2 each contain subordinate elementary items A, B, C, D and E (but they appear in different order within the two group items), then the command:

```
MOVE CORRESPONDING G1 TO G2.
```

moves A from G1 to A in G2, B from G1 to B in G2, and so on, regardless of the relative positions of the elementary data items. If there were an elementary item F in G1 only, the MOVE CORRESPONDING would not move it to G2, since there is no counterpart of F in G2. You can also do this:

```
MOVE C IN G1 TO C OF G2.
```

where the IN and OF are synonymous and interchangeable. The effect of this data item *qualification* is that you are allowed define more than one data item of a given name in the DATA division, provided they are subordinate to and qualified by different group data items. In example I've given, there are two group items, G1 and G2. Both have subordinate elementary data items called C but, because of the qualification, there is no ambiguity.

Redefining and renaming data items

Suppose you defined a (probably group) data item of alphanumeric data class and later you wanted arithmetically to add one to the contents of that data item. How could you do it? The answer lies in temporarily treating the alphanumeric item as numeric for purpose of the addition.

COBOL provides two verbs for *looking at data storage in a different way*: REDEFINES and RENAMES. Of these, REDEFINES is commonly used and pretty much indispensable; RENAMES, on the other hand, isn't very elegant and its use is frowned upon. In this section, I'll mention RENAMES but concentrate on REDEFINES.

REDEFINES

Before I enumerate the major rules governing use of REDEFINES, here's an example of its use. In the program DATEIO.CBL earlier in this chapter, there is a group data item for storing a date:

```
01 WS-DATE.
    02 WS-DATE-YY  PIC 99.
    02 WS-DATE-MM  PIC 99.
    02 WS-DATE-DD  PIC 99.
```

Because it's a group data item, it's inherently of alphanumeric data class. If we wanted to add one to the date, you can't simply do:

```
ADD 1 TO WS-DATE.
```

The COBOL compiler rejects this, complaining that the ADD must have a numeric operand. Instead, we redefine WS-DATE like this:

```
01 WS-DATE.
    02 WS-DATE-YY  PIC 99.
    02 WS-DATE-MM  PIC 99.
    02 WS-DATE-DD  PIC 99.
01 WS-DATE-N REDEFINES WS-DATE PIC 9(6).
```

WS-DATE-N maps the same area in memory as WS-DATE, but treats the data stored there as a numeric quantity. It's now OK to write:

```
ADD 1 TO WS-DATE-N.
```

The date is incremented by one which, notice, gives a correct result because the date is stored in *yymmdd* form. 971209, representing 9th December, 1997 is correctly incremented to 971210.

Strictly, where you redefine a data item such as WS-DATE, you're redefining the data class (type) of WS-DATE by mapping another name onto the memory area represented by WS-DATE. This remapping takes place starting at the first character position of WS-DATE. As I show in Chapter 5, you can define a file with more than one record specified at the 01 level. The second and subsequent record specifications are effective redefinitions of the first, again starting at the first character position.

A redefinition must be the same length as or shorter than the area it remaps; you could redefine WS-DATE just to get a numeric representation of the year and month:

```
01 WS-DATE.
   02 WS-DATE-YY  PIC 99.
   02 WS-DATE-MM  PIC 99.
   02 WS-DATE-DD  PIC 99.
01 WS-YYMM REDEFINES WS-DATE PIC 9999.
```

Redefinitions can be used anywhere in the DATA division: in the WORKING-STORAGE section as shown, or as part of file definitions. The REDEFINES clause always immediately follows a previous definition of the same storage area. No other data items may intervene except those subordinate to a group item, in this case, WS-DATE, being redefined. It's illegal, therefore, to write:

```
01 WS-DATE.
   02 WS-DATE-YY        PIC 99.
   02 WS-DATE-MM        PIC 99.
   02 WS-DATE-DD        PIC 99.
01 SOME-OTHER-ITEM      PIC X.
01 WS-DATE-N REDEFINES WS-DATE PIC 9(6).
```

The level numbers of the redefined and redefining items must be the same. You can repeat redefinitions:

```
01 WS-DATE.
   02 WS-DATE-YY        PIC 99.
   02 WS-DATE-MM        PIC 99.
   02 WS-DATE-DD        PIC 99.
01 WS-DATE-N REDEFINES WS-DATE PIC 9(6).
01 WS-YYMM REDEFINES WS-DATE   PIC 9999.
```

but note that the REDEFINES clauses always refer to the original data item definition.

You can also nest REDEFINES clauses:

```
01 WS-DATE.
    02 WS-DATE-YY PIC 99.
    02 WS-DATE-MM PIC 99.
    02 WS-DATE-DD PIC 99.
01 WS-DATE-N REDEFINES WS-DATE.
    02 WS-YYMM.
        03 WS-DATE-YY  PIC 99.
        03 WS-DATE-MM  PIC 99.
    02 WS-YYMM-N REDEFINES WS-YYMM.
    02 WS-DATE-DD.
```

You can't put a VALUE clause within a REDEFINES, but it's OK to place it in the item being redefined. So, the code following is valid:

```
01 WS-DATE.
    02 WS-DATE-YY PIC 99 VALUE 97.
    02 WS-DATE-MM PIC 99 VALUE 12.
    02 WS-DATE-DD PIC 99 VALUE 09.
01 WS-DATE-N REDEFINES WS-DATE PIC 9(6).
```

while this isn't:

```
01 WS-DATE.
    02 WS-DATE-YY PIC 99 VALUE 97.
    02 WS-DATE-MM PIC 99 VALUE 12.
    02 WS-DATE-DD PIC 99 VALUE 09.
01 WS-DATE-N REDEFINES WS-DATE.
 * Wrong VALUE clause following!!
    02 WS-DATE-YY-2    PIC 99 VALUE 99.
        .
```

RENAMES

The RENAMES clause, specified as a 66 level, works like this. Consider a group data item:

```
01 PAYROLL-DATA.
    02 PR-NAME.
        03 PR-FNAME           PIC X(15).
        03 PR-MNAME           PIC X(10).
        03 PR-LNAME           PIC X(10).
    02 PR-NUMBERS.
        03 PR-NAT-INS         PIC X(10).
        03 PR-TAX-FREE        PIC 9999V99.
    66 PR-ID-DATA RENAMES PR-LNAME THRU PR-NAT-INS.
```

Now, PR-ID-DATA is equivalent to a group definition made at the 02 level containing as subordinate data items PR-LNAME and PR-NAT-INS. In simple cases, RENAMES can be convenient. Otherwise, however, it tends to be confusing and you're encouraged to avoid using it.

70

Arithmetic

COBOL isn't suited for heavy-duty mathematical calculations of the type commonly carried out in languages such as C and (especially) Fortran. It is good, though, for basic business-level arithmetic. When it comes down to it, business mathematics rarely goes beyond multiplication and division unless, perhaps, you're an insurance actuary or spend your time doing compound-interest calculations. The COBOL arithmetic verbs are these:

ADD   SUBTRACT   MULTIPLY   DIVIDE   COMPUTE

The last of these allows you to write algebraic-type arithmetic statements of the type favoured by C and Fortran, for example $A = B * C / D$. The others – more common in conventional COBOL usage – allow simpler but more verbose and expressive arithmetic calculations.

The general forms of these five statements are too complex and long to give here, so what follows is a set of representative examples:

COBOL Statement	Explanation
ADD A TO B.	(B contains the sum of A and B)
ADD A TO B GIVING C.	(C contains the sum of A and B, B unchanged)
ADD A TO B GIVING X Y.	(X and Y contain the sum of A and B, A and B unchanged)
SUBTRACT A FROM B.	(B is reduced by the amount A)
SUBTRACT A FROM B GIVING C.	(Result of B - A placed in C, A and B unchanged.
SUBTRACT A B FROM C.	(C is reduced by the sum of A and B, A and B unchanged)
MULTIPLY A BY B.	(B contains A * B, A unchanged)
MULTIPLY A BY B GIVING C.	(C contains A * B, A and B unchanged)
MULTIPLY A BY 1.73205 GIVING B ROUNDED.	(Result is rounded to fit B, A unchanged)
MULTIPLY A BY 1.73205 GIVING B ROUNDED C ROUNDED.	(Result is rounded to fit B and C, A unchanged)
DIVIDE A INTO B.	(B is assigned B/A, A unchanged)
DIVIDE A INTO B C ROUNDED.	(B is assigned B/A, A unchanged, C is assigned B/A rounded)
DIVIDE A BY B GIVING C.	(C is assigned A/B, A and B unchanged).
COMPUTE ROUNDED A = B * C / D.	(A is assigned B * C / D, rounded, B, C and D unchanged)

Here's a program, PAYROLL.CBL, which illustrates conventional COBOL arithmetic statements. It takes as input your yearly gross income and tax-free allowance and calculates your monthly net pay using an approximation to UK tax rules.

PAYROLL.CBL

```
**********************************************************************
*                                                                    *
* Calculates net monthly pay based on input of yearly income, an     *
* assumed tax-free allowance UK tax rates and National Insurance.*
*                                                                    *
**********************************************************************
 IDENTIFICATION DIVISION.
 PROGRAM-ID. PAYROLL.

 ENVIRONMENT DIVISION.
 CONFIGURATION SECTION.
 SPECIAL-NAMES.
     CURRENCY SIGN IS "£".
 DATA DIVISION.
 WORKING-STORAGE SECTION.
 01 WS-GROSS-YR          PIC 9(6).
 01 WS-GROSS-MTH         PIC 9(6)V99.
 01 WS-TAX-ALL-YR        PIC 9(6)V99.
 01 WS-TAX-ALL-MTH       PIC 9(6)V99.
 01 WS-TAXABLE-MTH       PIC 9(6)V99.
 01 WS-TAX-MTH           PIC 9(6)V99.
 01 WS-NAT-INS-MTH       PIC 9(6)V99.
 01 WS-NET-PAY-MTH       PIC 9(6)V99.
 01 WS-NET-PAY-YTD       PIC 9(6)V99 VALUE ZERO.
 01 WS-DISPLAY-NET-MTH   PIC £££,££9.99.
 01 WS-DISPLAY-NET-YTD   PIC £££,££9.99.

 PROCEDURE DIVISION.
 GET-INCOME-DETAILS.
     DISPLAY "Enter Yearly Gross Income " NO ADVANCING.
     ACCEPT WS-GROSS-YR.
     DIVIDE WS-GROSS-YR BY 12 GIVING WS-GROSS-MTH ROUNDED.
     DISPLAY "Enter Yearly Tax Free Allowance " NO ADVANCING.
     ACCEPT WS-TAX-ALL-YR.
     MOVE WS-TAX-ALL-YR TO WS-TAX-ALL-MTH.
     DIVIDE 12 INTO WS-TAX-ALL-MTH ROUNDED.
     SUBTRACT WS-TAX-ALL-MTH FROM WS-GROSS-MTH
         GIVING WS-TAXABLE-MTH.
     MULTIPLY WS-TAXABLE-MTH BY 0.4
         GIVING WS-TAX-MTH.
```

WS-NET-PAY-YTD initialised to zero.

```
        MULTIPLY WS-GROSS-MTH BY 0.09
             GIVING WS-NAT-INS-MTH.
        SUBTRACT WS-TAX-MTH WS-NAT-INS-MTH FROM WS-GROSS-MTH
             GIVING WS-NET-PAY-MTH.
        ADD WS-NET-PAY-MTH TO WS-NET-PAY-YTD.

    DISPLAY-INTERMEDIATE-DETAILS.
        DISPLAY "Monthly Gross Pay " WS-GROSS-MTH.
        DISPLAY "Monthly Tax Allowance " WS-TAX-ALL-MTH.
        DISPLAY "Monthly Taxable Pay " WS-TAXABLE-MTH.
        DISPLAY "Monthly Tax " WS-TAX-MTH.
        DISPLAY "Monthly National Insurance " WS-NAT-INS-MTH.

    DISPLAY-INCOME-DETAILS.
        DISPLAY " ".
        MOVE WS-NET-PAY-MTH TO WS-DISPLAY-NET-MTH.
        DISPLAY "Net Monthly Pay " WS-DISPLAY-NET-MTH.
        MOVE WS-NET-PAY-YTD TO WS-DISPLAY-NET-YTD.
        DISPLAY "Net Pay Year To Date " WS-DISPLAY-NET-YTD.

    PROGRAM-END.
        STOP RUN.
```

It's easiest to see what PAYROLL.CBL does by inspecting its output:

```
Enter Yearly Gross Income 50000
Enter Yearly Tax Free Allowance 10000
Monthly Gross Pay 00416667
Monthly Tax Allowance 00083333
Monthly Taxable Pay 00333334
Monthly Tax 00133333
Monthly National Insurance 00037500

Net Monthly Pay  £2,458.34
Net Pay Year To Date  £2,458.34
```

First, the monthly gross pay is calculated (notice the rounding!). The effect of using ROUNDED is simple: if numbers to the right of the decimal point must be truncated, and if the leftmost truncated digit is 5 or greater, the rightmost remaining digit is incremented by one. In this case, therefore, 416666 becomes 416667, the trailing two digits being after the assumed decimal point. From this a mount, tax at 40% and National Insurance at 9% are deducted. The result is your net pay.

Notice that I initialised the data item WS-NET-PAY-YTD to zero. In COBOL, you can't depend on a data item defined in WORKING-STORAGE having any particular value; an uninitialised data item has an *undefined* value. To use such a data item, especially in arithmetic, before initialising it is usually a serious mistake. WS-NET-PAY-YTD is the only data item in PAYROLL.CBL not to be initialised in one way or another before it is used. If it is not explicitly initialised to zero, execution of the ADD statement of which it is an operand causes a runtime error. The data class of WS-NET-PAY-YTD is numeric but the group item of which it is a member is, necessarily, alphabetic. Accordingly, WS-NET-PAY-YTD may initially contain blanks or other alphabetic characters; using this as an operand of ADD will cause an arithmetic *exception*.

Golden rule: initialise all data items, by assignment or with the VALUE clause, before using them for arithmetic or any other processing.

I don't show all the possibilities of arithmetic statements either in PAYROLL.CBL or in the preceding table. Only some ROUNDED options are used, while REMAINDER and ON SIZE ERROR don't appear at all. In general, you may optionally use any combination of the three options (REMAINDER for division only) in any COBOL arithmetic statement. Again, rather than enumerating in text all the possibilities of these options, I've included a program (opposite) to display their effect. Aptly enough, it's called ODDSUMS.CBL. It illustrates most of the rounding, remainder and size-error possibilities. This is the output:

```
Result of addition too large
Can't store square root of 30000000
Unrounded root of 3 is 00017320
Rounded root of 3 is 00017321
Dividend 00020833 Remainder 000000040
Dividend 0002 Remainder 0001
```

The first output line from the program itself:

```
Result of addition too large
```

shows the ON SIZE ERROR option in effect. The size of WS-RESULT to the left of the assumed decimal point is only four numeric characters, not enough to store 1000000. This condition is called numeric *overflow*. If the ADD statement used 1000 instead, it would not occur. Trying to get the square root of 300000000 invokes ON SIZE ERROR also; the whole-number part of the result is too large to be held in WS-RESULT.

74

```
***********************************************************************
*                                                                     *
*   Illustrates ROUNDED REMAINDER and ON SIZE ERROR options.          *
*                                                                     *
***********************************************************************
     IDENTIFICATION DIVISION.
     PROGRAM-ID. ODDSUMS.

     ENVIRONMENT DIVISION.

     DATA DIVISION.
     WORKING-STORAGE SECTION.
     01 WS-RESULT    PIC 9999V9999 VALUE ZEROS.
     01 WS-R         PIC 9999V99999 VALUE ZEROS.
     01 WS-INT1      PIC 9999.
     01 WS-INT2      PIC 9999.

     PROCEDURE DIVISION.
     DO-ODD-SUMS.
         ADD 1000000 TO WS-RESULT
            ON SIZE ERROR DISPLAY "Result of addition too large".
         COMPUTE WS-RESULT = 3 ** .5
            ON SIZE ERROR DISPLAY "Can't store square root of 3".
         COMPUTE WS-RESULT = 300000000 ** .5
            ON SIZE ERROR
            DISPLAY "Can't store square root of 30000000".
         COMPUTE WS-RESULT = 3 ** .5
         DISPLAY "Unrounded root of 3 is " WS-RESULT.
         COMPUTE WS-RESULT ROUNDED = 3 ** .5
         DISPLAY "Rounded root of 3 is " WS-RESULT.
         DIVIDE 25 BY 12 GIVING WS-RESULT REMAINDER WS-R.
         DISPLAY "Dividend " WS-RESULT " Remainder " WS-R.
         DIVIDE 25 BY 12 GIVING WS-INT1 REMAINDER WS-INT2.
         DISPLAY "Dividend " WS-INT1 " Remainder " WS-INT2.

     PROGRAM-END.
         STOP RUN.
```

Having insufficient decimal points of precision does not cause overflow. The square root of 3 is (approx.) 1.732050808. The fractional part of this doesn't fit in the four positions specified in WS-RESULT to the right of the assumed decimal point. Nevertheless, the ON SIZE ERROR condition doesn't arise; the number is simply right-truncated to 1.7320. In the next line, using ROUNDED, the root is given as 1.7321.

In the final two lines of output, you can see that the REMAINDER option really only makes sense when used in the division of two whole numbers. 25/12 gives a somewhat obscure remainder of 0.00040 when the data items being assigned and used for the remainder are fractional. When they are whole numbers, the remainder is the predictable 1.

COMPUTE and operator precedence

You will recall the arithmetic operators: unary + and -; + (addition); - (subtraction); * (multiplication); / (division); and ** (exponentiation). An operator must be written with at least one space on either side. This is to avoid confusion: in COBOL, A-B is a data item name, while A - B (used with COMPUTE) is an arithmetic subtraction.

The precedence of operators is a standard one. Unary + and - are highest, followed by **, then * and /, and finally + and -. Here are a few simple examples, which assume that data items A, B and C respectively have the initial values 5, 6 and 7.

Expression	Value
A + B - C	4
A - B + C	6
A * B + C	37
A + B * C	47
A ** C - A	78120
A ** B / C	2232.14...
A * - B + C	-23

Using parentheses overrides precedence: A * (B + C) has the value 65, not 37. Where the precedence of operators is the same, parentheses make no difference: A + (B - C) still has the value 4.

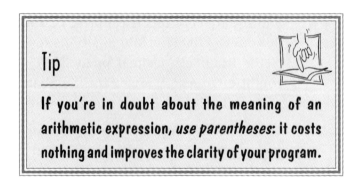

Tip

If you're in doubt about the meaning of an arithmetic expression, *use parentheses*: it costs nothing and improves the clarity of your program.

Working with tables

In Chapter 2, I explain the rudiments of how COBOL handles repeating data in tables, or arrays. In this section, I go into a few more of the details and variations surrounding tables, looking particularly at how tables and the REDEFINES clause can be used together. The two example programs use the IF...GO TO verb combination to *traverse* tables. That gives simple code, but be aware that using PERFORM with tables is better practice. I explain PERFORM in Chapter 4.

The table definition:

```
03 WS-TAB PIC 9999 OCCURS 5.
```

means that there are five data items called WS-TAB, each representing a four-digit unsigned integer; the five data items occupy 20 consecutive character positions in memory; and the data items are referred to individually as WS-TAB(1)....WS-TAB(5). The numbers in brackets are subscripts, which run from 1 to the limit defined in the OCCURS clause. Note that to use TIMES, as in OCCURS 5 TIMES, is optional. The OCCURS limit must be a numeric constant – COBOL does not support variable array bounds. I look at indexes, as the alternative to subscripts, in the context of PERFORM in Chapter 4.

You can define a table of group items:

```
02 WS-TAB OCCURS 3.
    03 WS-ITEM1   PIC 99.
    03 WS-ITEM2   PIC XXX.
```

where each occurrence of WS-TAB occupies six character positions in memory and a subscript in the range 1 to 3 must be used to access WS-ITEM1 and WS-ITEM2. For example, WS-ITEM1(2) refers to the second of three such data items in the table. If you were to write this statement:

```
MOVE SPACES TO WS-TAB.
```

you'd generate a compiler message complaining about the absence of a subscript value: which instance of WS-TAB do you mean? You can avoid the problem by extending the group item definition:

```
01 WS-TAB.
    02 WS-TAB-DATA OCCURS 3.
        03 WS-ITEM1   PIC 99.
        03 WS-ITEM2   PIC XXX.
```

Now, the target of the `MOVE`, `WS-TAB`, is unambiguous. I also refer to this ambiguity in Chapter 2. The last group definition above is best from the standpoint of backward-compatibility: the COBOL-74 standard and many compilers do not support use of `OCCURS` at the `01` level:

```
* This code probably illegal
  01 WS-TAB OCCURS 3.
      02 WS-ITEM1     PIC 99.
      02 WS-ITEM2     PIC XXX.
```

In a table of group data items, such as `WS-TAB-DATA` above, you must not specify a `PICTURE` with the `OCCURS` clause. The two may only appear in the same definition where the data item defined is elementary:

```
* Wrong!
      02 WS-TAB PIC X(5) OCCURS 3.
          03 WS-ITEM1     PIC 99.
          03 WS-ITEM2     PIC XXX.

* This is OK
      02 WS-TAB OCCURS 3.
          03 WS-ITEM1     PIC 99 OCCURS 4.
          03 WS-ITEM2     PIC XXX.
```

Just as the subscript limit specified in the `OCCURS` clause must be a numeric constant, so there are restrictions on how you specify a subscript itself. You can use only a positive numeric constant, a simple numeric data item, or a combination of the two such as `WS-SUB` + 1, as a subscript. You must not use numeric constants or data items of value less than 1, a table entry or a general arithmetic expression as a subscript.

The next simple example program, `TABLE1.CBL`, illustrates some of the syntax and use of a simple table.

I ask the purists among you to show forbearance. The IF...GO TO sequence used here to implement the loop around the table is not best practice. Using PERFORM in a structured manner (Chapter 4) is better. But the code is simple, readable, saves me having to explain PERFORM now and is satisfactory for a small program. Also, in your travels as a COBOL programmer, you'll encounter masses of code like it.

TABLE1.CBL

```
*********************************************************************
*                                                                 *
*  This program illustrates simple table processing.              *
*                                                                 *
*********************************************************************
    IDENTIFICATION DIVISION.
    PROGRAM-ID. TABLE1.

    ENVIRONMENT DIVISION.

    DATA DIVISION.
    WORKING-STORAGE SECTION.
    01 INT-RATE-TABLE.
        02 INT-RATE-DATA OCCURS 10 VALUE ALL '53'.
            03 INT-PRINCIPAL        PIC 9(7).
            03 INT-RATE             PIC 99V999.
    01 WS-SUB                       PIC 999 COMP.

    PROCEDURE DIVISION.
    PROGRAM-START.
        MOVE 1 TO WS-SUB.

    DISPLAY-ELEMENTS.
        DISPLAY "Principal " WS-SUB " " INT-PRINCIPAL(WS-SUB).
        DISPLAY "Rate " WS-SUB " " INT-RATE(WS-SUB).
        IF WS-SUB GREATER THAN 4
            GO TO DISPLAY-TABLE.
        ADD 1 TO WS-SUB.
            GO TO DISPLAY-ELEMENTS.

    DISPLAY-TABLE.
        DISPLAY "The whole table " INT-RATE-TABLE.

    PROGRAM-END.
        STOP RUN.
```

The group table definition:

```
01 INT-RATE-TABLE.
    02 INT-RATE-DATA OCCURS 10 VALUE ALL '53'.
        03 INT-PRINCIPAL        PIC 9(7).
        03 INT-RATE             PIC 99V999.
```

specifies a table of ten elements, where each element contains subordinate whole-number and fractional data items. To illustrate use of the ALL figurative constant (see *The COBOL Alphabet* in Chapter 2), all 120 character positions occupied in memory by the table are initialised to alternating 5s and 3s. The paragraph DISPLAY-

ELEMENTS displays the numeric values for each of the first four table elements, while DISPLAY-TABLE displays the contents of the whole table by referring to the group data item INT-RATE-TABLE. The output results look like this:

```
Personal COBOL version 2.0 from Micro Focus
PCOBRUN V2.0.02  Copyright (C) 1983-1993 Micro Focus Ltd.
Principal 001 5353535
Rate 001 35353
Principal 002 5353535
Rate 002 35353
Principal 003 5353535
Rate 003 35353
Principal 004 5353535
Rate 004 35353
Principal 005 5353535
Rate 005 35353
The whole table 5353535353535353535353535353535353535353535353535353535353535353
5353535353535353535353535353535353535353535353535353535353535353535353535353
```

As with all group data items, INT-RATE-TABLE is of alphanumeric data class. This is why the VALUE ALL clause specifies '53' as an alphanumeric rather than a numeric initialising value. When the contents of the whole table are displayed at the end, you're looking at an alphanumeric value. By contrast, consider the first of the five loops executed in the paragraph DISPLAY-ELEMENTS. Here, the lines

```
Principal 001 5353535
Rate 001 35353
```

are displayed. INT-PRINCIPAL(1) is a numeric data item holding a whole number somewhat greater than five million. INT-RATE(1) is a numeric data item holding, because of the assumed decimal point, a fractional value just greater than 35. Five such numeric pairs are displayed.

Finally, notice that the data item used as the subscript, WS-SUB, is defined as COMPUTATIONAL for more efficient performance. The most appropriate use of COMPUTATIONAL is when you have a small, often-used numeric variable. Subscript data items qualify on both counts and are therefore often specified as COMPUTATIONAL.

Table iInitialisation

In `TABLE1.CBL`, I crudely initialised the whole table to the string '5353535…'. How would we do a real initialisation? The answer is shown in the following, very important, example, `TABLE2.CBL`:

TABLE2.CBL

```
******************************************************************
*                                                              *
*   Illustrates use of REDEFINES with table initialisation     *
*                                                              *
******************************************************************
 IDENTIFICATION DIVISION.
 PROGRAM-ID. TABLE2.

 ENVIRONMENT DIVISION.

 DATA DIVISION.
 WORKING-STORAGE SECTION.
 01  INT-RATE-TABLE.
     02 INT-RATE-DATA.
         03 FILLER PIC 9(7)          VALUE 1000.
         03 FILLER PIC 99V999        VALUE 3.5.
         03 FILLER PIC 9(7)          VALUE 5000.
         03 FILLER PIC 99V999        VALUE 4.5.
         03 FILLER PIC 9(7)          VALUE 10000.
         03 FILLER PIC 99V999        VALUE 5.0.
         03 FILLER PIC 9(7)          VALUE 50000.
         03 FILLER PIC 99V999        VALUE 6.5.
         03 FILLER PIC 9(7)          VALUE 100000.
         03 FILLER PIC 99V999        VALUE 7.5.
     02 FILLER REDEFINES INT-RATE-DATA.
         03 FILLER OCCURS 5.
             04 INT-PRINCIPAL        PIC 9(7).
             04 INT-RATE             PIC 99V999.
 01  WS-SUB       PIC 999 COMP.

 PROCEDURE DIVISION.
 PROGRAM-START.
     MOVE 1 TO WS-SUB.

 DISPLAY-ELEMENTS.
     DISPLAY "Principal " WS-SUB " " INT-PRINCIPAL(WS-SUB).
     DISPLAY "Rate " WS-SUB " " INT-RATE(WS-SUB).
     IF WS-SUB GREATER THAN 4
         GO TO PROGRAM-END.
     ADD 1 TO WS-SUB.
         GO TO DISPLAY-ELEMENTS.

 PROGRAM-END.
     STOP RUN.
```

> FILLER data items are just used to initialise memory with data.

> The memory is REDFINEd as a table with meaningful data names.

This is a characteristic example of how, in real COBOL-programming life, you'd give a table an initial set of values, using *static initialisation*. In the group item INT-RATE-DATA, the subordinate elementary data items are each given initialising values. Here, they are money amounts each associated with a (fractional) interest rate. But this initialisation is of individual data items. In order to treat the successive pairs of data items as a table, we redefine INT-RATE-DATA with the lines:

```
02 FILLER REDEFINES INT-RATE-DATA.
   03 FILLER OCCURS 5.
```

Here, we're only interested in the data items – INT-PRINCIPAL and INT-RATE – that are members of the table. We don't care about the name of the redefining table, nor about the names of the elementary data items within INT-RATE-DATA. Whatever we don't care about, we can refer to as FILLER, instead of specifying individual data names. In fact we can leave the names out altogether, even the FILLER:

```
02 INT-RATE-DATA.
   03 PIC 9(7)      VALUE 1000.
   03 PIC 99V999    VALUE 3.5.
   03 PIC 9(7)      VALUE 5000.
   03 PIC 99V999    VALUE 4.5.
   03 PIC 9(7)      VALUE 10000.
   .
```

but that the definition is clearer where every data item has a name of some kind, which is why I use FILLER in preference to nothing.

Keep in mind that the REDEFINES clause does not use new memory for a new data-item definition. It simply enables you to look at an existing definition in a different way, this time as a table. Here's the output that TABLE2.CBL produced when I executed it:

```
Personal COBOL version 2.0 from Micro Focus
PCOBRUN V2.0.02  Copyright (C) 1983-1993 Micro Focus Ltd.
Principal 001 0001000
Rate 001 03500
Principal 002 0005000
Rate 002 04500
Principal 003 0010000
Rate 003 05000
Principal 004 0050000
Rate 004 06500
Principal 005 0100000
Rate 005 07500
```

To keep the program to a reasonable length, I've reduced the `OCCURS` subscript limit to `5`, which is the number of times the loop in the paragraph `DISPLAY-ELEMENTS` is executed. So why test for `GREATER THAN 4`? If I used the `GREATER THAN 5`, `WS-SUB` would increase to 6 and the program would stop with an array-bounds exception:

```
         .
Principal 005 0100000
Rate 005 07500
Principal 006 TABLE2 Segment RT : Error 153 at COBOL PC
0048
Description : Subscript out of range
```

Effectively, you run off the end of the table in memory. This is potentially a very serious programming error and you should take great care not to let it happen. One of the reasons for the superiority of the `PERFORM` statement over the `IF...GO TO` sequence above is that `PERFORM` provides better control over subscripts and indexes.

Finally, here's a simple example of a multi-dimensional (in this case, two-dimensional) table definition. Suppose that, with each principal amount and interest rate, there were associated a number of currency-conversion rates for dollars, pounds, euros, ECUs, that sort of thing. This requires our holding a table within a table:

```
03 FILLER OCCURS 5.
    04 INT-PRINCIPAL   PIC 9(7).
    04 INT-RATE        PIC 99V999.
    04 INT-CONV        PIC 99V99 OCCURS 4.
```

As before, we use `WS-SUB` as the subscript. To access `INT-PRINCIPAL` in the second table element, `WS-SUB` must have the value 2 and we refer to the required value with `INT-PRINCIPAL(WS-SUB)`. To access the third currency-conversion amount within the second table element, we have to write `INT-CONV(WS-SUB, 3)`.

To explore all the ramifications of multi-dimensional tables, and tables of variable size (see `OCCURS DEPENDING` in your system's documentation) is beyond the scope of this text. In principle, as you can see from the `INT-CONV` table-within-a-table example, manipulating multi-dimensional tables with subscripts is simply a logical extension of the same process for one-dimensional tables. If you want to try your hand at it, there's a relevant exercise at the end of this chapter.

String handling

File-handling, not text-processing, has traditionally been COBOL's greatest strength. By default, COBOL treats a data item such as:

```
01 WS-TEXT    PIC 9(6) VALUE "PQRSTU".
```

as a single entity and doesn't allow you any more *granularity* than that: you can't access, say, the fourth character, S, directly. With tables and REDEFINES, we can remedy this:

```
01 WS-TEXT      PIC 9(6) VALUE "PQRSTU".
01 WS-CHAR-TAB REDEFINES WS-TEXT.
   02 WS-CHAR  PIC X OCCURS 6.
```

Now, WS-CHAR(4) has the value S.

All very fine, you might say, but a bit clumsy and not the kind of string-handling facilities that would give COBOL programmers the same power as their C or Pascal counterparts. Isn't there some better way? The answer, happily is 'Yes'; COBOL-85 provides three verbs and the technique of *reference modification* to improve its built-in string-handling.

The verbs are INSPECT, STRING and UNSTRING. INSPECT can find and (optionally) replace text within a string. STRING joins separate pieces of text (say words) into one text entity (say a sentence). UNSTRING splits a string into separate pieces. Reference modification allows you to 'lift' a *substring* from the middle of a string.

Rather than explain each technique separately and illustrate its operation with a separate program, I've included a single program, STRING1.CBL, which exercises them all. However, INSPECT, STRING and UNSTRING have so many options that I can't hope in this section to be exhaustive. You should regard the usages shown in the program as being the most common but, for all possible variations, you'll have to refer to your system's documentation and be prepared to experiment.

```
******************************************************************
*                                                                *
*   Combines conventional string-handling techniques with the    *
*   STRING, UNSTRING, INSPECT and reference-modification commands *
*                                                                *
******************************************************************
     IDENTIFICATION DIVISION.
     PROGRAM-ID. STRING1.

     ENVIRONMENT DIVISION.

     DATA DIVISION.
     WORKING-STORAGE SECTION.
     01 WS-TEXT-LINE         PIC X(40) VALUE
                    "To be or not to be, that is the question".
     01 WS-TEXT-TABLE REDEFINES WS-TEXT-LINE.
        02 WS-CHAR           PIC X OCCURS 40.
     01 WS-SUB               PIC 999 COMP.
     01 WS-HITS              PIC 999.
     01 WS-TOKEN-TABLE.
        02 WS-T              PIC X(10) OCCURS 10.

     PROCEDURE DIVISION.
     PROGRAM-START.
         MOVE 1 TO WS-SUB.
         DISPLAY "Text string is: " NO ADVANCING.

     DISPLAY-CHAR-BY-CHAR.
         DISPLAY WS-CHAR(WS-SUB) NO ADVANCING.
         IF WS-SUB EQUALS 40
             GO TO PATTERN-SEARCH.
         ADD 1 TO WS-SUB.
             GO TO DISPLAY-CHAR-BY-CHAR.

     PATTERN-SEARCH.
         DISPLAY " ".
         MOVE ZERO TO WS-HITS.
         INSPECT WS-TEXT-LINE TALLYING WS-HITS FOR ALL "be".
         DISPLAY "Number of hits is: " WS-HITS.
         INSPECT WS-TEXT-LINE REPLACING ALL " " BY ".".
         DISPLAY "Dot-delimited text string is: " WS-TEXT-LINE.

     SUBSTRING-SEARCH.
         DISPLAY "Text string, positions 21-24: " WS-TEXT-LINE(21:4).

     SPLIT-TEXT.
         UNSTRING WS-TEXT-LINE DELIMITED BY "." INTO
             WS-T(1), WS-T(2), WS-T(3), WS-T(4), WS-T(5),
             WS-T(6), WS-T(7), WS-T(8), WS-T(9), WS-T(10).
         DISPLAY "Broken text string is: " WS-TOKEN-TABLE.
```

Uses subscripts to display the string character-by-character

Searches for a pattern and counts occurrences

Replace spaces with full-stops

Splits text into words delimited by the full stops inserted earlier.

```
JOIN-TEXT.
    MOVE SPACES TO WS-TEXT-LINE.
    STRING
        WS-T(1) DELIMITED BY SPACE,
        " " DELIMITED BY SIZE,
        WS-T(2) DELIMITED BY SPACE,
        " " DELIMITED BY SIZE,
        WS-T(3) DELIMITED BY SPACE,
        " " DELIMITED BY SIZE,
        WS-T(4) DELIMITED BY SPACE,
        " " DELIMITED BY SIZE,
        WS-T(5) DELIMITED BY SPACE,
        " " DELIMITED BY SIZE,
        WS-T(6) DELIMITED BY SPACE,
        " " DELIMITED BY SIZE,
        WS-T(7) DELIMITED BY SPACE,
        " " DELIMITED BY SIZE,
        WS-T(8) DELIMITED BY SPACE,
        " " DELIMITED BY SIZE,
        WS-T(9) DELIMITED BY SPACE,
        " " DELIMITED BY SIZE,
        WS-T(10) DELIMITED BY SPACE,
        " " DELIMITED BY SIZE
    INTO WS-TEXT-LINE.
    DISPLAY "Rejoined text line is: " WS-TEXT-LINE.

PROGRAM-END.
    STOP RUN.
```

> Rejoins all the words, delimited by blanks, into a string of the original form

All operations are carried out on WS-TEXT-LINE or copies or redefinitions of it. This data item is initialised to the text of a famous line from Hamlet. The paragraph DISPLAY-CHAR-BY-CHAR uses the table redefinition of WS-TEXT-LINE to display, character by character, all the text. This is conventional COBOL text processing but is, as I've noted, somewhat clumsy and inflexible.

The paragraph PATTERN-SEARCH uses the INSPECT verb first to search for a pattern – the word "be" – and count the number of occurrences; and second to replace all blank characters with full-stops.

The paragraph SUBSTRING-SEARCH lifts a substring of text from WS-TEXT-LINE. Specifically, in specifying WS-TEXT-LINE(21:4) it extracts the text starting at position 21 and, including that position, for four characters thereafter. Counting starts from 1 and the character 'T' of "To be...". The string extracted is the word "that".

Next we get into the UNSTRING/STRING pair. First, in paragraph SPLIT-TEXT, the UNSTRING verb takes each separate word of the quotation and assigns it to a member of the table WS-TOKEN-TABLE. The delimiting character used is the full-stop (placed there by the second INSPECT statement) that separates the words from each other in WS-TEXT-LINE. The group data item WS-TOKEN-TABLE, which contains all of the table entries, is then used to display the 'broken text'.

The last act of STRING1.CBL is to rejoin (concatenate) all the broken text using the STRING verb. The STRING statement shown is quite complex. In short, if all the words – DELIMITED BY SPACE, which eliminates all trailing spaces from each word – were simply joined, they would not be separated by spaces as they were in the original quotation. To achieve space-separation, we must insert a literal space, " ", after each constituent data item of the concatenation and specify that it is to be delimited by its size, that is, one character width. This forces insertion of a space between the individual words.

The displayed results when I ran the program were these:

```
Personal COBOL version 2.0 from Micro Focus
PCOBRUN V2.0.02  Copyright (C) 1983-1993 Micro Focus Ltd.
Text string is: To be or not to be, that is the question
Number of hits is: 002
Dot-delimited text string is: To.be.or.not.to.be,.that.is.the.question
Text string, positions 21-24: that
Broken text string is: To       be       or       not       to
be,      that     is       the      question
Rejoined text line is: To be or not to be, that is the question
```

To do a full treatment of string processing and all the possibilities of the techniques that I have mentioned in this section would require a book in its own right. With a little thought, you should be able to see how to write really useful programs with these string-processing commands. Examples include text search and replace systems; input text validation; mailing lists of edited names and addresses; and interactive enquiry programs.

Exercises

1   See if you can write a screen I/O program similar to SCRNIO1.CBL (see *ACCEPT* and *DISPLAY* at the start of this chapter) which displays four numeric menu options. The user must select one of these; if correct, the input is acknowledged; if in error, an error-message is generated. *Hint: see the section of Level 88 definitions in Chapter 2.*

2   Write a version of PAYROLL.CBL (see *Arithmetic*, in this chapter) that does exactly the same payroll calculations but uses only the COMPUTE command to do so, in place of the conventional COBOL arithmetic statements seen in PAYROLL.CBL.

3   Write a version of TABLE2.CBL (see *Table initialisation*, in this chapter) which incorporates the table INT-CONV within the main interest-rate table, initialises the nested table with some data and then displays its contents along with the interest rate data. As I hinted in this chapter, the two-dimensional table definition will look like this:

```
03 FILLER OCCURS 5.
      04 INT-PRINCIPAL     PIC 9(7).
      04 INT-RATE          PIC 99V999.
      04 INT-CONV          PIC 99V99 OCCURS 4.
```

4 Control Flow

Structuring your COBOL program

In the first three chapters, and particularly Chapters 2 and 3, I concentrate on what you might think of as the details of the COBOL language: the small stuff that you have to know to be able to write a COBOL program at all. In this chapter, we become more concerned with the Big Picture: how you design and structure a real COBOL program. Because of the size of this book and the range of topics to be covered, all the programs I've included are small ones. In a real, production, COBOL environment, it would be hard to find a program smaller than at least 500 to 1,000 lines. The point is that you can't expect to write programs of that size and greater without planning the program's design and *structure*.

For example, in Chapter 3, I acknowledge that using the IF...GO TO sequence to create loops, is really not very good practice. It's OK for illustrative programs but, in general, use of PERFORM is preferable. Why? Anyone who has tried to modify a 3,000-line unstructured GO TO-ridden COBOL program knows the answer. An unstructured program of that size becomes what is often referred to as *spaghetti code*: it's nearly impossible to unravel or understand. Worse, make a change in one place and something will break in an apparently unrelated part of the program. These problems are caused by a lack of structure and modularity that leads to unmaintainable code.

In the 1950s and 1960s, almost all programs were written in an unstructured manner, and the syntax of COBOL, although it has been improved in COBOL-85, reflects the practices of the time. IF...GO TO was for long the *only* way to implement loops and execute *subprograms*; the PERFORM and CALL verbs were later additions. Also, COBOL is not inherently block-structured, as are C, Pascal and PL/1: it in fact encourages use of the GO TO. COBOL has no mechanism for defining *local variables* – variables that are restricted in use to only a small part of the program. Everything is defined in the DATA division and all data items are visible throughout the program.

Even allowing for these shortcomings, however, COBOL programs can be written in a structured and disciplined way. The prize of doing so is that maintainable programs result, and low cost of maintenance is a huge issue for today's IT and software development managers. The means of doing so are the subject of this chapter. Chapters 5 and 6 then move on to COBOL's central application, file processing, taking care to use the structuring techniques outlined here.

Structured programming

In 1968, a famous computer scientist named Edgar Dijkstra made a proposal to the Association for Computing Machinery (ACM) that unconditional transfers of control (the GO TO to you and me!) should not be used in programming. This proposal led to the development of a set of practices that collectively became known as *structured programming* or, sometimes, *modular programming*. Today (even with the rise of the newer *object-oriented* programming techniques), nobody dissents from the essential tenets inherent in the structured programming approach. These are:

● Programs should be written with a top-down, hierarchical, structure;

● Programs (and subprograms, or modules) should have one entry point and one point of exit;

● Modules should be short, self-contained and have one well-defined design goal;

● Only basic programming constructs should be used;

● Inputs and outputs should be clearly defined;

● Programs should be written in a readable style.

Modules

Consider the first three of these points. They mean, in essence, that a COBOL – or any other – program should be a set of modules rather than a monolithic body of code. These modules should be predictable in the way they start and finish execution; they should be small and they should each do one simple job well. Finally, the modules should be organised in a hierarchy. To illustrate, suppose we want to write a payroll program. You won't get very far if, without thought, you just start coding right away. Instead, you need a structured design:

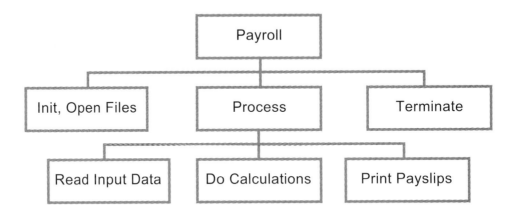

Each of the boxes represents a code module. The highest box in the hierarchy is 'Payroll'. Its function is subdivided into three subsidiary boxes. It doesn't have to be three; it could be more or fewer. However, every problem and process has a start, middle and end and this is often a good approach to take in your program design: in this case 'Init', 'Process' and 'Terminate'. Further down, the 'Do Calculations' module obviously concerns the whole business of calculation of tax and insurance; it needs to be refined into a further set of subsidiary modules.

This process of refinement – sometimes called *stepwise refinement* – is how you should approach the design and writing of your COBOL programs. You write a top-level module that starts the three main subsidiary modules. When you come to the 'Process' step, you don't dive in right away and write all the payroll code in one go. Instead, you call a module to perform the 'Process' part and then move on to 'Terminate', leaving the details of 'Process' until later. Similarly, within the 'Process' module, when you arrive at the point of 'Do Calculations', you make a call to a module of that name, move on and leave the details until later.

Stepwise refinement is a process by which you isolate areas of complexity and successively decompose them into manageable chunks. Maybe six or seven module levels down the hierarchy, you arrive at a point when no further decomposition is needed. Then you're finished, at least for that part of the overall program.

In COBOL, the modules that I've referred to are implemented as paragraphs, SECTIONs or independent programs. Within a given program, a SECTION is the largest modular entity, usually containing a number of paragraphs. Ideally, modules should be small (no more than 50 lines of code); should have low *coupling* (be as independent as possible of all other modules); should have high *strength* (be a coherent, one-function logical entity). Crucially, you should be able to treat a module as a *black box*: a reusable piece of code that you know works and that you can just drop into your program without prior inspection. In the real world, this kind of reusability is an aspiration rarely fully achieved. If you ever fully realise all these goals, try walking on water; you probably won't get your feet wet.

Programming constructs

The basic programming constructs are *sequence*, *selection*, *iteration* and *case*. Sequence means simply having statements execute in order of their appearance. Selection, in COBOL, means using the IF verb. Iteration means using the IF...GO TO sequence or, preferably, PERFORM. Case (multi-way selection) can be done with GO TO DEPENDING (see *The dreaded* GO TO, later in this chapter), but the EVALUATE verb was introduced by COBOL-85 specially for the purpose and is therefore preferred.

In principle, modules should have as few inputs and outputs as possible. They should be clearly specified as either inputs or outputs. In no case should an input data item then be used for output. Finally, SECTION, paragraph and data item names should conform to a reasonable system of naming conventions. I look at naming recommendations for COBOL later in this chapter.

The IF statement

IF is COBOL's primary means of changing the sequential flow of execution of your program's statements. This is its general operation:

```
IF <condition> [THEN]
   <do something>.
```

Here, I've used angle-brackets to indicate that the item within is to be replaced by something else. In the case of <condition> this might be something like WS-VAL GREATER THAN ZERO. Square brackets, as ever, mean that the item within is optional.

There are two more accurate general forms of IF: the first from the COBOL-74 Standard and the second, defined by COBOL-85. One of the major weaknesses of the earlier standard was its failure adequately to specify where complex statements like IF end. COBOL-85 rectifies this for IF by providing the END-IF terminator. However, both forms are in widespread use, so I introduce you in this section to both.

Apart from the differences in specification of the two standards, there's a multitude of other options that come with IF: the syntax of the statement itself; the kinds of conditions that can be tested; and the comparisons, simple and *compound*, that can be carried out. Many textbooks try to explain most or all of the options with program examples. I don't do this, partly for reasons of space and partly because IF is a rather intuitive verb: given its general forms and a few examples, you should be able yourself to figure out many of the uses to which it can be put.

The COBOL-74 general format of the IF statement is this:

```
IF <condition> {<statements-a>, NEXT SENTENCE}
   [ELSE {<statements-b>, NEXT SENTENCE}].
```

Here's a fictitious code example:

```
IF WS-VAL IS EQUAL TO ZERO
   MOVE 1 TO WS-VAL
   DISPLAY "Zero division, divisor value 1 assumed" WS-AMT
ELSE
   DIVIDE WS-VAL INTO WS-AMT
   DISPLAY "Amount: " WS-AMT.
```

If WS-VAL is zero, the two statements up to but not including the ELSE are executed; those after the ELSE are not. If WS-VAL is not zero, the opposite is the case. The indenting of the two pairs of lines is desirable but only for readability; it has no effect on how the code executes. As a reasonable alternative, we could write:

```
IF WS-VAL IS EQUAL TO ZERO
    NEXT SENTENCE
ELSE
    DIVIDE WS-VAL INTO WS-AMT
    DISPLAY "Amount: " WS-AMT.
```

Here, when WS-VAL is zero, the NEXT SENTENCE is effectively a *null statement*: a do-nothing and skip the statements subject to the ELSE following. The ELSE clause is optional; you could have just:

```
IF WS-VAL IS EQUAL TO ZERO
    MOVE 1 TO WS-VAL
DISPLAY "Zero division, divisor value 1 assumed" WS-AMT.
```

Note in all cases that the whole IF statement is terminated by a full-stop. The positioning of this full-stop is vital; in this piece of code:

```
IF WS-VAL IS EQUAL TO ZERO
    MOVE 1 TO WS-VAL
    DISPLAY "Zero division, divisor value 1 assumed" WS-AMT
ELSE
    DIVIDE WS-VAL INTO WS-AMT.
    DISPLAY "Amount: " WS-AMT.
```

The message "Amount: ", because of the (wrongly) preceding full-stop is displayed whether the IF condition is true or false. The real difficulty with the COBOL-74 IF arises when you nest IF statements:

```
IF WS-VAL IS EQUAL TO ZERO
    MOVE 1 TO WS-VAL
    DISPLAY "Zero division, divisor value 1 assumed" WS-AMT
ELSE
    IF WS-AMT IS LESS THAN 1000
        DIVIDE 5 INTO WS-AMT
    ELSE
        DIVIDE WS-VAL INTO WS-AMT
    DISPLAY "Amount: " WS-AMT.
```

The question here is: do we or don't we put a full-stop after the second-last line of code? It is, after all, the last line in the enclosed IF statement and, as such, should have a full-stop. On the other hand, if that full-stop were to terminate the whole enclosing IF statement, the "Amount: " message would be wrongly displayed. Unfortunately, both alternatives are likely to be wrong. If you place a full-stop at the end of the second-last line, you terminate the whole enclosing IF statement and "Amount: " is always displayed. If you don't, "Amount: " will only be displayed in the case of WS-VAL being non-zero and less than 1000 – probably not what is intended. In COBOL-74, there's no neat solution for this dilemma, which is why COBOL-85 contains a major change.

This is the COBOL-85 general format of the IF statement:

```
IF <condition> [THEN] {<statements-a>, NEXT SENTENCE}
   {
   ELSE <statements-b>… END-IF,
   ELSE NEXT SENTENCE,
   END-IF
   }
```

It isn't as complex as it seems. A superficial change is the inclusion of the noise-word THEN, which is not part of the COBOL-74 specification. The major beneficial effect is to eliminate the Catch-22 type problem we encountered with the COBOL-74 nested IFs. The problem code, with a COBOL-85 compiler, would be written thus:

```
IF WS-VAL IS EQUAL TO ZERO THEN
    MOVE 1 TO WS-VAL
    DISPLAY "Zero division, divisor value 1 assumed" WS-AMT
ELSE
    IF WS-AMT IS LESS THAN 1000 THEN
       DIVIDE 5 INTO WS-AMT
    ELSE
       DIVIDE WS-VAL INTO WS-AMT
    END-IF
    DISPLAY "Amount: " WS-AMT
END-IF
```

Notice, no full-stops at all! The enclosed IF is unambiguously terminated by its END-IF, as is the enclosing IF statement. The DISPLAY "Amount: "... statement is now, correctly, subject to the ELSE clause of the enclosing IF statement, where previously it was either executed always or was subject to both IFs.

That's the difficult aspect of IF disposed of, really. We now need to look at the conditions that can be tested and how those conditions can be grouped into *compound conditions*.

IF conditions

COBOL provides three kinds of general condition tests:

- The relation condition, for example IF A IS EQUAL TO B and its algebraic equivalent, IF A = B

- The class condition, for example IF A IS NOT NUMERIC

- The sign condition, for example IF A IS POSITIVE

COBOL also allows you to combine condition tests, into compound conditions, using the relations AND, OR and NOT.

Relation conditions

Here is the full set of relation conditions, given with their algebraic equivalents and with noise-words (that's the optional ones!) indicated:

Condition	Algebraic Equivalent
A IS [NOT] GREATER THAN B	A IS [NOT] > B
A IS [NOT] LESS THAN B	A IS [NOT] < B
A IS [NOT] EQUAL TO B	A IS [NOT] = B
A IS GREATER THAN OR EQUAL TO B	A IS >= B
A IS LESS THAN OR EQUAL TO B	A IS <= B

These are self-explanatory, at least for numeric operands:

```
01 WS-NUM1          PIC 99V9       VALUE 12.3.
01 WS-NUM2          PIC 999V99     VALUE 12.4.
```

An IF statement comparing the two:

```
IF WS-NUM1 IS LESS THAN WS-NUM2
```

yields a true result: statements subject to the IF will be executed. In the verbose forms given above, any word not underlined is a noise-word and may be omitted. I could have written the last comparison:

```
IF WS-NUM LESS WS-NUM2
```

Numeric comparisons are straightforward: the numeric, not the alphanumeric, representations of the operands are compared. In the example above, WS-NUM1 and WS-NUM2 hold their values in memory respectively as 123 and 01240. In the numeric comparison, these are treated simply as the numeric quantities 12.3 and 12.4, and *not* as the alphanumeric strings 123 and 01240.

By contrast, any comparison of alphanumeric data items is done on a left-to-right, character-by-character basis according to the *collating sequence* of the executing computer. The collating sequence is the sort order of the characters that make up the system's character set. Most systems today use the ASCII sequence which, in ascending order is SPACE; some punctuation characters; numeric 0 – 9; special and punctuation characters; lowercase 'a' – 'z'; and uppercase 'A' – 'Z'. According to this sequence, alphanumeric '01240' would evaluate as *less than* '123'. Similarly, because of two leading spaces, ' ABC' would evaluate as less than 'ABC'.

Mostly, you'll use your common sense and compare only like with like: numeric with numeric and alphanumeric with alphanumeric. Sometimes though, you won't be able to avoid a mixed comparison of numerics and alphanumerics and you need to know how the comparison is handled. There are several detailed rules surrounding mixed comparisons, which can be summarised thus: *any mixed numeric-alphanumeric comparison is treated as a purely alphanumeric comparison*, with the numeric operand being first converted in memory to its alphnumeric (DISPLAY) equivalent. So, if you choose to compare the data items:

```
01 WS-NUM1     PIC XXX VALUE '123'.
01 WS-NUM2     PIC 9(5) VALUE 897.
```

you should be aware that the comparison will be an alphanumeric one between the text strings '123' and '00897'. WS-NUM1 is reported as being greater than WS-NUM2.

Finally, a fractional integer or literal value may only be compared with another numeric value. If you try to compare a numeric fraction with an alphanumeric value, you'll get a compiler message complaining about the comparison.

Class conditions

The class condition tests that COBOL gives you are NUMERIC, ALPHABETIC, ALPHABETIC-LOWER and ALPHABETIC-UPPER. Here's a program, CLASSCON.CBL, that illustrates a number of the possibilities:

```
***********************************************************************
*   Tests the numeric and alphabetic class conditions              *
***********************************************************************
    IDENTIFICATION DIVISION.
    PROGRAM-ID. CLASSCON.

    ENVIRONMENT DIVISION.

    DATA DIVISION.
    WORKING-STORAGE SECTION.
    01 WS-NUM              PIC S9(6) VALUE -123.
    01 WS-ALPHANUM         PIC X(6) VALUE '123456'.
    01 WS-ALPHA            PIC A(6) VALUE 'abcdef'.

    PROCEDURE DIVISION.
    CLASS-TEST.
        IF WS-NUM IS NUMERIC THEN
            DISPLAY WS-NUM " is numeric".
*       Next test rejected by compiler
*       IF WS-NUM IS NOT ALPHABETIC THEN
*           DISPLAY WS-NUM " is not alphabetic".
        IF WS-ALPHANUM NUMERIC THEN
            DISPLAY WS-ALPHANUM " is numeric".
        IF WS-ALPHA NOT NUMERIC THEN
            DISPLAY WS-ALPHA " is not numeric".
        IF WS-ALPHA IS ALPHABETIC-LOWER THEN
            DISPLAY WS-ALPHA " is lower-case alphabetic".

    PROGRAM-END.
        STOP RUN.
```

> Message from the compiler – generated by doing an **ALPHABETIC** test on a numeric data item.

A signed numeric data item is judged to have NUMERIC contents if it holds all numeric characters and (optionally) a minus-sign. An alphanumeric data item is NUMERIC if all the characters of its contents are in the range zero to 9. The three ALPHABETIC tests should only be applied to alphanumeric or alphabetic data items.

The output results of CLASSCON.CBL are these:

```
000123- is numeric
123456 is numeric
abcdef is not numeric
abcdef is lower-case alphabetic
```

The ALPHABETIC test is true if all characters in the operand are upper- or lower-case alphabetic or blank. ALPHABETIC-LOWER is true if all characters are lower-case alphabetic or blank. ALPHABETIC-UPPER is true if all characters are upper-case alphabetic or blank.

Sign conditions

The sign conditions are used to check the positive, negative or zero status of a signed numeric data item. The tests used are these:

```
IF <data item> IS [NOT] {POSITIVE, NUMERIC, ZERO}
```

You can't use these tests on a data item of non-numeric (not PIC 9) class. If you do, the compiler will stop you. If you define a data item:

```
01 WS-NUM     PIC 9(6).
```

and then test it:

```
IF WS-NUM IS ZERO.....
```

You get an arithmetic exception when you try to execute the program. You can't depend on the value of a data item defined in WORKING-STORAGE being zero. It must be initialised before testing. Let's do this:

```
COMPUTE WS-NUM = 4 - 5.
```

What happens when you test this for being NEGATIVE?

```
IF WS-NUM NEGATIVE...
```

The result is false. WS-NUM isn't signed and so the result of the expression 4 - 5 is stored in it as the positive number 1. Only when you give WS-NUM the PICTURE specification PIC S9(6) does the test work.

Compound conditions

You can test more than one assertion with a single IF statement. Suppose we have two data items, defined and initialised like this:

```
01 WS-NUM1       PIC 999 VALUE 4.
01 WS-NUM2       PIC 999 VALUE 5.
```

The result of these compound tests are all true:

```
IF (WS-NUM1 = 4) AND (WS-NUM2 EQUAL 5)
IF (WS-NUM1 = 4) OR (WS-NUM2 EQUAL 3)
IF NOT (WS-NUM = 6)
```

The parentheses are unnecessary, but aid clarity. When compound tests become complex enough, you'll find it useful to use parentheses to be sure of the meaning of the comparisons. The logical *negation*, NOT, is unlikely to be used in this manner. It's more likely that you would do something like this when reading records from a file:

```
READ INPUT-FILE
   AT END WS-EOF = 1
   NOT AT END PERFORM PROCESS-RECORD
END-READ.
```

Inverted tests such as NOT AT END were introduced with COBOL-85. I look at PERFORM in detail later, but you should be able to sense the meaning of the usage in the example. END-READ (like END-IF) was introduced by COBOL-85 to make clear where the READ statement, possibly having many subordinate tests, is terminated.

Here's a real beauty that shows the perils of carelessly using compound conditions. The program's function is to ascertain that a given number, WS-A, is *not* equal to either of two other numbers, WS-B and WS-C.

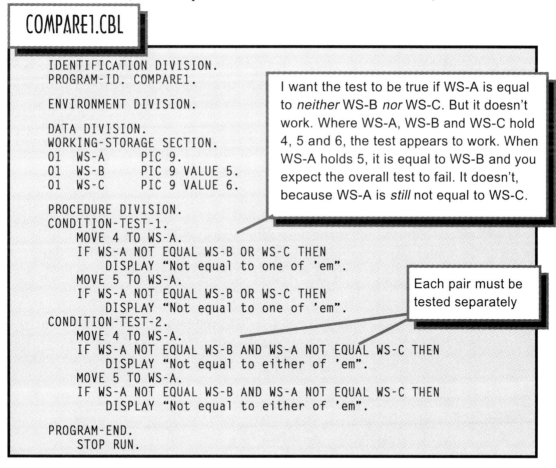

COMPARE1.CBL

```
IDENTIFICATION DIVISION.
PROGRAM-ID. COMPARE1.

ENVIRONMENT DIVISION.

DATA DIVISION.
WORKING-STORAGE SECTION.
01   WS-A      PIC 9.
01   WS-B      PIC 9 VALUE 5.
01   WS-C      PIC 9 VALUE 6.

PROCEDURE DIVISION.
CONDITION-TEST-1.
     MOVE 4 TO WS-A.
     IF WS-A NOT EQUAL WS-B OR WS-C THEN
         DISPLAY "Not equal to one of 'em".
     MOVE 5 TO WS-A.
     IF WS-A NOT EQUAL WS-B OR WS-C THEN
         DISPLAY "Not equal to one of 'em".
CONDITION-TEST-2.
     MOVE 4 TO WS-A.
     IF WS-A NOT EQUAL WS-B AND WS-A NOT EQUAL WS-C THEN
         DISPLAY "Not equal to either of 'em".
     MOVE 5 TO WS-A.
     IF WS-A NOT EQUAL WS-B AND WS-A NOT EQUAL WS-C THEN
         DISPLAY "Not equal to either of 'em".

PROGRAM-END.
     STOP RUN.
```

I want the test to be true if WS-A is equal to *neither* WS-B *nor* WS-C. But it doesn't work. Where WS-A, WS-B and WS-C hold 4, 5 and 6, the test appears to work. When WS-A holds 5, it is equal to WS-B and you expect the overall test to fail. It doesn't, because WS-A is *still* not equal to WS-C.

Each pair must be tested separately

The displayed output of the program is this:

```
Not equal to one of 'em
Not equal to one of 'em
Not equal to either of 'em
```

The dreaded GO TO

GO TO unconditionally transfers execution control from one part of your program to another. Occasionally, GO TO used well can be of benefit. This is why it or an equivalent statement is found in most programming languages. GO TO used extensively and indiscriminately is a disaster that will turn your programs into spaghetti.

What are the desirable uses of GO TO? First, in illustrative programs of the sort in this book. These are too small to take on spaghetti-like characteristics and the GO TO can be a force for clarity of meaning.

Second (and better), you've written a disciplined 2,000-line program. The program is in execution, seven levels of PERFORMs deep, and it encounters a logical disaster. The input file from which you're getting your data is corrupt and you must bail out of the program *now*. It's too difficult to retrace all the PERFORMs and exit gracefully, so you GO TO a paragraph called 999-EXIT, which contains the statement STOP RUN.

The GO TO statement has two general forms. Here's the simple one.

```
GO TO <paragraph-name>.
```

This unconditionally transfers control of program execution to the named paragraph, which might be 5,000 lines away. This is part of the GO TO problem, which leads me to give you a tip: if you're going to use GO TO, name your paragraphs so that they appear in alphabetic order.

The second form of GO TO is this:

```
GO TO <paragraph-name>... DEPENDING ON <identifier>.
```

To explain how this is used, I define and initialise a numeric data item:

```
01 WS-SWITCH        PIC 99 VALUE 2.
```

Now, here's the GO TO DEPENDING:

```
GO TO PARA-A PARA-B PARA-C PARA-D
    DEPENDING ON WS-SWITCH.
```

This transfers execution to the first line in the paragraph PARA-B. This is because the value of WS-SWITCH is 2. If that value were 1, the target of the GO TO would be PARA-A; if 3, the target would be PARA-C, and so on. If the value of WS-SWITCH falls outside the number of paragraphs specified, the statement does nothing – execution *falls through* to the next statement. GO TO DEPENDING has been made obsolete by the EVALUATE verb, introduced by COBOL-85 (see page 121).

CALL: Programs calling programs

Recall that the PROCEDURE division of a COBOL program is made up of SECTIONs, paragraphs, sentences and statements, in descending order of size and complexity. You can transfer execution control between these entities using verbs such as PERFORM and GO TO.

A COBOL program can be made up of several *program file*s: full individual COBOL programs between which execution control may be transferred. The verb used to transfer control between programs is CALL. When you're developing real, full-size, production COBOL programs, the code will inevitably get to such a size that you'll want to break it into more than one program file.

Broadly, programs-calling-programs fall into three classifications:

● Programs that make simple calls on other, separate, programs;

● Programs that call other separate programs passing *parameters* to the called programs;

● Nested programs, all in one program file, that call each other.

Below, I give examples of programs in each of the three classifications. I've pointed out that the reason why we want programs to call other programs is to stop any individual program becoming too large. And, for a short, *Made Simple*, book like this, size is the problem here. For reasons of space, I've kept all the following examples as short as I can, and I don't cover all possible options. Nonetheless the three sets of programs should give you a useful template which will help you develop your own real-life code.

Simple CALL

The simplest variation is where we want a (top-level) program to call one or more (sub) programs, execute the subprograms and return to the points in the top-level program from which they were called. The three COBOL programs that follow, TOPPROG.CBL, SUBPROG1.CBL and SUBPROG2.CBL show the calling sequence in action.

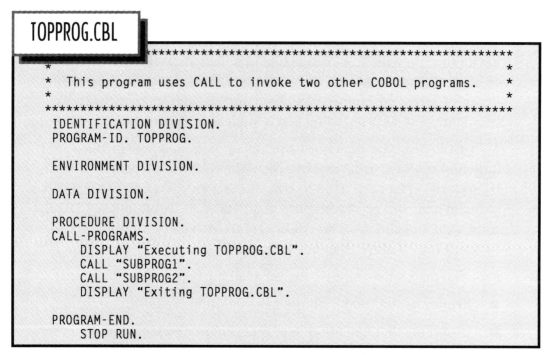

```
TOPPROG.CBL
      ************************************************************
      *                                                        *
      *  This program uses CALL to invoke two other COBOL programs.  *
      *                                                        *
      ************************************************************
       IDENTIFICATION DIVISION.
       PROGRAM-ID. TOPPROG.

       ENVIRONMENT DIVISION.

       DATA DIVISION.

       PROCEDURE DIVISION.
       CALL-PROGRAMS.
           DISPLAY "Executing TOPPROG.CBL".
           CALL "SUBPROG1".
           CALL "SUBPROG2".
           DISPLAY "Exiting TOPPROG.CBL".

       PROGRAM-END.
           STOP RUN.
```

The only purpose of topprog.cbl is to display a message, call the two subprograms, display another message and exit. Here's subprog1.cbl:

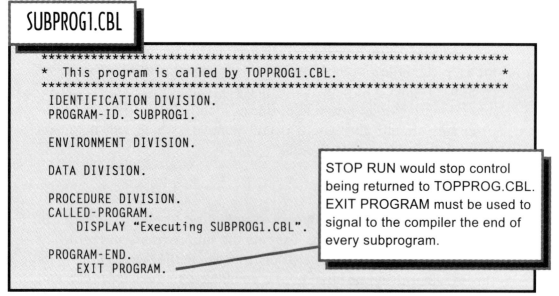

```
SUBPROG1.CBL
      ************************************************************
      *  This program is called by TOPPROG1.CBL.                *
      ************************************************************
       IDENTIFICATION DIVISION.
       PROGRAM-ID. SUBPROG1.

       ENVIRONMENT DIVISION.

       DATA DIVISION.

       PROCEDURE DIVISION.
       CALLED-PROGRAM.
           DISPLAY "Executing SUBPROG1.CBL".

       PROGRAM-END.
           EXIT PROGRAM.
```

STOP RUN would stop control being returned to TOPPROG.CBL. EXIT PROGRAM must be used to signal to the compiler the end of every subprogram.

All that subprog1.cbl does is to display its own message and return to the statement in topprog.cbl after the one from which it is called. That's the call to subprog2.cbl, which is next:

```
*********************************************************************
*  This program  is called by TOPPROG.CBL.                        *
*********************************************************************
   IDENTIFICATION DIVISION.
   PROGRAM-ID. SUBPROG2.

   ENVIRONMENT DIVISION.

   DATA DIVISION.

   PROCEDURE DIVISION.
   CALLED-PROGRAMS.
       DISPLAY "Executing SUBPROG2.CBL".

   PROGRAM-END.
       EXIT PROGRAM.
```

With Personal COBOL, you compile each of these programs separately then run the topprog intermediate code file using the command line PCOBRUN TOPPROG. This was displayed result when I ran it:

```
Personal COBOL version 2.0 from Micro Focus
PCOBRUN V2.0.02  Copyright (C) 1983-1993 Micro Focus Ltd.
Executing TOPPROG.CBL
Executing SUBPROG1.CBL
Executing SUBPROG2.CBL
Exiting TOPPROG.CBL
```

TOPPROG.CBL starts executing, calls the two subprograms which display their own messages, and then displays the 'Exiting...' message just before the STOP RUN. The program names used in the CALLs must be those in the PROGRAM-ID clauses of the called programs. In turn, these names should be the same as the prefix of the actual program name on the computer. For example, SUBPROG1 matches SUBPROG1.CBL. Personal COBOL doesn't insist on this symmetry, but many compilers do and it's good practice to match the names.

When you write it – or use it – you may not know if a program is to be a top-level program or a subprogram. How then do you know whether to use EXIT PROGRAM or STOP RUN? The answer is to use both:

```
   PROGRAM-EXIT.
       EXIT PROGRAM.
   PROGRAM-STOP.
       STOP RUN.
```

These paragraphs are placed where the processing of the program file has finished. First, `EXIT PROGRAM` is executed. If the program is a called one, control is returned to the caller. If it is not, `EXIT PROGRAM` is ignored, `STOP RUN` is executed and all execution for all programs in the suite stops. It's recommended that you make `EXIT PROGRAM` and `STOP RUN` the only lines in the paragraphs they belong to. This is an aid to clarity, but is not required by most compilers.

CALL with parameters

The simple calling sequence I've just shown has its uses, but we can extend its capability by passing data between the calling and called programs. This is done with the `CALL USING` statement together with the `LINKAGE SECTION` in the called program. Here's the example code. The top-level program is again called `TOPPROG.CBL`; it calls only one subprogram, `SUBPROG1.CBL`, with one parameter.

The parameter is `WS-PARMS`. The literal "`Initialising text string`" is moved to it before the call to `SUBPROG1.CBL`. The call passes `WS-PARMS` 'across the gap' to `SUBPROG1.CBL`.

The top-level program, `TOPPROG.CBL`, passes the contents of its data item `WS-PARMS` to the data item of the same name found in the `LINKAGE SECTION` of `SUBPROG1.CBL`. The names don't have to correspond like this but it could, marginally, be regarded as good practice that they should do so.

Once executing in `SUBPROG1.CBL`, we display a message, reassign `WS-PARMS` with the literal "`Assigned text string`" and use `EXIT PROGRAM` to return control to `TOPPROG.CBL`. There, when we display `WS-PARMS`, we find it has the value assigned to it in `SUBPROG1.CBL`. The displayed output from the execution of the two programs is this:

```
Personal COBOL version 2.0 from Micro Focus
PCOBRUN V2.0.02  Copyright (C) 1983-1993 Micro Focus Ltd.
Executing TOPPROG.CBL
Calling SUBPROG1.CBL with Initialising text string
Executing SUBPROG1.CBL with Initialising text string
Returned from SUBPROG1.CBL with Assigned text string
Exiting TOPPROG.CBL
```

TOPPROG.CBL

```
**********************************************************************
*                                                                    *
*    This program uses CALL to invoke one other COBOL program,       *
*    passing  a parameter by means of the USING clause.              *
*                                                                    *
**********************************************************************
     IDENTIFICATION DIVISION.
     PROGRAM-ID. TOPPROG.

     ENVIRONMENT DIVISION.

     DATA DIVISION.
     WORKING-STORAGE SECTION.
     01  WS-PARMS    PIC X(50).

     PROCEDURE DIVISION.
     CALL-PROGRAMS.
         DISPLAY "Executing TOPPROG.CBL".
         MOVE "Initialising text string" TO WS-PARMS.
         DISPLAY "Calling SUBPROG1.CBL with " WS-PARMS.
         CALL "SUBPROG1" USING WS-PARMS.
         DISPLAY "Returned from SUBPROG1.CBL with " WS-PARMS.
         DISPLAY "Exiting TOPPROG.CBL".

     PROGRAM-END.
         STOP RUN.
```

> Output parameter sent to **SUBPROG1**.

> Parameter changed on return from **SUBPROG1**, shown here

SUBPROG1.CBL

```
**********************************************************************
*    This program is called by TOPPROG.CBL.                          *
**********************************************************************
     IDENTIFICATION DIVISION.
     PROGRAM-ID. SUBPROG1.

     ENVIRONMENT DIVISION.

     DATA DIVISION.
     WORKING-STORAGE SECTION.
     LINKAGE SECTION.
     01  WS-PARMS    PIC X(50).

     PROCEDURE DIVISION USING WS-PARMS.
     DISPLAY-PARMS.
         DISPLAY "Executing SUBPROG1.CBL with " WS-PARMS.
         MOVE "Assigned text string" TO WS-PARMS.

     PROGRAM-END.
         EXIT PROGRAM.
```

> Input parameter received from **TOPPROG** here.

Nested program CALL

The last of the three ways in which you can call one program from another is by nesting the code of the called program within the code of the calling program. This raises a range of possibilities that are beyond the scope of this book. I point these out in describing the simple implementation that follows. This time, there's only one program file, again TOPPROG.CBL; SUBPROG1.CBL is nested within it.

TOPPROG.CBL

```
****************************************************
*                                                  *
* This uses CALL to invoke one other COBOL program nested within *
* the source code. It also introduces the GLOBAL attribute.    *
*                                                  *
****************************************************
 IDENTIFICATION DIVISION.
 PROGRAM-ID. TOPPROG.

 ENVIRONMENT DIVISION.

 DATA DIVISION.
 WORKING-STORAGE SECTION.
 01  WS-PARMS     PIC X(50) GLOBAL.

 PROCEDURE DIVISION.
 CALL-PROGRAMS.
     DISPLAY "Executing TOPPROG.CBL".
     MOVE "Initialising text string" TO WS-PARMS
     DISPLAY "Calling SUBPROG1.CBL with " WS-PARMS.
     CALL "SUBPROG1".
     DISPLAY "Returned from SUBPROG1.CBL with " WS-PARMS.
     DISPLAY "Exiting TOPPROG.CBL".

 PROGRAM-END.
     STOP RUN.

*********************** SUBPROG1.CBL ***********************
 IDENTIFICATION DIVISION.
 PROGRAM-ID. SUBPROG1.

 PROCEDURE DIVISION.
 DISPLAY-PARMS.
     DISPLAY "Executing SUBPROG1.CBL with " WS-PARMS.
     MOVE "Assigned text string" TO WS-PARMS.

 PROGRAM-END.
     EXIT PROGRAM.

 END PROGRAM SUBPROG1.
 END PROGRAM TOPPROG.
```

Nested program
SUBPROG

The nested program SUBPROG1.CBL extends from the comment-line containing that name to the line END PROGRAM SUBPROG1. The enclosing program TOPPROG.CBL extends from the first line of code to the line END PROGRAM TOPPROG. The END PROGRAM delimiter is necessary here to mark the end of the source code of a nested program. It is different in meaning from EXIT PROGRAM, which ends execution of a (non-nested) CALLed program. Unlike the STOP RUN and EXIT PROGRAM statements, END PROGRAM must start in Area A (between columns 8 and 11).

Thanks to the fact that WS-PARMS is qualified GLOBAL at the point of its definition, the value assigned to WS-PARMS in TOPPROG.CBL is available within the PROCEDURE division of SUBPROG1.CBL. When changed there, the changed value is reflected in TOPPROG.CBL after the point of the call to SUBPROG1.CBL.

If WS-PARMS were not GLOBAL, it would not be visible (in *scope*) in SUBPROG1.CBL. Instead, we'd have to use CALL USING and the LINKAGE section as before.

There are very many ways of nesting COBOL programs. Imagine a top-level program P1, containing two nested programs P2 and P3. Suppose that P2 contains the nested programs P4 and P5. In this arrangement of nesting two levels deep, you'll find that you can't call P4 directly from P1. P1 must call P2 which in turn calls P4. To get around this restriction, you can qualify P4 as COMMON in its PROGRAM-ID clause:

```
PROGRAM-ID.    P4 COMMON.
```

Now any program in the hierarchy down to P4 may call it. P4 (or any other COBOL program), however, cannot call itself.

All this has major implications for the scope of GLOBAL data items – where they are visible and usable. Here, however, a *Made Simple* text must leave it; I refer you to your system's documentation.

The PERFORM statement

Where CALL is used for inter-program calls, PERFORM is used to treat SECTIONs and paragraphs within the PROCEDURE division of a single program effectively as subprograms. You can use PERFORM at a given point in your program to transfer execution control to, to execute, and to return from a block of code elsewhere in the program.

The limitations of PERFORM compared to CALL: PERFORM is restricted in use to one program; you can't pass parameters; and you can't have data local to a PERFORMed procedure, as you can with a CALLed program.

PERFORM may not be quite as powerful as CALL, but it's everywhere, it's good practice to use it and it's vital that you are familiar with it. If MOVE is the most commonly used COBOL verb, PERFORM probably occupies (an admittedly distant) second position. Use PERFORM well and you get modular, easily-manageable COBOL programs that satisfy many aspects of the structured-programming wish-list which I present at the start of this chapter.

The PERFORM statement has several variants. With PERFORM, you can:

1 From a point in code execute an out-of-line paragraph or paragraphs (a body of code), effectively as a subprogram;

2 Execute an out-of-line SECTION containing a number of paragraphs;

3 Execute an out-of-line body of code a fixed number of times;

4 Execute an out-of-line body of code until some condition is satisfied;

5 Repeatedly execute a number of lines of code in-line; this is an elegant loop construction;

6 Execute an out-of-line body of code a number of times, specifying variable values for each iteration.

Sounds complex? At least these descriptions are English and not as obscure as the COBOL-85 general formats for PERFORM. In this and the next section, I present examples of all of these usages of PERFORM. This section covers items 1 and 2; the next section implements the rest in the context of table processing.

Simple PERFORM

The simplest variant of the PERFORM statement is this:

```
PERFORM <paragraph-name>.
```

When this statement is encountered, control of execution is transferred to the start of the paragraph named following the PERFORM verb. That's the same as the behaviour of GO TO. Crucially, when it has finished executing the out-of-line paragraph, PERFORM returns control to the next statement after itself. With GO TO, you transfer control into the wild blue yonder, as it were, and you have no way of knowing what will happen after the transfer. With PERFORM, you're assured that control will return to the start-point after the required code is PERFORMed. The fact that it returns control in this way makes PERFORM far superior to GO TO as a control-flow mechanism.

This program, PERFORM1.CBL, shows simple operation of PERFORM:

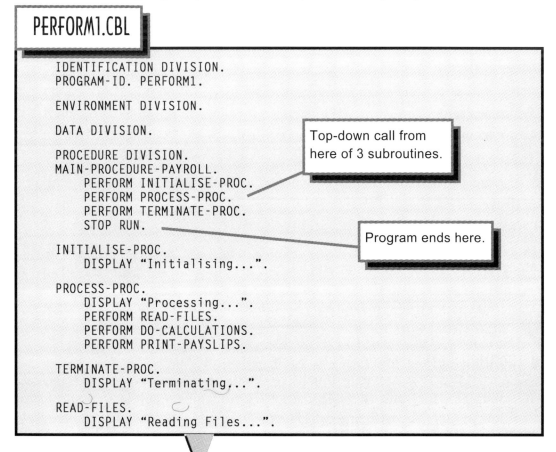

PERFORM1.CBL

```
IDENTIFICATION DIVISION.
PROGRAM-ID. PERFORM1.

ENVIRONMENT DIVISION.

DATA DIVISION.

PROCEDURE DIVISION.
MAIN-PROCEDURE-PAYROLL.
    PERFORM INITIALISE-PROC.
    PERFORM PROCESS-PROC.
    PERFORM TERMINATE-PROC.
    STOP RUN.

INITIALISE-PROC.
    DISPLAY "Initialising...".

PROCESS-PROC.
    DISPLAY "Processing...".
    PERFORM READ-FILES.
    PERFORM DO-CALCULATIONS.
    PERFORM PRINT-PAYSLIPS.

TERMINATE-PROC.
    DISPLAY "Terminating...".

READ-FILES.
    DISPLAY "Reading Files...".
```

Top-down call from here of 3 subroutines.

Program ends here.

```
DO-CALCULATIONS.
    DISPLAY "Doing Calculations...".

PRINT-PAYSLIPS.
    DISPLAY "Printing Payslips...".
```

This looks a bit different from any of the programs you've seen in this book up to now. For example, STOP RUN is no longer at the end of that program. It isn't a start-at-the-beginning, end-at-the-end kind of program. Look at it closely, and you'll see that PERFORM1.CBL is a very structured program. In fact, this is an implementation of the block diagram that I show earlier as an example of structured design.

In the paragraph MAIN-PROCEDURE-PAYROLL, there are three PERFORM statements immediately followed by STOP RUN. Each of these executes the paragraph it names and returns. That's it; that's the program, at its highest level. The rest is refinement, and is implemented in the paragraphs PERFORMed in MAIN-PROCEDURE-PAYROLL.

Consider one of these paragraphs, PROCESS-PROC. This in turn has three PERFORM statements that execute three further, lower-level paragraphs and return. When these three paragraphs have finished executing, PROCESS-PROC returns control to MAIN-PROCEDURE-PAYROLL. Execution stops there with STOP RUN.

Here's the output displayed when PERFORM1.CBL is run:

```
Initialising...
Processing...
Reading Files...
Doing Calculations...
Printing Payslips...
Terminating...
```

You should trace this output to understand fully how all the PERFORM statements work together.

PERFORM THROUGH

With PERFORM and THROUGH (or THRU), you can execute many out-of-line paragraphs with one call. The program PERFORM2.CBL does this, producing the same results as PERFORM1.CBL.

```
PERFORM2.CBL

        IDENTIFICATION DIVISION.
        PROGRAM-ID. PERFORM2.

        ENVIRONMENT DIVISION.

        DATA DIVISION.

        PROCEDURE DIVISION.
        MAIN-PROCEDURE-PAYROLL.
            PERFORM INITIALISE-PROC THROUGH TERMINATE-PROC.
            STOP RUN.

        INITIALISE-PROC.
            DISPLAY "Initialising...".

        PROCESS-PROC.
            DISPLAY "Processing...".
            PERFORM READ-FILES THRU PRINT-PAYSLIPS.

        TERMINATE-PROC.
            DISPLAY "Terminating...".

        READ-FILES.
            DISPLAY "Reading Files...".

        DO-CALCULATIONS.
            DISPLAY "Doing Calculations...".

        PRINT-PAYSLIPS.
            DISPLAY "Printing Payslips...".
```

> Executes all the paragraphs from INITIALISE-PROC through to TERMINATE-PROC. There can be any number of paragraphs between the named pair – all will be performed.

PERFORM a SECTION

An improvement on PERFORM2.CBL is to group the paragraph-sequences into SECTIONs within the PROCEDURE division. The code gets even more structured, becoming a set of true functional modules – some with many paragraphs – instead of a jumble of paragraphs. I strongly recommend this use of PERFORM, for the organisation and structure it imposes on programs. PERFORM3.CBL follows on page 114.

I've marked off the two code SECTIONs with comment lines. They are MAIN-PROCEDURE-PAYROLL, MAIN-LINE and MAIN-PROCESSING. The last two are terminated by paragraphs containing only an EXIT verb. To perform a section, you simply use the section name:

    PERFORM MAIN-LINE

which automatically includes all the paragraphs within MAIN-LINE.

```
      IDENTIFICATION DIVISION.
      PROGRAM-ID. PERFORM3.

      ENVIRONMENT DIVISION.

      DATA DIVISION.

      PROCEDURE DIVISION.
**************Program entry point*********
      MAIN-PROCEDURE-PAYROLL SECTION.
          PERFORM MAIN-LINE.
          STOP RUN.

**************Top level logic module*********
      MAIN-LINE SECTION.
      INITIALISE-PROC.
          DISPLAY "Initialising...".

      PROCESS-PROC.
          DISPLAY "Processing...".
          PERFORM MAIN-PROCESSING.

      TERMINATE-PROC.
          DISPLAY "Terminating...".

      MAIN-LINE-EXIT.
          EXIT.

**************Main Processing module*********
      MAIN-PROCESSING SECTION.
      READ-FILES.
          DISPLAY "Reading Files...".

      DO-CALCULATIONS.
          DISPLAY "Doing Calculations...".

      PRINT-PAYSLIPS.
          DISPLAY "Printing Payslips...".

      MAIN-PROCESSING-EXIT.
          EXIT.
```

Why the EXIT paragraphs? It's a useful convention (but isn't necessary) that explicitly denotes where the PERFORMed paragraphs end. When using PERFORM THROUGH, if the final paragraph is an EXIT paragraph, it's easier to add paragraphs to the executed sequence without changing the calling PERFORM statement. The EXIT verb must be on its own in a paragraph. Once again, the results displayed by this program are unchanged from its earlier versions.

PERFORM used with tables

This section looks at PERFORM in the context of table processing. I present code examples for each of the PERFORM variants 3, 4, 5 and 6 listed on page 110. In Chapter 3, there's some elementary table processing that involves looping through the tables' elements using subscripts. The loops are implemented in TABLE2.CBL (see *Working with tables* in Chapter 3) with the IF… GO TO combination:

```
PROGRAM-START.
    MOVE 1 TO WS-SUB.

DISPLAY-ELEMENTS.
    DISPLAY "Principal " WS-SUB " " INT-PRINCIPAL(WS-SUB).
    DISPLAY "Rate " WS-SUB " " INT-RATE(WS-SUB).
    IF WS-SUB GREATER THAN 4
        GO TO DISPLAY-TABLE.
    ADD 1 TO WS-SUB.
    GO TO DISPLAY-ELEMENTS.
```

which, as I acknowledge in Chapter 3, is OK but far inferior to PERFORM as a mechanism for implementing the loop. The examples that follow show all the main uses of PERFORM with tables; the result is better, more elegant and more maintainable code.

TIMES and UNTIL

You can perform a body of code a fixed number of times or until a particular condition arises. Here's the first of a set of examples derived from the program TABLE2.CBL, found in Chapter 3. It's called TABLE41.CBL and demonstrates use of PERFORM with the TIMES option.

The loop is implemented much more cleanly than in Chapter 3 using a repeated PERFORM. The paragraph DISPLAY-ELEMENTS is executed a fixed 5 times and the subscript data item WS-SUB is kept in step.

Notice that WS-SUB starts at zero and must be increased by one in DISPLAY-ELEMENTS *before* the elements are displayed. If ADD 1 TO WS-SUB. were the last rather than the first sentence in the paragraph, we'd get a subscript-out-of-range error through trying to access table element zero. It's easy to get the order of checking and incrementing loop limits wrong. You must exercise care here, and take advantage of the advanced PERFORM variants used in the examples that follow.

TABLE41.CBL

```
***********************************************************************
*                                                                     *
*  This program traverses a table using a repeated PERFORM.           *
*                                                                     *
***********************************************************************
 IDENTIFICATION DIVISION.
 PROGRAM-ID. TABLE41.

 ENVIRONMENT DIVISION.

 DATA DIVISION.
 WORKING-STORAGE SECTION.
 01  INT-RATE-TABLE.
     02 INT-RATE-DATA.
         03 FILLER PIC 9(7)           VALUE 1000.
         03 FILLER PIC 99V999         VALUE 3.5.
         03 FILLER PIC 9(7)           VALUE 5000.
         03 FILLER PIC 99V999         VALUE 4.5.
         03 FILLER PIC 9(7)           VALUE 10000.
         03 FILLER PIC 99V999         VALUE 5.0.
         03 FILLER PIC 9(7)           VALUE 50000.
         03 FILLER PIC 99V999         VALUE 6.5.
         03 FILLER PIC 9(7)           VALUE 100000.
         03 FILLER PIC 99V999         VALUE 7.5.
     02 FILLER REDEFINES INT-RATE-DATA.
         03 FILLER OCCURS 5.
             04 INT-PRINCIPAL         PIC 9(7).
             04 INT-RATE              PIC 99V999.

 01  WS-SUB      PIC 999 COMP.

 PROCEDURE DIVISION.
 PROGRAM-START.
     MOVE ZERO TO WS-SUB.
     PERFORM DISPLAY-ELEMENTS 5 TIMES.

 PROGRAM-END.
     STOP RUN.

 DISPLAY-ELEMENTS.
     ADD 1 TO WS-SUB.
     DISPLAY "Principal " WS-SUB " " INT-PRINCIPAL(WS-SUB).
     DISPLAY "Rate " WS-SUB " " INT-RATE(WS-SUB).
```

The PERFORM a fixed number of TIMES technique is a little inflexible: what if the subscript limit is other than 5? You can use a variable limit in the PERFORM statement:

```
PERFORM DISPLAY-ELEMENTS WS-SUB-LIMIT TIMES.
```

where WS-SUB-LIMIT must be defined as a numeric data item containing the current TIMES limit. A good alternative is to use PERFORM UNTIL:

```
PERFORM DISPLAY-ELEMENTS UNTIL WS-SUB EQUALS WS-SUB-LIMIT.
```

There's an exercise at the end of this chapter in which you're asked to implement TABLE41.CBL with this flavour of PERFORM.

Whichever way you choose to do it – with TIMES or UNTIL – the displayed result on execution of TABLE41.CBL is this:

```
Principal 001 0001000
Rate 001 03500
Principal 002 0005000
Rate 002 04500
Principal 003 0010000
Rate 003 05000
Principal 004 0050000
Rate 004 06500
Principal 005 0100000
Rate 005 07500
```

PERFORM in-line

It's possible to use PERFORM to loop over an in-line body of code. Up to now, all uses of PERFORM that I've shown have executed an out-of-line body of code such as a SECTION or one or more paragraphs. In COBOL-74, this was the only way you could use PERFORM; COBOL-85 introduces this mechanism:

```
PROCEDURE DIVISION.
DISPLAY-ELEMENTS.
    PERFORM VARYING WS-SUB FROM 1 BY 1
        UNTIL WS-SUB EQUALS 5
        DISPLAY "Principal " WS-SUB " " INT-PRINCIPAL(WS-SUB)
        DISPLAY "Rate " WS-SUB " " INT-RATE(WS-SUB)
    END-PERFORM.

PROGRAM-END.
    STOP RUN.
```

This code is from the program TABLE42.CBL. Because everything up to the PROCEDURE division is unchanged from TABLE41.CBL, I've left all that stuff out. The code

```
PERFORM VARYING WS-SUB FROM 1 BY 1
    UNTIL WS-SUB EQUALS 5
```

actually doesn't specify a paragraph to PERFORM. What it does do is iterate a data item, WS-SUB, between the specified limits and, on each iteration, execute all the code up to the point where END-PERFORM is encountered. This is extremely useful. Now you've got a general technique for implementing loops in-line. You don't have to resort to the IF... GO TO combination of TABLE2.CBL. Neither do you have to put the code to be looped over in a separate paragraph so that it can be executed by a PERFORM call. You may find that this is the variant of PERFORM that you use most often.

This is a COBOL-85 PERFORM...END-PERFORM construct. The END-PERFORM is necessary. A full-stop in its place won't work. If you use a full-stop at the end of any of the enclosed statements, that won't work either and you'll get complaining compiler messages. Take care, then, not to terminate any of the enclosed statements with a full-stop.

When TABLE42.CBL runs, it displays this output:

```
Principal 001 0001000
Rate 001 03500
Principal 002 0005000
Rate 002 04500
Principal 003 0010000
Rate 003 05000
Principal 004 0050000
Rate 004 06500
```

Why did the loop stop at 4? The reason is that PERFORM by default checks the loop limit *before* executing its enclosed DISPLAY statements. To make its check the limits *after* it executes the statements, you need to change the syntax of the PERFORM slightly:

```
PERFORM WITH TEST AFTER
    VARYING WS-SUB FROM 1 BY 1
    UNTIL WS-SUB EQUALS 5
        DISPLAY "Principal " WS-SUB " " INT-PRINCIPAL(WS-SUB)
        DISPLAY "Rate " WS-SUB " " INT-RATE(WS-SUB)
END-PERFORM.
```

Now, WITH TEST AFTER ensures that the UNTIL is not tested until after the two DISPLAYs are executed. The contents of all five table elements are now displayed. For the opposite effect, you can use the WITH TEST BEFORE clause but, as it's the default, you'll never need to.

Out-of-line PERFORM VARYING

In this, the most advanced PERFORM variant, an out-of-line body of code is repeatedly executed, the repetition being governed by the values of a data item varying between the limits set in the PERFORM statement. It's easiest to understand by looking at an example:

TABLE43.CBL

```
****************************************************************
*                                                              *
*   Traverses a table using an out-of-line PERFORM and INDEXes *
*                                                              *
****************************************************************
 IDENTIFICATION DIVISION.
 PROGRAM-ID. TABLE43.

 ENVIRONMENT DIVISION.

 DATA DIVISION.
 WORKING-STORAGE SECTION.
 01 INT-RATE-TABLE.
     02 INT-RATE-DATA.
         03 FILLER PIC 9(7)          VALUE 1000.
         03 FILLER PIC 99V999        VALUE 3.5.
         03 FILLER PIC 9(7)          VALUE 5000.
         03 FILLER PIC 99V999        VALUE 4.5.
         03 FILLER PIC 9(7)          VALUE 10000.
         03 FILLER PIC 99V999        VALUE 5.0.
         03 FILLER PIC 9(7)          VALUE 50000.
         03 FILLER PIC 99V999        VALUE 6.5.
         03 FILLER PIC 9(7)          VALUE 100000.
         03 FILLER PIC 99V999        VALUE 7.5.
     02 FILLER REDEFINES INT-RATE-DATA.
         03 RATE-TABLE OCCURS 5 INDEXED BY RATE-INDEX.
             04 INT-PRINCIPAL  PIC 9(7).
             04 INT-RATE       PIC 99V999.

 01  WS-SUB   PIC 999 COMP.

 PROCEDURE DIVISION.
 PROGRAM-MAIN.
     PERFORM DISPLAY-ELEMENTS
         VARYING RATE-INDEX FROM 1 BY 1
         UNTIL RATE-INDEX EQUALS 5.

 PROGRAM-END.
     STOP RUN.

 DISPLAY-ELEMENTS.
     SET WS-SUB TO RATE-INDEX.
     DISPLAY "Principal " WS-SUB " " INT-PRINCIPAL(RATE-INDEX).
     DISPLAY "Rate " WS-SUB " " INT-RATE(RATE-INDEX).
```

This time, we're using an indexed, as opposed to a subscripted, table. We need to vary the index whilst looping over the table. You're not allowed use arithmetic on INDEXes along the lines of

```
ADD 1 TO RATE-INDEX.
```

Notice that RATE-INDEX isn't defined anywhere in the DATA division with a PICTURE clause. To increment it, you must use the special form

```
SET RATE-INDEX UP BY 1.
```

Instead of repeatedly doing this, it's better to use PERFORM VARYING:

```
PERFORM DISPLAY-ELEMENTS
    VARYING RATE-INDEX FROM 1 BY 1
    UNTIL RATE-INDEX EQUALS 5.
```

All the statements in DISPLAY-ELEMENTS are repeatedly executed. RATE-INDEX can only be used as an index on the table; you can't add to it, otherwise access it or DISPLAY it. Therefore, we have to maintain the data item WS-SUB to display the loop count. The SET statement shown is the only way of extracting the value in RATE-INDEX for display.

The number of restrictions on using INDEXes raises the question: why not just use subscripts instead? The COBOL INDEX mechanism was implemented to increase the internal efficiency of table-handling. In general, using an INDEXed table is at least as fast as, and usually faster than, using the subscripted equivalent. This is particularly so when INDEXes are used in conjunction with the SEARCH verb:

```
SEARCH ALL RATE-TABLE
    AT END DISPLAY "Finished Search"
WHEN PRINCIPAL(RATE-INDEX) > 100000
    DISPLAY "Quote special interest rate"
END SEARCH.
```

Considerations of space preclude my looking further at SEARCH here, but you should be able to get the sense of its meaning. As regards INDEX, in our era of supercomputers on desks, there's now a school of thought which holds that internal efficiency gains of the INDEX mechanism aren't worth the cost of its inflexibility. I'm inclined to agree and to recommend that you use subscripts in preference to INDEXes.

The EVALUATE statement

EVALUATE is the COBOL-85 alternative, for complex condition-testing, to the cascade of nested IF statements. Where you have to make a complex multi-way test, you should use EVALUATE in preference to sequences of IFs and ELSEs. Here's an example, EVALUAT1.CBL, of EVALUATE in action:

EVALUAT1.CBL

```
*********************************************************************
*                                                                 *
*   This program  demonstrates a simple EVALUATE statement.       *
*                                                                 *
*********************************************************************
      IDENTIFICATION DIVISION.
      PROGRAM-ID. EVALUAT1.

      ENVIRONMENT DIVISION.

      DATA DIVISION.
      WORKING-STORAGE SECTION.
      01  WS-DAYNO     PIC 9.

      PROCEDURE DIVISION.
      ENTER-DATA.
          DISPLAY "Enter day number " NO ADVANCING.
          ACCEPT WS-DAYNO.

      TEST-DATA.
          EVALUATE WS-DAYNO
              WHEN 1
                  DISPLAY "Monday"
              WHEN 2
                  DISPLAY "Tuesday"
              WHEN 3
                  DISPLAY "Wednesday"
              WHEN 4
                  DISPLAY "Thursday"
              WHEN 5
                  DISPLAY "Friday"
              WHEN 6 THRU 7
                  DISPLAY "Weekend!!!"
              WHEN OTHER
                  DISPLAY "Invalid day number entered"
          END-EVALUATE.

      PROGRAM-END.
          STOP RUN.
```

It should be fairly obvious to you what this program does. The first paragraph accepts into WS-DAYNO a number input by the user. WS-DAYNO is EVALUATEd in the next paragraph and an action taken depending on its value. I ran the program in sequence three times, with the following results (my input in boldface):

```
Personal COBOL version 2.0 from Micro Focus
PCOBRUN V2.0.02  Copyright (C) 1983-1993 Micro Focus Ltd.
Enter day number 5
Friday
Personal COBOL version 2.0 from Micro Focus
PCOBRUN V2.0.02  Copyright (C) 1983-1993 Micro Focus Ltd.
Enter day number 6
Weekend!!!
Personal COBOL version 2.0 from Micro Focus
PCOBRUN V2.0.02  Copyright (C) 1983-1993 Micro Focus Ltd.
Enter day number 8
Invalid day number entered
```

The tests need not be in numeric order as shown. Only one test can be successful on any EVALUATE operation. If a given test is included twice and is successful, only the first one has its associated statement(s) executed. WHEN OTHER does not have to be included but, if it is, it must be the last test.

The main alternative form of EVALUATE is EVALUATE TRUE, in which complex tests can be made on any data item:

```
EVALUATE TRUE
      WHEN (WS-DAYNO < 1) OR (WS-DAYNO > 7)
          DISPLAY "Invalid day number entered"
      WHEN (WS-DAYNO > 0) AND (WS-DAYNO < 6)
          DISPLAY "Weekday"
      WHEN (WS-DAYNO = 6) OR (WS-DAYNO = 7)
          DISPLAY "Weekend!!!"
END-EVALUATE.
```

In this case, EVALUATE is entered and any condition for any data item can be tested within the EVALUATE ...END-EVALUATE pair.

122

Naming conventions

In every real-life COBOL programming environment, you'll find that there are conventions in place according to which you must write your code. Their purpose is to ensure that your code is readable, consistent with other programs on the site and easily maintainable.

There are no universally-accepted COBOL naming conventions. What is universally-accepted is that any conventions you do use should be consistently applied. In a sense, it doesn't matter too much what the conventions are, provided they are predictable and always used. All I can do here is give a set of recommendations which are widely accepted as good practice and to which you should adhere if no other standards are in place at your location.

- Be consistent. Whatever naming scheme you adopt, use it all the time. Much of the value of a naming convention lies in its predictability.

- Don't use COBOL names that are too long; such names impair the readability of your code. Restrict names to 30 characters or less.

- Prefix input file, record and data names with the letter 'I' as well as a system identifier. For example, the input payroll transaction file could be called I-PR-TRANS-FILE. Output files should be similarly prefixed 'O' and input-output files 'IO'.

- Data items defined in WORKING-STORAGE should be prefixed 'WS', followed by a system identifier. For example, in the stock-control system, you might use WS-SC-STOCK-ON-HAND.

- Number-off SECTION and paragraph names in alphabetic order. If you have written a program of 500 paragraphs, whoever succeeds you in maintaining it will thank you. SECTIONs in the payroll program might be named A-PR-INIT, B-PR-PROCESS and C-PR-TERMINATE at the top level. A SECTION called from B-PR-PROCESS might be BA-PR-READ-FILES. Another level down would have the prefix BAA, and so on. Within a given section, paragraphs should be named, e.g. BA-000-START, BA-010-READ, and so on. The final paragraph in a SECTION will be something like BA-999-EXIT.

- Finally, although it's not strictly to do with naming, you should use indentation to make obvious the meaning of your program's code.

Exercises

1   Write a variant of `table41.cbl` (see *PERFORM used with tables*) which stops the loop on the table's elements using a `PERFORM UNTIL` statement.

2   Write a program, `topprog.cbl`, which accepts two numbers as user input, and passes three parameters to a program called `addnos.cbl`. Two of the parameters are for the numbers and the third is for the result of the addition of the numbers done by `addnos.cbl`.

Identation styles

The two statements following are semantically identical:

```
IF A = B THEN ADD 1 TO B DISPLAY "B Incremented" END-IF.

IF A = B THEN
    ADD 1 TO B
    DISPLAY "B Incremented"
END-IF.
```

but it's easy to see that the second form is preferable. The indentation conventions I use in this book are a reasonable guideline that you should follow.

5 Sequential file I/O

File concepts

Files are at the heart of COBOL programming. You can think of all the stuff in the first four chapters as being a kind of preparation – the bits and pieces, or 'plumbing' – that you need to take advantage of COBOL's powerful file-processing capabilities. The sample programs in this and the next chapter use the techniques of structure and control flow shown in Chapter 4, as well as a version of the naming conventions mentioned there.

As I point out in Chapter 1, files are repositories of data. They are organised as sequences or collections of records. In COBOL, this organisation can be of three kinds: sequential, indexed and relative.

● With sequential organisation, you access the records one after the other in the order they appear.

● Indexed files allow so-called *random access* (a misnomer, because there's absolutely nothing random about COBOL); you read the file, accessing records using a *key* that uniquely identifies one record. Such a key might be your name or (more likely) employee or National Insurance number. Key access allows the indexed file to be accessed in an *apparently* random fashion.

● Relative files contain numbered records and, given those numbers, you can read the file's records in any order you want.

This chapter deals only with the techniques of defining, setting up and using COBOL sequential files. Chapters 6 covers indexed and relative files.

In COBOL, for every file that you want to use, you must provide a physical definition and a logical definition. The physical definition is placed in the ENVIRONMENT division; computer systems vary in the ways they implement disk, tape and printer files, so this is an appropriate place for it. The logical definition is found in the DATA division.

Having defined the file, there are four ways in which you can open it and get at the data therein: you can open for *input*, for *output*, for *input-output* and *extend*.

- Input mode means that you're going to read the file.

- Output implies writing.

- Input-output means to open the file for both reading and writing (or for *in-situ update*, as some classical scholars would have it).

- EXTEND mode allows you with sequential files to append and write data to the end of an existing file.

You can't delete records from a COBOL sequential file. All you can do by way of a substitute is to mark a record deleted: put a big X or some equivalent in the record so that programs that access that record later 'know' that it has been 'deleted'. At some point later on, you actually remove all the 'deleted' records by creating a new version of the sequential file that contains only the non-'deleted' records.

One of the major reasons-for-existence of COBOL is for producing printed reports. To make a COBOL program print a report, you need a printer and an associated *print file*. A print file is a kind of sequential file and I explain how to implement it in this chapter as well.

Nowadays users of computers (particularly PCs or other small ones) tend to equate 'file' with 'disk file'. But there's a whole world of mainframes and minis out there that also use *serial* devices such as magnetic tape for large-scale archival storage. Look at your next UNIX or mainframe system and you'll find a print *spooler*: a mechanism for *buffering* and storing many print files for output. (Trivia: *spool* stands for Simultaneous Peripheral Operations On Line). The way in which files are specified in COBOL programs reflect this orientation towards large-scale-computing.

Defining a file

Physical definition

You define the physical characteristics of a file in your COBOL program in the FILE-CONTROL paragraph of the INPUT-OUTPUT section of the ENVIRONMENT division. FILE-CONTROL is the first of two paragraphs specified in the INPUT-OUTPUT section:

```
ENVIRONMENT DIVISION.
   ...
INPUT-OUTPUT SECTION.
FILE-CONTROL.
   ...
I-O-CONTROL.
   ...
```

The I-O-CONTROL paragraph is optional – it includes definitions for tape devices and record buffering – but FILE-CONTROL is not. You use the SELECT statement in the FILE-CONTROL paragraph to specify the physical characteristics of a file that your COBOL program will use. SELECT is written in Area B: between columns 12 and 72. SELECT has a large number of options, but it's worth summarising them here. This is the general form of SELECT for sequential files:

```
SELECT [OPTIONAL] <file-name>
   ASSIGN TO {<implementor-name-1>, <literal-1>}
   [RESERVE <integer-1> {AREA, AREAS}]
   [[ORGANIZATION IS] SEQUENTIAL]
   [PADDING CHARACTER IS {<data-name-1>, <literal-2>}]
   [RECORD DELIMITER IS {STANDARD-1, <implementor-name-2>}]
   [ACCESS MODE IS SEQUENTIAL]
   [FILE STATUS IS <data-name-2>].
```

As usual, everything in square brackets can be left out, depending on the characteristics of the file you're defining. The curly braces contain lists of alternatives. Anything underlined must be used in full if it is used at all. I've given this full general form because it's useful. COBOL programmers are often unsure of what the SELECT options are, whether or not they are optional, and in what order they are used. The order of options shown in the general form is the only one that you can be sure will work with all COBOL-85 compilers. Refer to the general form if you're in doubt.

The minimum you need physically to define a sequential file is this:

```
SELECT <file-name>
    ASSIGN <physical file name>.
```

which doesn't look so bad, does it? In this minimal case, the way that the SELECT statement would actually appear in your program is this:

```
SELECT O-PAYROLL-MASTER
    ASSIGN "seqpmast.dat".
```

where O-PAYROLL-MASTER is an example identifier used within the program to represent the physical (on your system's disk or other peripheral device) file called SEQPMAST.DAT.

A typical use of SELECT, when defining a sequential file, is this:

```
SELECT OPTIONAL O-PAYROLL-MASTER
    ASSIGN "seqpmast.dat"
    ORGANIZATION IS SEQUENTIAL
    ACCESS MODE IS SEQUENTIAL
    FILE STATUS IS WS-O-PR-STATUS.
```

SELECT OPTIONAL (OPTIONAL is optional!) means that, if the file is opened for input (reading) and it doesn't exist, both the OPEN and subsequent READ statements will work but will retrieve no data.

When it is first written, the file seqpmast.dat will be organised sequentially – every record written to the file after all existing records. ORGANIZATION IS SEQUENTIAL is the default, so you can leave it out, but it's usual to include it for clarity. Also, note the North American spelling (the 'Z' in ORGANIZATION), which is necessary: the equivalent British 'S' will not do.

There are three possibilities in COBOL for file ORGANIZATION: SEQUENTIAL, INDEXED and RELATIVE. You must pick one and get it right first time: once a data file is created with a given physical ORGANIZATION, you cannot subsequently change it.

Unlike ORGANIZATION, ACCESS MODE can vary after the physical file has been created. For example, you can create a file with ORGANIZATION INDEXED, run one program that uses the file with ACCESS MODE IS SEQUENTIAL, and then run another that specifies ACCESS MODE IS INDEXED. All this means is that you are, on the one hand, looking sequentially at the records of a physically-indexed file while, on the other, you are using the full indexed capabilities of the file to read its records 'randomly'.

ACCESS MODE IS SEQUENTIAL means that, when your program reads the file, records will be accessed in the physical order that they appear in the file. Again, this is the default and can be left out.

FILE STATUS refers to a data item, WS-O-PR-STATUS, defined in the WORKING-STORAGE section, which is assigned a numeric code after every OPEN, CLOSE, READ, WRITE, REWRITE, DELETE and START statement executed. It is a very good idea to include this, as it allows you to diagnose errors that may happen when you're doing file I/O operations. The FILE STATUS values found in the associated variable can be summarised thus:

Status Code	Meaning
'00'	Successful execution of preceding command
'1' first character	Unsuccessful execution: AT END
'2' first character	Unsuccessful execution: INVALID KEY
'3' first character	Unsuccessful execution: file missing or corrupt
'4' first character	Unsuccessful execution: illogical operation
'9' first character	Implementation-defined error

The '2' errors (INVALID KEY), by definition only occur with indexed files, which are the subject of Chapter 6. '00' is defined as success, so the least you will usually do is to test the FILE STATUS data item for being NOT EQUAL TO ZERO. If it isn't zero, something went wrong on the last I/O operation. If it's '30' or upwards, the error is serious. If it's less than '30', you can often ignore the error. The full list of I/O status codes for sequential file I/O operations is shown opposite.

You can usually omit the remaining SELECT options. It's possible to RESERVE multiple areas for records in memory so that reading a file is made more efficient. This was more relevant in the past than it is now. Today's operating systems usually look after this kind of read-buffering for you, so you need not explicitly specify it in your program.

Status Code	Meaning
'00'	Successful execution of preceding command
'04'	Unexpected record size on READ
'05'	File doesn't exist on OPEN
'07'	Tape-drive options in disk-file definitions
'10'	READ failed AT END of file, or with SELECT OPTIONAL
'30'	'Permanent', system-level error
'34'	Out of space on WRITE
'35'	Non-OPTIONAL file doesn't exist on OPEN
'37'	System prohibits you from OPENing file
'38'	OPEN error; file previously CLOSEd WITH LOCK
'39'	OPEN error; file attributes in the program do not match those of the file
'41'	OPEN error: file already open
'42'	CLOSE error: file not open
'43'	Operation out of sequence (e.g. REWRITE must be preceded by READ)
'44'	Size error on REWRITE
'46'	READ failure after previous READ failure
'47'	Can't READ from file opened OUTPUT or EXTEND
'48'	Can't WRITE to file opened INPUT
'49'	Must open file I-O to use REWRITE
'9n'	Compiler-specific error

The PADDING CHARACTER is for any space on the physical device (tape, disk) not filled by the file records when they are written: let it default to whatever the system chooses. It won't hurt you. RECORD DELIMITER refers to tape devices and the formats by which records are separated from each other. You only need to know its internal details if you have to do something like write a C program to interpret a file produced by a COBOL program. If in doubt, use STANDARD-1, but ignore this in most cases.

Logical definition

Now that you're in a position to use the SELECT statement, you need to know how to specify the file logically – making a link with the physical definition – so that your program can use the file. You make the logical definition using an FD level 'number' in the FILE section of the DATA division. The FILE section precedes the WORKING-STORAGE section within the DATA division:

```
DATA DIVISION.
FILE SECTION.
      .
      .
WORKING-STORAGE SECTION.
      .
      .
LINKAGE SECTION.
```

I specify the general form of the SELECT statement quite accurately above, so that you know all the options, as well as the order in which they are used. It's less useful to give the general form of the FD for sequential files: there are many little-used specifications which would tend to confuse rather than clarify.

The FD must start in Area A: between columns 8 and 11. Almost everything is optional. Here's an example of an absolute minimum FD specification:

```
FD O-PAYROLL MASTER.
01 O-PR-RECORD.
      02............ .
```

O-PAYROLL-MASTER is the identifier that the COBOL program uses to refer to the file. It's associated with the name of the file on disk or tape, SEQPMAST.DAT, by the earlier SELECT statement. The logical file definition consists also of one or more record definitions, made at the 01 level immediately following the full-stop terminating the FD.

This is a more typical FD specification for a sequential file:

```
FD O-PAYROLL MASTER
      BLOCK CONTAINS 20 RECORDS
      LABEL RECORDS ARE STANDARD
      RECORD CONTAINS 113 CHARACTERS.

01 O-PR-RECORD.
      02...
```

The BLOCK CONTAINS option specifies that records are to read from the file 20 at a time, a buffering technique which, depending on the characteristics of the system you're using, may improve your program's file-access performance. As I explain in Chapter 1 (*Your first real COBOL program*), LABEL RECORDS ARE STANDARD refers to tape files. It isn't needed at all for disk files and is included only for compatibility with older programs. As you'll see, for a printer – where labels are not relevant – we'll use LABEL RECORDS ARE OMITTED.

The RECORD CONTAINS option is more important. In the form shown above, it specifies that the maximum record-length is 113 characters. If a record is defined which is longer, the part after 113 characters will be truncated when a record is written to the file or read from it. Multiple records can be specified at the 01 level. This is, as I point out in Chapter 3 (*Redefining and renaming data items*) as if REDEFINES were quietly used to respecify the file's record format. Three record definitions at the 01 level don't use three times the space; they just allow you to look at the same record space in three different ways. If you use multiple record specifications of different lengths, you might write the RECORD CONTAINS entry like this:

```
RECORD CONTAINS 73 TO 211 CHARACTERS.
```

where no record is shorter than 73 characters or longer than 211.

Accessing file data

The next step is to use the OPEN, CLOSE, READ, WRITE and REWRITE verbs to allow you access to files that you have defined.

You must open a file before you can read from it or write to it. You should close the file when you no longer require it, although STOP RUN will probably (it should, according to the COBOL-85 Standard) close the file for you at the end of the program. In general, you should keep files open for the shortest possible time: having a large number of files permanently open for a lengthy executing program is inefficient and may lock out other programs trying to access them.

OPEN

This is the general form of OPEN for sequential files:

    OPEN {INPUT, OUTPUT, I-O, EXTEND} <file-name> [REVERSED].

Where you want to read records from a file, you must open the file for INPUT or I-O (input-output). If you open a file in INPUT mode and it does not exist, it is not created. Instead, an error is generated, unless you specified the physical definition of the file with SELECT OPTIONAL.

Open the file for OUTPUT if you want to write to it. Open the file I-O if you intend to use the REWRITE statement to update records in place. Be aware that every REWRITE you use must be immediately preceded by a corresponding READ statement. If a file does not exist, opening it in OUTPUT or I-O mode will create it. Opening a file for OUTPUT destroys the data in any existing file of the same name. If, instead, you want to append records at the end of an existing file – after all its existing records – then open the file in EXTEND mode.

The following statement opens a file for output:

    OPEN OUTPUT O-PAYROLL-MASTER.

where O-PAYROLL-MASTER is the identifier used in the FD to refer to the disk file seqpmast.dat. When you open a sequential file in this way, subsequent READ operations will retrieve the records from the file, start to end, in the order they appear. You could read the file from back to front using this OPEN statement:

    OPEN OUTPUT O-PAYROLL-MASTER REVERSED.

although there won't be many applications where you'll need to do so.

CLOSE

Compared to OPEN, CLOSE is easy. Close the file with the statement:

```
CLOSE O-PAYROLL-MASTER.
```

Depending on the system, this may or may not mean that the file data has all actually been written to disk. UNIX does a form of *write-behind*: it tells the program that it has written the data to disk but in fact has only buffered the data in memory for later writing. In practice, the 'later' write to disk is almost immediate but remember that it may be later and that this is outside the control of your program.

If you use the form:

```
CLOSE O-PAYROLL-MASTER WITH LOCK.
```

It means that, while the program is executing, you can't open the file again; you must restart the program.

READ

Here's the general form of the READ statement for sequential files:

```
READ <file-name> [NEXT] [RECORD] [INTO <identifier-1>]
    [AT END <statement-1>]
    [NOT AT END <statement-2>]
[END-READ].
```

Usually, you'll take the default record and identifier – the 01 level following the FD – and write something like this:

```
READ I-PAYROLL-MASTER AT END
    MOVE "Y" TO WS-I-END-FILE.
```

You can, equivalently, write:

```
READ I-PAYROLL-MASTER AT END
    MOVE "Y" TO WS-I-END-FILE
    END-READ.
```

This is the preferred form, having been introduced with COBOL-85. Its advantage over the earlier, COBOL-74 version of READ is that it specifies clearly where the READ sentence ends. In both, the MOVE statement is executed once, when the end of file is reached after reading all its records. The NOT AT END option is available, and can be used in conjunction with AT END. Using NOT AT END causes its subject statement(s) to be executed every time a record is read from the file.

Using NEXT RECORD has no effect for sequential files but can be used for readability. If you use the INTO <identifier-1> option, the data read from the file is moved to that identifier instead of the default file record. You need to ensure that the identifier can accommodate all the data stored in a record being read from the file.

WRITE

Here's the general form for WRITE for sequential files:

```
WRITE <record-name> [FROM <identifier-1>]
   [{BEFORE, AFTER} ADVANCING {PAGE, <integer-1> LINES}]
   [AT {EOP, END-OF-PAGE} <statement-1>]
   [NOT AT {EOP, END-OF-PAGE} <statement-2>]
[END-WRITE].
```

Unless you're printing, with sequential files you'll almost always use something like:

```
WRITE O-PR-RECORD.
```

where O-PR-RECORD is a 01-level record name associated with an FD representing a file that you have already opened for OUTPUT. Remember:*you READ a file name but you WRITE a record name.*

If you use the FROM <identifier-1> option, the data in that identifier is copied to the output record before the record is written. It's up to you to be sure that this move makes sense.

Pretty much all the other options have to do with printing. Even with the simple WRITE of a single record, you can use END-WRITE although it smacks of overkill. If you use all the print options, (see page 144), you should end the WRITE statement with END-WRITE.

REWRITE

If you remember that you must always READ a record immediately before you REWRITE it, the rest is easy. Here's the general form of REWRITE for sequential files:

```
REWRITE <record-name> [FROM <identifier-1>].
```

Having previously read a record from a file opened in I-O mode, you can REWRITE that record, presumably having changed its contents. This updates the file in place. If you use the FROM <identifier-1> option, it's up to you to ensure that the data in that identifier fits in the allotted record space in the file.

136

File-update application

And now, after all that good stuff, we at last get to write a proper file processing application. It's made up of two programs. The first, SEQWRITE.CBL, creates a payroll file full of employee information input by the user. The second, SEQUPD.CBL, does a simple update-in-place of that file. Here's the file-creation program:

SEQWRITE.CBL

```
****************************************************************
*                                                              *
*    This program initialises the payroll master file from user-*
*    input data. File organization is sequential.              *
*                                                              *
****************************************************************
     IDENTIFICATION DIVISION.
     PROGRAM-ID. SEQWRITE.

     ENVIRONMENT DIVISION.

     INPUT-OUTPUT SECTION.
     FILE-CONTROL.
         SELECT OPTIONAL O-PAYROLL-MASTER
             ASSIGN TO "SEQPMAST.DAT"
             ORGANIZATION IS SEQUENTIAL
             ACCESS MODE IS SEQUENTIAL
             FILE STATUS IS WS-O-PR-STATUS.

     DATA DIVISION.
     FILE SECTION.
     FD  O-PAYROLL-MASTER
         BLOCK CONTAINS 20 RECORDS
         LABEL RECORDS ARE STANDARD
         RECORD CONTAINS 113 CHARACTERS.
     01  O-PR-RECORD.
         02 FILLER              PIC X(113).

     WORKING-STORAGE SECTION.
     01  WS-PR-RECORD.
         02 WS-PR-NAME          PIC X(20).
         02 WS-PR-EMPNO         PIC X(8).
         02 WS-PR-EMPTYPE       PIC X.
         02 WS-PR-GRADE         PIC 99.
         02 WS-PR-AGE           PIC 999.
         02 WS-PR-GENDER        PIC X.
         02 WS-PR-REFNO         PIC 9999.
         02 WS-PR-ADDR          PIC X(30).
```

> As the field detail is collected into WS-PR-RECORD, O-PR-RECORD need only be a FILLER of the record size.

```
         02 WS-PR-EMPDATE.
            03 WS-PR-CCYY     PIC 9999.
            03 WS-PR-MM       PIC 99.
            03 WS-PR-DD       PIC 99.
         02 WS-PR-PAY         PIC 9(6)V99.
         02 WS-PR-BONUS       PIC 9(6)V99.
         02 WS-PR-CAR         PIC X(20).

     01  WS-O-OUTPUT-FINISHED PIC X VALUE "N".
     01  WS-O-CONTINUE-INPUT  PIC X.
     01  WS-O-PR-STATUS       PIC XX.

     PROCEDURE DIVISION.
     A-MAIN-LINE SECTION.
     A-000-MAIN.
         PERFORM AA-INITIALISE.
         PERFORM AB-PROCESS UNTIL WS-O-OUTPUT-FINISHED = "Y".
         PERFORM AC-TERMINATE.

     A-999-EXIT.
         STOP RUN.

     AA-INITIALISE SECTION.
     AA-000-OPEN.
         OPEN OUTPUT O-PAYROLL-MASTER.
         IF WS-O-PR-STATUS NOT EQUAL ZERO THEN
             DISPLAY "Error " WS-O-PR-STATUS
                 " opening payroll master file."
             GO TO A-999-EXIT
         END-IF.

     AA-999-EXIT.
         EXIT.

     AB-PROCESS SECTION.
     AB-000-GET-DATA.
         MOVE SPACES TO WS-PR-RECORD.
         DISPLAY "Enter Employee name: " NO ADVANCING.
         ACCEPT WS-PR-NAME.
         DISPLAY "Enter Employee number: " NO ADVANCING.
         ACCEPT WS-PR-EMPNO.
         DISPLAY "Enter Employee type (H/S/C): " NO ADVANCING.
         ACCEPT WS-PR-EMPTYPE.
         DISPLAY "Enter Employee grade (1-30): " NO ADVANCING.
         ACCEPT WS-PR-GRADE.
         DISPLAY "Enter Employee age: " NO ADVANCING.
         ACCEPT WS-PR-AGE.
         DISPLAY "Enter Employee gender (M/F): " NO ADVANCING.
         ACCEPT WS-PR-GENDER.
```

Classic three part program: initialise, process and terminate, with the SECTIONs PERFORMed from here.

Because the AB-PROCESS section deals with one record on every execution, it is executed in a loop.

User prompted for payroll/personnel data, which is stored in a holding area in the WORKING-STORAGE section.

```
        DISPLAY "Enter Employee address: " NO ADVANCING.
        ACCEPT WS-PR-ADDR.
        DISPLAY "Enter Employee hire date (CCYYMMDD): " NO ADVANCING.
        ACCEPT WS-PR-EMPDATE.
        DISPLAY "Enter Employee pay: " NO ADVANCING.
        ACCEPT WS-PR-PAY.
        DISPLAY "Enter Employee bonus: " NO ADVANCING.
        ACCEPT WS-PR-BONUS.
        DISPLAY "Enter Employee car: " NO ADVANCING.
        ACCEPT WS-PR-CAR.

AB-010-MOVE-DATA.
        MOVE WS-PR-RECORD TO O-PR-RECORD.

AB-020-WRITE-RECORD.
        WRITE O-PR-RECORD.
        IF WS-O-PR-STATUS NOT EQUAL ZERO THEN
            DISPLAY "Error " WS-O-PR-STATUS " writing employee "
                WS-PR-EMPNO " to payroll master file."
            GO TO A-999-EXIT
        END-IF.

AB-030-CONTINUE.
        DISPLAY "Enter more data? Y/N: " NO ADVANCING.
        ACCEPT WS-O-CONTINUE-INPUT.
        IF (WS-O-CONTINUE-INPUT NOT = "y") AND
           (WS-O-CONTINUE-INPUT NOT = "Y") THEN
            MOVE "Y" TO WS-O-OUTPUT-FINISHED.

AB-999-EXIT.
        EXIT.

AC-TERMINATE SECTION.
AC-000-CLOSE.
        CLOSE O-PAYROLL-MASTER.

AC-999-EXIT.
        EXIT.
```

> When each record's input is complete, WS-PR-RECORD is moved to O-PR-RECORD and the record is written to file.

> Any reply other than "y" or "Y" ends the loop.

> The file is closed and the program stops.

This program is simply in a different order to anything you've seen before in this book. It's longer – constrained by the *Made Simple* space requirements, it's as short as I can make it – but COBOL is verbose and there is only so much you can do. The program is designed and written in a very structured, top-down manner. GO TO has almost disappeared, except where I use it to exit after an OPEN or WRITE error. I've introduced naming conventions, and how (to use the North American vernacular!).

Notice the hierarchical and sequenced way in which the sections and paragraphs are named: `A-000-MAIN`, `AA-INITIALISE`, `AA-000-OPEN`, and so on. This makes finding sections and paragraphs easy. The convention also gives structure and organisation; using it will make your programs better. A shortcoming is that, if you go, say, eight levels of `PERFORM`s down, you can end up with paragraphs names like `BACEADAA-000-READ`. However, having extensively used the scheme in real, commercial-strength applications, I've found that it usually doesn't come to that. If the program is very large and the naming does get unwieldy, the convention is not difficult to adapt to circumstances.

What you see when you run `SEQWRITE.CBL` is a long `DISPLAY/ACCEPT` sequence, similiar to those shown earlier in this book.

Writing to the file happens behind the scenes; if you look, after running the program, you'll notice that a file called `SEQPMAST.DAT`, containing all the data you entered, exists in the same system directory as the source-code file `SEQWRITE.CBL`. With a sequential file, the data can be seen in (relatively!) plain-text. When I ran `SEQWRITE.CBL`, I entered data for four people. This is what it looks like in the disk file:

```
Conor Sexton        1234    C10029M     Rathfarnham, Dublin, Ireland.
199511090100000000000000Bubble Car          Mike Cash           2345
S25039M     Jordan Hill, Oxford, UK.
198712120500000000500000Ferrari Testarossa  Rebecca Hammersley  5643
S10023F     Summertown, Oxford, UK.         199601010250000000250000E-
type Jag           Peter Dixon          0089    S30045M     Blenheim,
Oxford, UK         198504010900000001000000Mercedes S600
```

After every file I/O operation except `CLOSE`, the `FILE STATUS` is checked for error. This is excellent practice, giving the program a graceful exit (and giving you a means of diagnosis) after an I/O error. The test done on the file-status data item is the crude `NOT-EQUAL ZERO`. In real applications, you might choose to be more selective, but not-zero is still a good blanket test for the presence of error.

Updating a sequential file

As the second part of our sequential-file application, we take the file created by `SEQWRITE.CBL`, `SEQPMAST.DAT`, and update it. Here, I could present a fully-fledged interactive update program that would prompt the user for update information about a record, search `SEQPMAST.DAT` for that record and then update it in place. This program would be rather large. Quite apart from space considerations, I've found that the very fact of a program being large can obscure the essence of the technique that it's trying to illustrate.

Therefore, in this section, I go for a much shorter, non-interactive update program, `SEQUPD.CBL`. All this program does is open and read `SEQPMAST.DAT` and update the first record in that file. Less useful than a fully-fledged interactive update program, it does show the essential use of the `REWRITE` verb in updating a file in place. Here's the program:

SEQUPD.CBL

```
*********************************************************************
*                                                                  *
*   This program updates a payroll master file record in place.    *
*   File organization is sequential.                               *
*                                                                  *
*********************************************************************
 IDENTIFICATION DIVISION.
 PROGRAM-ID. SEQUPD.

 ENVIRONMENT DIVISION.

 INPUT-OUTPUT SECTION.
 FILE-CONTROL.
     SELECT OPTIONAL IO-PAYROLL-MASTER
         ASSIGN TO "SEQPMAST.DAT"
         ORGANIZATION IS SEQUENTIAL
         ACCESS MODE IS SEQUENTIAL
         FILE STATUS IS WS-IO-PR-STATUS.

 DATA DIVISION.
 FILE SECTION.
 FD IO-PAYROLL-MASTER
     BLOCK CONTAINS 20 RECORDS
     LABEL RECORDS ARE STANDARD
     RECORD CONTAINS 113 CHARACTERS.
 01 IO-PR-RECORD.
     02 FILLER       PIC X(113).
```

```
WORKING-STORAGE SECTION.
01  WS-PR-RECORD.
    02  WS-PR-NAME        PIC X(20).
    02  WS-PR-EMPNO       PIC X(8).
    02  WS-PR-EMPTYPE     PIC X.
    02  WS-PR-GRADE       PIC 99.
    02  WS-PR-AGE         PIC 999.
    02  WS-PR-GENDER      PIC X.
    02  WS-PR-REFNO       PIC 9999.
    02  WS-PR-ADDR        PIC X(30).
    02  WS-PR-EMPDATE.
        03  WS-PR-CCYY    PIC 9999.
        03  WS-PR-MM      PIC 99.
        03  WS-PR-DD      PIC 99.
    02  WS-PR-PAY         PIC 9(6)V99.
    02  WS-PR-BONUS       PIC 9(6)V99.
    02  WS-PR-CAR         PIC X(20).

01  WS-IO-PR-STATUS       PIC XX.

PROCEDURE DIVISION.
A-MAIN-LINE SECTION.
A-000-MAIN.
    PERFORM AA-INITIALISE.
    PERFORM AB-PROCESS.
    PERFORM AC-TERMINATE.

A-999-EXIT.
    STOP RUN.

AA-INITIALISE SECTION.
AA-000-OPEN.
    OPEN I-O IO-PAYROLL-MASTER.
    IF WS-IO-PR-STATUS NOT EQUAL ZERO THEN
        DISPLAY "Error " WS-IO-PR-STATUS
            " opening payroll master file."
        GO TO A-999-EXIT
    END-IF.

AA-999-EXIT.
    EXIT.

AB-PROCESS SECTION.
AB-000-READ-DATA.
    READ IO-PAYROLL-MASTER.
    IF WS-IO-PR-STATUS NOT EQUAL ZERO THEN
        DISPLAY "Error " WS-IO-PR-STATUS
            " reading payroll master file."
        GO TO A-999-EXIT
    END-IF.
```

OPEN the file in I-O mode for update

```
AB-010-UPDATE-FIRST-RECORD.
    MOVE IO-PR-RECORD TO WS-PR-RECORD.
    MOVE ZEROS TO WS-PR-EMPNO.
    MOVE WS-PR-RECORD TO IO-PR-RECORD.
    REWRITE IO-PR-RECORD.
    IF WS-IO-PR-STATUS NOT EQUAL ZERO THEN
        DISPLAY "Error " WS-IO-PR-STATUS " writing employee "
            WS-PR-EMPNO " to payroll master file."
        GO TO A-999-EXIT
    END-IF.

AB-999-EXIT.
    EXIT.

AC-TERMINATE SECTION.
AC-000-CLOSE.
    CLOSE IO-PAYROLL-MASTER.

AC-999-EXIT.
    EXIT.
```

Update the first
record in place.

When you run this program, there is no visible interaction. It opens the file `seqpmast.dat`, reads its first record, moves zeros to the employee-number field of that record and then REWRITEs the record (in AB-010-UPDATE-FIRST-RECORD). The file is thereby updated in place. Incidentally, moving zeros in this way to an important field like WS-PR-EMPNO could be treated as logical deletion of the record. As I've pointed out, you can't actually delete a record from a sequential file but you could adopt a convention that would regard records with employee-number zero as having been deleted.

This program, SEQUPD.CBL, is very similar to SEQWRITE.CBL which created its input file, SEQPMAST.DAT. The way that file is used is a little different, in that it's OPENed I-O so that its records can be updated in place. The naming convention used for the file's logical definition reflects this difference: the prefix 'IO' is used in place of 'O' in the earlier program. In the PROCEDURE division, the initialise-process-terminate structure introduced in SEQWRITE.CBL is little changed. The section and paragraph naming conventions are much the same also.

Printer files

We've now created a sequential file, initialised it with payroll/employee data, read the first record from the same file back into memory and updated that record in place. Now, we need to read all the records from the file SEQPMAST.DAT and send some information from each record to the printer for output as a report.

As a real-world COBOL programmer, you'll spend a surprising proportion of your time specifying report formats and writing or modifying COBOL programs to produce those reports. You may find that the COBOL Report Writer is available in your environment. This partially automates the business of specifying and producing reports. The focus of this section, however, is to get you into the nuts and bolts of how produce simple printed output from a COBOL program.

The essence of the thing is that, in COBOL, the printer is treated as a sequential file pretty much like any other. This file can, of necessity, only be OPENed for OUTPUT. (Try reading from a printer!). The exact specifications used in the SELECT statement for the printer file definition are system-dependent. For example, in Personal COBOL, you refer to the printer here as PRINTER. Using a different version of COBOL, (Ryan McFarland) RM/COBOL-85, you have to use PRINTER "PRN". So, if you're using yet another COBOL environment, you'll have to refer to your system documentation for information on printer specification. The program, SEQPRINT.CBL, is shown opposite.

This, again, is quite a long program, but it has very much the same structure as its two predecessors in this chapter. It's organised in three sections for initialisation, processing and termination. The section and paragraph naming conventions are those I've already explained.

Two files are SELECTed: the payroll file, seqpmast.dat, and the printer file. Access to both is SEQUENTIAL. It doesn't make sense to SELECT a printer file with any other kind of access. The payroll file is given the identifier I-PAYROLL-MASTER in the FD. The print file is called O-PAYROLL-PRINT. By now, you can probably guess from these names that the payroll file will be opened in input mode and the printer file in output mode.

```
***********************************************************************
*                                                                     *
*   Reads the payroll master file and prints its contents.           *
*                                                                     *
***********************************************************************
    IDENTIFICATION DIVISION.
    PROGRAM-ID. SEQPRINT.

    ENVIRONMENT DIVISION.
    CONFIGURATION SECTION.
    SPECIAL-NAMES.
        CURRENCY SIGN IS "£".

    INPUT-OUTPUT SECTION.
    FILE-CONTROL.
        SELECT OPTIONAL I-PAYROLL-MASTER
            ASSIGN TO "SEQPMAST.DAT"
            ORGANIZATION IS SEQUENTIAL
            ACCESS MODE IS SEQUENTIAL
            FILE STATUS IS WS-I-PR-STATUS.

        SELECT O-PAYROLL-PRINT
            ASSIGN TO PRINTER
            ORGANIZATION IS SEQUENTIAL
            FILE STATUS IS WS-O-PR-PRINT-STATUS.

    DATA DIVISION.
    FILE SECTION.
    FD  I-PAYROLL-MASTER
        BLOCK CONTAINS 20 RECORDS
        LABEL RECORDS ARE STANDARD
        RECORD CONTAINS 113 CHARACTERS.
    01  I-PR-RECORD.
        02 FILLER               PIC X(113).

    FD  O-PAYROLL-PRINT
        LABEL RECORDS ARE OMITTED
        RECORD CONTAINS 80 CHARACTERS.
    01  O-PR-PRINT-RECORD.
        02 FILLER               PIC X(80).

    WORKING-STORAGE SECTION.
    01  WS-PR-RECORD.
        02 WS-PR-NAME           PIC X(20).
        02 WS-PR-EMPNO          PIC X(8).
        02 WS-PR-EMPTYPE        PIC X.
        02 WS-PR-GRADE          PIC 99.
        02 WS-PR-AGE            PIC 999.
        02 WS-PR-GENDER         PIC X.
        02 WS-PR-REFNO          PIC 9999.
        02 WS-PR-ADDR           PIC X(30).
```

> Printer files are of SEQUENTIAL organisation. Their exact specification is system-dependent

> The printer file has no LABEL RECORDS attribute.

145

```
        02 WS-PR-EMPDATE.
            03 WS-PR-CCYY      PIC 9999.
            03 WS-PR-MM        PIC 99.
            03 WS-PR-DD        PIC 99.
        02 WS-PR-EMPDATE-N REDEFINES WS-PR-EMPDATE PIC 9(8).
        02 WS-PR-PAY          PIC 9(6)V99.
        02 WS-PR-BONUS        PIC 9(6)V99.
        02 WS-PR-CAR          PIC X(20).

   01  WS-PR-PRINT-HEADER.
        02 FILLER             PIC X(25) VALUE SPACES.
        02 WS-PR-PRINT-TEXT   PIC X(29) VALUE
                              "ABC Company. Payroll Records.".
        02 FILLER             PIC X(26) VALUE SPACES.

   01  WS-PR-PRINT-RECORD.
        02 WS-PR-PRINT-NAME        PIC X(20).
        02 FILLER                  PIC XX.
        02 WS-PR-PRINT-EMPNO        PIC X(8).
        02 FILLER                  PIC XX.
        02 WS-PR-PRINT-GRADE        PIC Z9.
        02 FILLER                  PIC XX.
        02 WS-PR-PRINT-EMPDATE      PIC 9999/99/99.
        02 FILLER                  PIC XX.
        02 WS-PR-PRINT-PAY          PIC £££,££9.99.
        02 FILLER                  PIC X(22).

   01  WS-I-END-FILE              PIC X VALUE "N".
   01  WS-I-PR-STATUS             PIC XX.
   01  WS-O-PR-PRINT-STATUS       PIC XX.

   PROCEDURE DIVISION.
   A-MAIN-LINE SECTION.
   A-000-MAIN.
        PERFORM AA-INITIALISE.
        READ I-PAYROLL-MASTER AT END
        MOVE "Y" TO WS-I-END-FILE.
        PERFORM AB-PROCESS UNTIL WS-I-END-FILE = "Y".
        PERFORM AC-TERMINATE.

   A-999-EXIT.
        STOP RUN.

   AA-INITIALISE SECTION.
   AA-000-OPEN.
        OPEN INPUT I-PAYROLL-MASTER.
        IF WS-I-PR-STATUS NOT EQUAL ZERO THEN
            DISPLAY "Error " WS-I-PR-STATUS
                " opening employee master file."
            GO TO A-999-EXIT
        END-IF.
```

Print record for report header

Print record, with edit fields, maps a line of printed output.

Print a line for each input file record.

```
          OPEN OUTPUT O-PAYROLL-PRINT.
          IF WS-O-PR-PRINT-STATUS NOT EQUAL ZERO THEN
              DISPLAY "Error " WS-O-PR-PRINT-STATUS
                  " opening printer file."
              GO TO A-999-EXIT
          END-IF.

          MOVE SPACES TO WS-PR-PRINT-RECORD.
          MOVE WS-PR-PRINT-HEADER TO O-PR-PRINT-RECORD.
          WRITE O-PR-PRINT-RECORD BEFORE ADVANCING 2.
          IF WS-O-PR-PRINT-STATUS NOT EQUAL ZERO THEN
              DISPLAY "Error " WS-O-PR-PRINT-STATUS
              " writing to printer file."
              GO TO A-999-EXIT
          END-IF.

  AA-999-EXIT.
      EXIT.

  AB-PROCESS SECTION.
  AB-000-MOVE-DATA.
      MOVE I-PR-RECORD TO WS-PR-RECORD.

  AB-010-PRINT-RECORD.
      MOVE WS-PR-NAME TO WS-PR-PRINT-NAME.
      MOVE WS-PR-EMPNO TO WS-PR-PRINT-EMPNO.
      MOVE WS-PR-GRADE TO WS-PR-PRINT-GRADE.
      MOVE WS-PR-EMPDATE-N TO WS-PR-PRINT-EMPDATE.
      MOVE WS-PR-PAY TO WS-PR-PRINT-PAY.
      MOVE WS-PR-PRINT-RECORD TO O-PR-PRINT-RECORD.
      WRITE O-PR-PRINT-RECORD.
      IF WS-O-PR-PRINT-STATUS NOT EQUAL ZERO THEN
          DISPLAY "Error " WS-O-PR-PRINT-STATUS
              " writing to printer file."
          GO TO A-999-EXIT
      END-IF.

  AB-020-READ-DATA.
      READ I-PAYROLL-MASTER AT END
      MOVE "Y" TO WS-I-END-FILE.

  AB-999-EXIT.
      EXIT.

  AC-TERMINATE SECTION.
  AC-000-CLOSE.
      CLOSE I-PAYROLL-MASTER.
      CLOSE O-PAYROLL-PRINT.

  AC-999-EXIT.
      EXIT.
```

First, print a header for the report.

Set up the output record and write it to the printer file.

147

The payroll-file record specification is of the familiar 113 characters, while the printer record is 80 characters long. Why 80? Because it's a good width for the paper (European A4) that fits in my laser printer! In fact, 80 is usually a good print-record length for standard loose-sheet paper, while 132 is normal for continuous wide-listing (*fanfold*) paper.

The holding-area for input-file records in WORKING-STORAGE is the same WS-PR-RECORD found in the earlier two programs. This is where all the payroll-file field detail is found; it's enough in the file record specification itself, I-PR-RECORD, just to specify the record as a FILLER of length 113.

Notice that, in the case of the printer file, there are two holding areas (and therefore effectively two record definitions) in WORKING-STORAGE. As I've pointed out earlier, we could alternatively have two record specifications at the 01 level within the FD for the printer file. We need two record specifications because, in a normal print report, you find lines of different formats. In this (simple) case, I allow for a header line at the top of the report and a series of detailed columnar-data lines following.

The record specification within the printer file FD, O-PR-PRINT-RECORD, contains simply a FILLER of length 80. When we want a report header, we move the data item WS-PR-PRINT-HEADER from WORKING-STORAGE to O-PR-PRINT-RECORD and then WRITE the record. When we want a detail line, we fill up WS-PR-PRINT-RECORD with the required data from the current payroll-file record, move it to O-PR-PRINT-RECORD and then WRITE the record. You can see that, after the header is written, two lines are skipped to leave some space between the header and the detail lines on the printed output. If you omit the BEFORE ADVANCING option, the default advance when writing to the printer file is of one line.

Printing detail lines is what is repeatedly done by SEQPRINT.CBL. The second SECTION, AA-INITIALISE, opens the two files and writes the fixed-text header record to the printer. AB-PROCESS moves the required data from the payroll file record to the detail print record in

WORKING-STORAGE, moves that data item to O-PR-PRINT-RECORD and writes the record to the printer.

One quirk which I'll mention is the use of REDEFINES to specify the date of employment as a numeric PIC 9(8). For the slashes to appear in the edited output-date field, you must a move a numeric quantity to that field. WS-PR-EMPDATE, being a group item, is alphanumeric; hence the need for the redefinition.

AB-PROCESS is called until there are no more records left in the input payroll file. AC-TERMINATE closes the two files.

When you run SEQPRINT.CBL, you get a printed report that looks something like this:

```
                     ABC Company. Payroll Records.

Conor Sexton        1234    10      1995/11/09      £10,000.00
Mike Cash           2345    25      1987/12/12      £50,000.00
Rebecca Hammersley  5643    10      1996/01/01      £25,000.00
Peter Dixon         0089    30      1985/04/01      £90,000.00
```

In real COBOL applications, reports are more complex than this, involving sub-headers, sub-totals, page-breaks and all kinds of other details. What I've shown, however, should give you enough grounding in sequential and printer files to be able to do further development yourself.

Exercises

1   Generate a sequential payroll file the same as that specified in this chapter using `SEQWRITE.CBL`.

2   Modify the program `SEQWRITE.CBL` so that you can add records to the existing file (`seqpmast.dat`) by `OPEN`ing it in `EXTEND` mode.

3   Write a program, derived from `SEQUPD.CBL` which accepts user input of an employee number and a numeric amount representing a pay rise. Search for that employee in the file. If it exists, increase the pay figure by the amount input. If it does not exist, report an error.

4   Write a program, derived from `SEQPRINT.CBL`, which produces report output only for those employees earning more than £20,000 and working for the company since 1st January, 1992.

6 Indexed file I/O

Defining an indexed file

Many of the general concepts of COBOL file processing are addressed in Chapter 5. In this chapter, I look at what's involved in defining, creating and using indexed files. At its end, I summarise the characteristics of relative files, which are very similar to indexed files in their definition and operation. But first, a little more 'concept' stuff.

If your organisation had to produce a million printed statements based on the debtors' ledger file, you would by choice access the file sequentially and print the statements record-by-record. Even if some of your customers didn't owe money, you could just test for that and skip them while sequentially processing the debtors' file.

Many applications can't work in this sequential fashion. Imagine that someone telephones your organisation to make an enquiry on their account. There are a million accounts. Computers are fast, but you can't just hunt through the million records from the top. On average, you'll have to read 500,000 records to find the one you want and this amount of work is unlikely to fit in the required two-second response time. Smarter searching is needed; this is what indexed files provide.

Some terms: indexed access is also called *random access* and *direct access*. Strictly, the way in which an indexed file is read is *indexed sequential*: you go to a certain point in the file and read sequentially from there. This gives rise to the term *indexed sequential access method* and the associated acronym *ISAM*.

In essence, an indexed file is *two* files: the data file and an index file. The data file contains the data records; the index file contains shortest-path information that allows the searching program to go 'directly' to the required record. This shortest-path information is based on a key value, specified on creating the file, that occurs within all its records.

There are many ways to implement file-search indexes; many are based on creation of a *binary tree*, and the required record is found with a *binary search*. Happily, most of us don't have to worry about the internals of COBOL indexing. We can just accept that, when we do an indexed read on an indexed file using a key, the associated record will be retrieved, if it exists. If it does not exist, an error is generated, whereupon we can take some action.

Physical definition

Indexed files are physically defined in the SELECT statement, as are sequential files. Here's the general form of SELECT for indexed files:

```
SELECT [OPTIONAL] <file-name>
    ASSIGN TO {<implementor-name-1>, <literal-1>}
    [RESERVE <integer-1> {AREA, AREAS}]
    [[ORGANIZATION IS] INDEXED]
    [ACCESS MODE IS {SEQUENTIAL, RANDOM, DYNAMIC}]
    RECORD KEY IS <data-name-1>
    [ALTERNATE RECORD KEY IS <data-name-2>
      [WITH DUPLICATES]]…
    [FILE STATUS IS <data-name-3>].
```

This isn't all that different from the sequential general form you can see in Chapter 5. The PADDING CHARACTER and RECORD DELIMITER specifications have disappeared, but they're no great loss. The newcomer is ALTERNATE RECORD KEY, which allows you the option of searching an indexed file using more than one key. Alternate keys can be duplicated in a file – different records sharing keys – if the WITH DUPLICATES option is specified. This means that you could have an employee file with a primary key (the main one, specified with RECORD KEY) being the employee number and a secondary key, the employee's name. The primary key must be unique to one record but there could be several records with the same secondary key. You can't define a primary key to be an alternate key. For now, I concentrate on implementing indexed files with a primary key.

All the other entries are in both the sequential and indexed SELECTs, with minor differences. The most important of these differences are:

- Using ORGANIZATION IS INDEXED when creating a file means the file will have an indexed structure and be fundamentally physically different from a sequential file. Once you've created an indexed file, it stays indexed: you can't convert it to sequential or any other type. Equally, once you've specified keys, they remain the keys for good. The only way to change keys is to re-create the file.

- Having created an indexed file, you're not limited to getting records by explicitly specifying key values before each read. You can, for example, read an indexed file in a sequential, random or dynamic (sequential and random!) manner. The way you control the manner of reading is with the ACCESS MODE specification.

The minimum you need physically to define an indexed file is this:

```
SELECT <file-name>
    ASSIGN <physical file name>
    ORGANIZATION INDEXED
    RECORD <key data item>.
```

This by default gives you ACCESS MODE SEQUENTIAL: you will have to read the file's records in sequence using the key specified. A more likely specification is:

```
SELECT OPTIONAL O-PAYROLL-MASTER
    ASSIGN "idxpmast.dat"
    ORGANIZATION IS INDEXED
    ACCESS MODE IS RANDOM
    RECORD KEY IS O-PR-EMPNO
    FILE STATUS IS WS-O-PR-STATUS.
```

Taken all together, this SELECT means that, when the program runs, the indexed file idxpmast.dat is created; that its primary key is the data item O-PR-EMPNO; that access to the file is 'random' using that key and the index; and that the status of all I/O operations on the file is recorded in the data item WS-O-PR-STATUS immediately after each operation. OPTIONAL, as ever, means that, if the file doesn't exist when you try to read it, you won't get an error message.

The categories of error-codes produced by I/O operations are these:

Status Code	Meaning
'00'	Successful execution of preceding command
'1' first character	Unsuccessful execution: AT END
'2' first character	Unsuccessful execution: INVALID KEY
'3' first character	Unsuccessful execution: file missing or corrupt
'4' first character	Unsuccessful execution: illogical operation
'9' first character	Implementation-defined error

The only newcomers with indexed files are those status codes that have the first character '2'. All the other status codes for indexed files are virtually identical with their sequential counterparts. See the longer table in Chapter 5 (*Defining a file*). Here's a table of the status codes that are specific to indexed file I/O:

Status Code	Meaning
'21'	Sequence error. Key value changed between READ and REWRITE or key values not in sequence on sequential WRITE to the file
'22'	Attempt to WRITE or REWRITE a record that would create a duplicate key (DUPLICATES not specified)
'23'	Record specified by key does not exist in the file
'24'	Attempt to write outside space allocated for the file; the system has placed a limit on your file's size

The only remaining SELECT option that I haven't covered in the context of indexed files is RESERVE... AREAS. If you specify:

    RESERVE 20 AREAS

you're asking the COBOL system to set aside enough space to hold 20 records in memory at the same time. The same mechanism is available for sequential files, and I give the same reservation here as I do in Chapter 5 about using it. The operating system probably takes the law into its own hands here, so don't bother using the RESERVE option.

Logical definition

Let's now look at the file definition (FD) entry necessary to provide a logical definition for your indexed file. Recall from Chapter 5 that one of the purposes of this definition is to provide a link between the physical file on a peripheral device – idxpmast.dat in this case – and a data name within the program. That data name is the one associated with the FD. A reasonable FD entry for this indexed file is:

```
FD O-PAYROLL MASTER
        BLOCK CONTAINS 20 RECORDS
        LABEL RECORDS ARE STANDARD
        RECORD CONTAINS 113 CHARACTERS.

    01 O-PR-RECORD.
        02...
```

A data item for the RECORD KEY (and alternate record keys, if any) specified in the SELECT corresponding to the FD must be found in the record(s) associated with the FD. In this case, O-PR-RECORD must contain a numeric or alphanumeric data item for the key O-PR-EMPNO. In all other ways, this FD has the same meaning as its sequential-file counterpart (see the end of *Defining a file*, Chapter 5).

Accessing file data

You've physically defined your indexed file with `ORGANIZATION IS INDEXED` and you've specified an `ACCESS MODE`. It's time now to look at the seven verbs that COBOL gives you for accessing, reading from and writing to indexed files. This is two more than with sequential access: the new ones are `DELETE` and `START`. Unlike with sequential files, you can `DELETE` records from indexed files. `START` allows you to specify a point in the indexed file to go to, after which access may be either sequential or dynamic (a combination of sequential and random).

The other verbs are familiar: `OPEN`, `CLOSE`, `READ`, `WRITE` and `REWRITE`. The behaviour of these verbs when used with indexed files is quite similar to that when they are used with sequential files. There are specific differences – such as the `INVALID KEY` clause with `READ`, `WRITE` and `REWRITE` – which I explain as we encounter them. However, pretty much all of the *general* aspects of behaviour of these verbs that I summarise in Chapter 5 for sequential files also hold true for indexed files. For example, `READ`ing an indexed (or any other) file won't create it; `OPEN`ing a file in `I-O` mode allows you both to `READ` from and `WRITE` to the file; to `CLOSE` an indexed file detaches it from the program and makes the file unavailable to the program; and `REWRITE` must immediately follow a corresponding `READ`.

Let's look at some of the behaviour of the access verbs that is specific to indexed files. In the remainder of this section, I summarise the characteristics of all seven verbs. You'll find examples of their use in the sections that follow in this chapter.

OPEN and CLOSE

The general form of `OPEN` for indexed files is this:

    OPEN {INPUT, OUTPUT, I-O, EXTEND} <file-name>.

Unlike with sequential files, there's no option to open the file `REVERSED` (at the end, and read the file backwards). Since the purpose of indexed files is mainly to be able to jump around the file reading records at 'random', reading sequentially in reverse order is not very useful and is not supported.

There are many combinations of syntax options for indexed files. To avoid getting confused with them all, think in terms of what you're OPENing an indexed file for. This is defined by the ACCESS MODE of the file. The ACCESS MODE, as we've seen, can be any of SEQUENTIAL, RANDOM and DYNAMIC. Of these, SEQUENTIAL and RANDOM are distinct in meaning; DYNAMIC means that you're reserving the right to access the file in either SEQUENTIAL or RANDOM mode.

If you want to READ a 'random' record from the file, you'll OPEN the file for INPUT, use key access and RANDOM or DYNAMIC access mode. If you want to go to a certain point in the file and read from there, you'll OPEN the file for INPUT, access records with the START verb and use SEQUENTIAL or DYNAMIC access mode.

To WRITE a record to the file, OPEN it for OUTPUT. If you're using SEQUENTIAL access mode, you'll have to write records in ascending key order – say employee numbers 2376, 4671 and 8902, in that order. With RANDOM access mode, the records can be written in any order. You can only WRITE duplicate records (and then only with alternate keys) if you use the DUPLICATES option in the SELECT statement defining the file.

To update a record in an indexed file, you must use REWRITE. To do this, you have to OPEN the file in I-O mode. If the file's ACCESS MODE is SEQUENTIAL or RANDOM, there are restrictions on what you can do. If the access mode is SEQUENTIAL, you can DELETE records from and REWRITE records to an indexed file opened I-O, but you can't WRITE a record to it. If the mode is RANDOM, you can't use the START verb with the file. By contrast, ACCESS MODE DYNAMIC lets you do pretty much anything with an indexed file. For an indexed file opened I-O, use DYNAMIC access mode to avoid the niggling restrictions I've pointed out.

A tabular summary of valid combinations of I/O statements and OPEN modes is given on the next page.

An indexed file accessed in DYNAMIC access mode is the most powerful file-access facility that COBOL gives you. There's a temptation to use it all the time and thereby avoid all usage restrictions. It's effectively

Access Mode	I/O Statement	Open Mode			
		INPUT	OUTPUT	I-O	EXTEND
SEQUENTIAL	READ	OK		OK	
	WRITE		OK		OK
	REWRITE			OK	
	START	OK		OK	
	DELETE			OK	
RANDOM	READ	OK		OK	
	WRITE		OK		
	REWRITE			OK	
	START				
	DELETE			OK	
DYNAMIC	READ	OK		OK	
	WRITE		OK	OK	
	REWRITE			OK	
	START	OK		OK	
	DELETE			OK	

a sequential and random-access file rolled into one. In my view, however, its very power can be a disadvantage. When you see a file opened with ACCESS MODE DYNAMIC, you have no information from that specification alone about what the file is to be used for. Is it going to be used sequentially or randomly? You don't know. Therefore, if you know that a file is *only* going to be read sequentially to produce, say, a lot of mailing labels, open it with SEQUENTIAL access mode. If you know that a file is going to be used *only* for ad-hoc on-line enquiry, open it RANDOM.

If you have a reason for going to a point in a file and reading sequentially from there, use DYNAMIC. For example, you might want records for all employee numbers higher than such-and-such or for those hired later than on a certain date. You can do this with DYNAMIC access and READ...NEXT. You can, as you'll see later in this chapter, also use the START and READ combination to do this. The point is, don't just use DYNAMIC as a blanket specification. Use the minimum specification that will do the job for you – it can help make your program more understandable.

The final file OPEN mode is EXTEND. With indexed files, EXTEND mode can only be used with SEQUENTIAL access and then only with the WRITE verb. This allows you to add records to the file but not to change or otherwise manipulate any that already exist.

Closing an indexed file is the same as closing a sequential file, usually CLOSE <filename>. For the LOCK option, see Chapter 5, *Accessing file data*.

READ

The general form of the READ statement for record retrieval by key from an indexed file is this:

```
READ <file-name> [NEXT] [RECORD] [INTO <identifier-1>]
    [KEY IS <data-name-1>]
    [INVALID KEY <statement-1>]
    [NOT INVALID KEY <statement-2>]
[END-READ].
```

For indexed files opened in SEQUENTIAL access mode, NEXT RECORD has no effect. For RANDOM access mode, it's invalid: each READ must be by key. You can use NEXT RECORD in DYNAMIC access mode. You READ a record with a key. After that READ, READ NEXT gets you the next (in sequence) record in the file.

Normally, a data record is read into the 01-level data items specified in a file's FD. You can optionally specify the appropriate group item in the FD with the INTO option. You can also read a record into another item, such as a WORKING-STORAGE temporary area, again using READ... INTO.

The default key is the primary key, found in the record definition and specified in the file's SELECT statement. With the KEY IS clause, you can specify an alternative at the point of reading from the file. This is done most often if alternate keys are defined; see *Indexed file enquiry* later in this chapter.

By far the most commonly-used options are the INVALID KEY/NOT INVALID KEY pair. If for some reason (see the error codes in *Defining an indexed file*, earlier in this chapter), the READ-with-a-key fails, the statement(s) subject to INVALID KEY are executed. If it succeeds, the statement(s) subject to NOT INVALID KEY are executed. An indexed file opened for SEQUENTIAL access uses the AT END/NOT AT END pair instead. You can test for errors on READ – or any other I/O verb – in a more general way by testing the FILE STATUS identifier instead of using INVALID KEY or AT END.

Syntactically, READ and the other I/O verbs can have END delimiters:

```
READ...........
    ...
END-READ.
```
or:
```
DELETE........
    ...
END-DELETE
```

The delimited form is an introduction of COBOL-85. COBOL-74 requires that you end the sentence with a full-stop rather than, say, END-REWRITE. COBOL-85 allows this too, but the newer, delimited, form is superior and I use it frequently in READ and the other I/O statements from now on.

WRITE and REWRITE

In the above table, you can find when it's appropriate to use WRITE and REWRITE. In general, WRITE places a new record in a file, indexed or otherwise; REWRITE updates an existing record. Here is the general form of WRITE:

```
WRITE <record-name> [FROM <identifier-1>]
    [INVALID KEY <statement-1>]
    [NOT INVALID KEY <statement-2>]
[END-WRITE].
```

and this is the equivalent for REWRITE:

```
REWRITE <record-name> [FROM <identifier-1>]
    [INVALID KEY <statement-1>]
    [NOT INVALID KEY <statement-2>]
[END-WRITE].
```

If either a keyed WRITE or REWRITE fails, the statements subject to the INVALID KEY option are executed, otherwise those subject to NOT

INVALID KEY are executed. As for READ, you can instead test the FILE STATUS identifier directly.

DELETE

DELETE can only be used on files opened in I-O mode. The verb uses a key to remove a record from an indexed file. Its general form is:

```
DELETE <file-name> [RECORD]
    [INVALID KEY <statement-1>]
    [NOT INVALID KEY <statement-2>]
[END-DELETE].
```

If the record to be DELETEd cannot be found in the index, the INVALID KEY option is invoked, otherwise the NOT INVALID KEY option, if it is included. Once again, you can instead test the FILE STATUS explicitly.

START

And, to finish (as it were!), we have START. START is used to go to a certain record in an indexed file, OPENed INPUT or I-O with either SEQUENTIAL or DYNAMIC access mode. READ then continues in key order from that point. First, you move a value to a key, then use START to go to the corresponding record in the file. Here's an example:

```
MOVE ZEROS TO I-PR-EMPNO.
START I-PAYROLL-MASTER
    KEY IS GREATER THAN I-PR-EMPNO
    INVALID KEY DISPLAY "Invalid key on START"
END-START.
```

The effect of this is that subsequent READ operations return all the records of the file in ascending sequence of the key I-PR-EMPNO. This is because the STARTing key is specified as zero and all actual key values in the file are higher than that. This mechanism effectively sorts the file and is a very powerful I/O feature of COBOL. You can, as an alternative, do something like this:

```
MOVE 5000 TO I-PR-EMPNO.
```

which, followed by START… GREATER THAN and successive READs, will return in key order all the records with a key value greater than 5000.

The general form of START is this:

```
START <file-name> [ KEY IS
        {
         EQUAL TO
         =
         GREATER THAN
         >
         NOT LESS THAN
         NOT <
         GREATER THAN OR EQUAL TO
         >=
        }
        <data-name> ]
    [INVALID KEY <statement-1>]
    [NOT INVALID KEY <statement-2>]
[END-START].
```

You should be able to sense the meaning of the comparison options: in essence, you can START reading the records of an indexed file either from (and including) a record accessed using a keyed READ, or from the next record in ascending key order. If no key value in the file meets the requirements of the comparison used, the INVALID KEY option is invoked, otherwise the NOT INVALID KEY option, if it is included. If the KEY specification and comparison are omitted, the comparison used is EQUAL TO.

Creating an indexed file

After working your way through all the necessary rules and general forms, you're now ready to examine some programs that implement indexed file I/O. Before doing anything else, you must first create an indexed file. The following program, `IDXWRITE.CBL`, sets up an indexed file called `IDXPMAST.DAT`, an indexed variant of the sequential payroll file seen in Chapter 5. The program accepts data from keyboard input and writes that data to the file. Here it is:

IDXWRITE.CBL

```
***************************************************************
*                                                             *
*   Initialises the payroll master file from user-input data. *
*                                                             *
***************************************************************

    IDENTIFICATION DIVISION.
    PROGRAM-ID. IDXWRITE.

    ENVIRONMENT DIVISION.

    INPUT-OUTPUT SECTION.
    FILE-CONTROL.
        SELECT OPTIONAL O-PAYROLL-MASTER
            ASSIGN TO "IDXPMAST.DAT"
            ORGANIZATION IS INDEXED
            ACCESS MODE IS SEQUENTIAL
            RECORD KEY IS O-PR-EMPNO
            ALTERNATE RECORD KEY IS O-PR-NAME
            FILE STATUS IS WS-PR-STATUS.

    DATA DIVISION.
    FILE SECTION.
    FD  O-PAYROLL-MASTER
        BLOCK CONTAINS 20 RECORDS
        LABEL RECORDS ARE STANDARD
        RECORD CONTAINS 113 CHARACTERS.
    01  O-PR-RECORD.
        02 O-PR-NAME        PIC X(20).
        02 O-PR-EMPNO       PIC X(8).
        02 FILLER           PIC X(85).

    WORKING-STORAGE SECTION.
    01  WS-PR-RECORD.
        02 WS-PR-NAME       PIC X(20).
```

> Indexed file, to be written sequentially by employee-number key.

163

```
      02 WS-PR-EMPNO        PIC X(8).
      02 WS-PR-EMPTYPE      PIC X.
      02 WS-PR-GRADE        PIC 99.
      02 WS-PR-AGE          PIC 999.
      02 WS-PR-GENDER       PIC X.
      02 WS-PR-REFNO        PIC 9999.
      02 WS-PR-ADDR         PIC X(30).
      02 WS-PR-EMPDATE.
          03 WS-PR-CCYY     PIC 9999.
          03 WS-PR-MM       PIC 99.
          03 WS-PR-DD       PIC 99.
      02 WS-PR-PAY          PIC 9(6)V99.
      02 WS-PR-BONUS        PIC 9(6)V99.
      02 WS-PR-CAR          PIC X(20).

01 WS-OUTPUT-FINISHED       PIC X VALUE "N".
01 WS-CONTINUE-INPUT        PIC X.
01 WS-PR-STATUS             PIC XX.

PROCEDURE DIVISION.
A-MAIN-LINE SECTION.
A-000-MAIN.
    PERFORM AA-INITIALISE.
    PERFORM AB-PROCESS UNTIL WS-OUTPUT-FINISHED = "Y".
    PERFORM AC-TERMINATE.

A-999-EXIT.
    STOP RUN.

AA-INITIALISE SECTION.
AA-000-OPEN.
    OPEN OUTPUT O-PAYROLL-MASTER.
    IF WS-PR-STATUS NOT EQUAL ZERO THEN
        DISPLAY "Error " WS-PR-STATUS
            " opening payroll master file."
        GO TO A-999-EXIT
    END-IF.

AA-999-EXIT.
    EXIT.

AB-PROCESS SECTION.
AB-000-GET-DATA.
    MOVE SPACES TO WS-PR-RECORD.
    DISPLAY "Enter Employee name: " NO ADVANCING.
    ACCEPT WS-PR-NAME.
    DISPLAY "Enter Employee number: " NO ADVANCING.
    ACCEPT WS-PR-EMPNO.
    DISPLAY "Enter Employee type (H/S/C): " NO ADVANCING.
```

```
        ACCEPT WS-PR-EMPTYPE.
        DISPLAY "Enter Employee grade (1-30): " NO ADVANCING.
        ACCEPT WS-PR-GRADE.
        DISPLAY "Enter Employee age: " NO ADVANCING.
        ACCEPT WS-PR-AGE.
        DISPLAY "Enter Employee gender (M/F): " NO ADVANCING.
        ACCEPT WS-PR-GENDER.
        DISPLAY "Enter Employee address: " NO ADVANCING.
        ACCEPT WS-PR-ADDR.
        DISPLAY "Enter Employee hire date (CCYYMMDD): " NO ADVANCING.
        ACCEPT WS-PR-EMPDATE.
        DISPLAY "Enter Employee pay: " NO ADVANCING.
        ACCEPT WS-PR-PAY.
        DISPLAY "Enter Employee bonus: " NO ADVANCING.
        ACCEPT WS-PR-BONUS.
        DISPLAY "Enter Employee car: " NO ADVANCING.
        ACCEPT WS-PR-CAR.

   AB-010-MOVE-DATA.
        MOVE WS-PR-RECORD TO O-PR-RECORD.

   AB-020-WRITE-RECORD.
        WRITE O-PR-RECORD INVALID KEY
            DISPLAY "Error " WS-PR-STATUS " writing employee "
                WS-PR-EMPNO " to payroll master file."
            GO TO A-999-EXIT
        END-WRITE.

   AB-030-CONTINUE.
        DISPLAY "Enter more data? Y/N: " NO ADVANCING.
        ACCEPT WS-CONTINUE-INPUT.
            IF (WS-CONTINUE-INPUT NOT = "y") AND
                    (WS-CONTINUE-INPUT NOT = "Y") THEN
                MOVE "Y" TO WS-OUTPUT-FINISHED.

   AB-999-EXIT.
        EXIT.

   AC-TERMINATE SECTION.
   AC-000-CLOSE.
        CLOSE O-PAYROLL-MASTER.

   AC-999-EXIT.
        EXIT.
```

> Use the primary key value to write a record that can later be directly retrieved

> Continue until user-input finished

This is quite a long program by our standards, but it's not very difficult. In essence, it iterates, building and writing file records, until told by the user to stop. On each loop, it accepts employee/personnel-type data input by the user, forms a record from that data and writes the record to the file. The difference with idxpmast.dat, for which ORGANIZATION IS INDEXED is specified, is that each record has two keys, specified in the SELECT statement, and written to the file along with all the other fields in the record.

For the file idxpmast.dat, the keys – from which the index file that accompanies the data file is built – are defined to be O-PR-EMPNO and O-PR-NAME. The primary key is O-PR-EMP-NO and the secondary or (in COBOL-speak) alternate key is O-PR-NAME. Each time data is accepted from the user in paragraph AB-000-GET-DATA, the key fields are assigned data values which can be used later to retrieve the record 'randomly' or by 'direct access'.

The critical body of code in IDXWRITE.CBL is this:

```
AB-010-MOVE-DATA.
    MOVE WS-PR-RECORD TO O-PR-RECORD.

AB-020-WRITE-RECORD.
    WRITE O-PR-RECORD INVALID KEY
        DISPLAY "Error " WS-PR-STATUS " writing employee "
          WS-PR-EMPNO " to payroll master file."
        GO TO A-999-EXIT
    END-WRITE.
```

In the code preceding this, the holding area WS-PR-RECORD, defined in WORKING-STORAGE, is filled up with data supplied by the user. The paragraph AB-010-MOVE-DATA moves WS-PR-RECORD to the file's record data item, O-PR-RECORD. The key data in WS-PR-EMPNO and WS-PR-NAME is moved with it, thereby assigning content to the record keys O-PR-EMPNO and O-PR-NAME. The WRITE statement in paragraph AB-020-WRITE-RECORD uses the primary key value to write the record in the file so that it can be later directly retrieved. If there's an error in the output operation, you get a message and the program terminates (by means of one of the few good uses of GO TO).

A cautionary note is in order here. You can see that the file idxpmast.dat in the program as shown is opened with ACCESS MODE IS SEQUENTIAL. This is fine; it's an accepted way to create indexed files. But, where the MODE is SEQUENTIAL, the records entered by the user in sequence must have primary keys in ascending order of value.

166

There must be no duplicates and every key must be greater (in the case of O-PR-EMPNO, numerically greater) than that of the last record written to the file. In practice, you'd usually create an indexed data file by copying data to it from another, sorted file. With ACCESS MODE SEQUENTIAL and the keys guaranteed to be in ascending order while the file is created, there is then no difficulty.

If you do enter a record with a primary key value less than that in some preceding record, you'll get an INVALID KEY error, and an underlying FILE STATUS code 21. An attempt to write a record containing a duplicate primary key results in an error and code 22.

A way of avoiding the problem altogether is to specify ACCESS MODE IS RANDOM in the SELECT statement. Then, you should be able to enter record data containing keys in any order. This works fine in Personal COBOL. However, it isn't allowed in all implementations of COBOL, so be warned.

Running this program in the Personal COBOL environment, the output is two program files, with no screen display other than that associated with user input. The program does not display the data records for you after they have been written to the file. Later programs in this chapter do this. The two files are IDXPMAST.DAT and IDXPMAST.IDX; the first being the data file and the latter the index file. It isn't beautiful, but you can see the data I entered from the raw text in IDXPMAST.DAT:

```
Sexton, Conor        1234     C15029M      Rathfarnham, Dublin, Ireland.
19951109010000000000000000Bubble Car           Cash, Mike          2456
S25039M    Jordan Hill, Oxford, UK.
19871212050000000000500000Ferrari Testarossa Hammersley, Rebecca 3769
S10023F    Summertown, Oxford, UK.       19960101025000000250000E-
type Jag         Dixon, Peter        5000     S29045M      Blenheim,
Oxford, UK.         19850401090000000001000000Mercedes S600
```

Sequential access to an indexed file

The simplest way of reading an indexed file is sequentially, in the key order in which the records were written to the file. With the program IDXSEQ.CBL, we sequentially access the four records written to the file idxpmast.dat and display their contents.

IDXSEQ.CBL

```
**********************************************************************
*                                                                    *
*   This program sequentially reads the payroll master file          *
*                                                                    *
**********************************************************************

    IDENTIFICATION DIVISION.
    PROGRAM-ID. IDXSEQ.

    ENVIRONMENT DIVISION.

    INPUT-OUTPUT SECTION.
    FILE-CONTROL.
        SELECT OPTIONAL I-PAYROLL-MASTER
            ASSIGN TO "IDXPMAST.DAT"
            ORGANIZATION IS INDEXED
            ACCESS MODE IS SEQUENTIAL
            RECORD KEY IS I-PR-EMPNO
            ALTERNATE RECORD KEY IS I-PR-NAME
            FILE STATUS IS WS-PR-STATUS.

    DATA DIVISION.
    FILE SECTION.
    FD  I-PAYROLL-MASTER
        BLOCK CONTAINS 20 RECORDS
        LABEL RECORDS ARE STANDARD
        RECORD CONTAINS 113 CHARACTERS.
    01  I-PR-RECORD.
        02 I-PR-NAME          PIC X(20).
        02 I-PR-EMPNO         PIC X(8).
        02 FILLER             PIC X(85).

    WORKING-STORAGE SECTION.
    01  WS-PR-RECORD.
        02 WS-PR-NAME         PIC X(20).
        02 WS-PR-EMPNO        PIC X(8).
        02 WS-PR-EMPTYPE      PIC X.
        02 WS-PR-GRADE        PIC 99.
        02 WS-PR-AGE          PIC 999.
        02 WS-PR-GENDER       PIC X.
        02 WS-PR-REFNO        PIC 9999.
```

> SEQUENTIAL access again, but here the indexed file will be OPENed for INPUT (reading).

168

```
        02 WS-PR-ADDR           PIC X(30).
        02 WS-PR-EMPDATE.
            03 WS-PR-CCYY       PIC 9999.
            03 WS-PR-MM         PIC 99.
            03 WS-PR-DD         PIC 99.
        02 WS-PR-PAY            PIC 9(6)V99.
        02 WS-PR-BONUS          PIC 9(6)V99.
        02 WS-PR-CAR            PIC X(20).
    01  WS-PR-EOF               PIC X VALUE "N".
    01  WS-PR-STATUS            PIC XX.

    PROCEDURE DIVISION.
    A-MAIN-LINE SECTION.
    A-000-MAIN.
        PERFORM AA-INITIALISE.
        PERFORM AB-PROCESS UNTIL WS-PR-EOF = "Y".
        PERFORM AC-TERMINATE.

    A-999-EXIT.
        STOP RUN.

    AA-INITIALISE SECTION.
    AA-000-OPEN.
        OPEN INPUT I-PAYROLL-MASTER.
        IF WS-PR-STATUS NOT EQUAL ZERO THEN
            DISPLAY "Error " WS-PR-STATUS
                " opening payroll master file."
            GO TO A-999-EXIT
        END-IF.

    AA-999-EXIT.
        EXIT.

    AB-PROCESS SECTION.
    AB-000-READ-RECORD.
        READ I-PAYROLL-MASTER
            AT END MOVE "Y" TO WS-PR-EOF
            NOT AT END
                MOVE I-PR-RECORD TO WS-PR-RECORD
                DISPLAY WS-PR-NAME " " WS-PR-EMPNO " "
                    WS-PR-PAY " " WS-PR-CAR
        END-READ.

    AB-999-EXIT.
        EXIT.

    AC-TERMINATE SECTION.
    AC-000-CLOSE.
        CLOSE I-PAYROLL-MASTER.

    AC-999-EXIT.
        EXIT.
```

OPEN the file to read it sequentially.

READ ... AT END indicates the indexed file is being read in sequential record order by key.

Display contents of each record as it is read.

Notice that the SELECT, FD and record definitions are the same as those made in the program IDXWRITE.CBL in the last section, except that some of the names reflect the fact that the file idxpmast.dat is this time opened INPUT to be read, as opposed to OUTPUT for file creation. Having defined the form of the indexed file – SELECT, records, keys and so on – you can't subsequently change it. You can use different data names and access modes all right, but if you want to change the basic structure of the file as it's expressed in terms of its ORGANIZATION and keys, you have to re-create the file. So, define your indexed files carefully and with an eye to the future.

Although the file's ORGANIZATION is INDEXED, we open it with ACCESS MODE IS SEQUENTIAL. Once we've OPENed idxpmast.dat for INPUT in paragraph AA-000-OPEN, we sequentially READ and DISPLAY the data contents of the file's records in AB-000-READ-RECORD. The display is effected from the NOT AT END clause of the READ statement; the contents of every record are displayed immediately it is read. When we have read all four records, the AT END option is invoked, we move "Y" to the end-of-file flag WS-PR-EOF, close the file and stop the program. The displayed output looks like this:

```
Personal COBOL version 2.0 from Micro Focus
PCOBRUN V2.0.02  Copyright (C) 1983-1993 Micro Focus Ltd.
Sexton, Conor        1234  01000000   Bubble Car
Cash, Mike           2456  05000000   Ferrari Testarossa
Hammersley, Rebecca  3769  02500000   E-type Jag
Dixon, Peter         5000  09000000   Mercedes S600
```

STARTing in the middle of the file

One of the main purposes of reading an indexed file sequentially is to go to a certain point in the file – employee number, invoice number, whatever – and then start reading the records in order from there. You do this with a combination of the START and READ verbs used on an indexed file opened with ACCESS MODE IS SEQUENTIAL either for INPUT or I-O. Here's a program, IDXSTART.CBL, that does the job:

```
*********************************************************************
*                                                                 *
* Uses START to read the payroll master file using alternate keys.*
*                                                                 *
*********************************************************************
       IDENTIFICATION DIVISION.
       PROGRAM-ID. IDXSTART.

       ENVIRONMENT DIVISION.

       INPUT-OUTPUT SECTION.
       FILE-CONTROL.
           SELECT OPTIONAL I-PAYROLL-MASTER
               ASSIGN TO "IDXPMAST.DAT"
               ORGANIZATION IS INDEXED
               ACCESS MODE IS SEQUENTIAL
               RECORD KEY IS I-PR-EMPNO
               ALTERNATE RECORD KEY IS I-PR-NAME
               FILE STATUS IS WS-PR-STATUS.

       DATA DIVISION.
       FILE SECTION.
       FD  I-PAYROLL-MASTER
           BLOCK CONTAINS 20 RECORDS
           LABEL RECORDS ARE STANDARD
           RECORD CONTAINS 113 CHARACTERS.
       01  I-PR-RECORD.
           02 I-PR-NAME          PIC X(20).
           02 I-PR-EMPNO         PIC X(8).
           02 FILLER             PIC X(85).

       WORKING-STORAGE SECTION.
       01  WS-PR-RECORD.
           02 WS-PR-NAME         PIC X(20).
           02 WS-PR-EMPNO        PIC X(8).
           02 WS-PR-EMPTYPE      PIC X.
           02 WS-PR-GRADE        PIC 99.
           02 WS-PR-AGE          PIC 999.
           02 WS-PR-GENDER       PIC X.
           02 WS-PR-REFNO        PIC 9999.
           02 WS-PR-ADDR         PIC X(30).
           02 WS-PR-EMPDATE.
               03 WS-PR-CCYY     PIC 9999.
               03 WS-PR-MM       PIC 99.
               03 WS-PR-DD       PIC 99.
           02 WS-PR-PAY          PIC 9(6)V99.
           02 WS-PR-BONUS        PIC 9(6)V99.
           02 WS-PR-CAR          PIC X(20).

       01  WS-PR-EOF             PIC X VALUE "N".
       01  WS-PR-STATUS          PIC XX.
```

171

```
PROCEDURE DIVISION.
A-MAIN-LINE SECTION.
A-000-MAIN.
    PERFORM AA-INITIALISE.
    PERFORM AB-PROCESS UNTIL WS-PR-EOF = "Y".
    PERFORM AC-TERMINATE.

A-999-EXIT.
    STOP RUN.

AA-INITIALISE SECTION.
AA-000-OPEN.
    OPEN INPUT I-PAYROLL-MASTER.
    IF WS-PR-STATUS NOT EQUAL ZERO THEN
        DISPLAY "Error " WS-PR-STATUS
            " opening payroll master file."
        GO TO A-999-EXIT
    END-IF.

AA-010-SET-KEY.
    MOVE SPACES TO WS-PR-RECORD.
    MOVE 2000 TO WS-PR-EMPNO.

AA-020-START.
    MOVE WS-PR-RECORD TO I-PR-RECORD.
    START I-PAYROLL-MASTER
        KEY IS GREATER THAN I-PR-EMPNO
        INVALID KEY DISPLAY "Invalid START key"
    END-START.

AA-999-EXIT.
    EXIT.

AB-PROCESS SECTION.
AB-000-READ-RECORD.
    READ I-PAYROLL-MASTER
        AT END MOVE "Y" TO WS-PR-EOF
        NOT AT END
            MOVE I-PR-RECORD TO WS-PR-RECORD
            DISPLAY WS-PR-NAME " " WS-PR-EMPNO " "
                WS-PR-PAY " " WS-PR-CAR
    END-READ.

AB-999-EXIT.
    EXIT.

AC-TERMINATE SECTION.
AC-000-CLOSE.
    CLOSE I-PAYROLL-MASTER.

AC-999-EXIT.
    EXIT.
```

Fill the working record with blanks and set the START key value.

Start reading records with key value above 2000.

Display part of each record

In `IDXSTART.CBL`, I've again `OPEN`ed the file `IDXPMAST.DAT` for `INPUT` using sequential access mode. The difference from the straight sequential read of all records done in the previous program, `IDXSEQ.CBL`, is that reading this time doesn't start at the top of the file.

By specifying an arbitrary starting-key value of `2000` in `AA-010-SET-KEY`, we `START` at the first record having a primary key greater than that value. Specifically, the `START` statement in paragraph `AA-020-START` brings the current read position to the first record with key in excess of `2000`; that key is `2456`. The first `READ` after the `START` – in paragraph `AB-000-READ-RECORD` – gets the data record. Once again, I've used the `NOT AT END` clause of the `READ` statement to display the record's contents. `AB-PROCESS SECTION` is then repeatedly called, and records from the file repeatedly read, until end-of-file is reached. In short, we read from the record with key value `2456` until the last record in the file. When you run this program, you get the following output:

```
Cash, Mike          2456   05000000 Ferrari Testarossa
Hammersley, Rebecca 3769   02500000 E-type Jag
Dixon, Peter        5000   09000000 Mercedes S600
```

If I had used a zero start-key value, instead of `2000`, all the records in the file would have been read and displayed in ascending key sequence. This is an effective sort of an indexed file and is a very powerful COBOL facility. You can take advantage of it as a substitute for the explicit use of the COBOL `SORT` verb. Using `SORT` on files involves a new type of file definition – the `SD` – and may also require the `MERGE` verb to combine existing files. Because of the usual *Made Simple* pressure of space, I don't deal with `SORT` any further in this book.

The `START`/`READ` combination is very powerful and commonly used in commercial COBOL programs. It offers a solution to a very general class of application such as finding all employees hired later than a certain date, or all invoices higher than a certain number. To search in this way on, say, the employee date, you must, at the point of creation of the indexed file, have specified the date as either a primary or as an alternate key. In the Exercises at the end of this chapter, you're invited to write a program using an alternate key to `START` reading a file sequentially.

If you want to update records found after a START, you must OPEN the file in I-O mode, using REWRITE to perform the record updates. ACCESS MODE must be either SEQUENTIAL or DYNAMIC; as you can see from idxstart.cbl, SEQUENTIAL is sufficient although less powerful than DYNAMIC, so I've used it here. If the file were opened with ACCESS MODE IS DYNAMIC, you could, in addition to the sequential access shown, also read records 'randomly' in any order. I cover ad-hoc enquiry of this kind in the next section.

READ... NEXT

You can achieve much the same effect as IDXSTART.CBL does in sequentially reading a file from a point not at its start by using ACCESS MODE IS DYNAMIC and READ with the NEXT option. The next program, IDXNEXT.CBL, does this. With the exception of the fact that ACCESS MODE is specified as DYNAMIC in the SELECT statement, the file and record definitions are the same as those found in IDXSTART.CBL, OPPOSITE. The file IDXPMAST.DAT is also OPENed for INPUT. To save space, I've just shown a part of the code from the PROCEDURE division.

In the paragraph AB-000-GET-KEY, we accept a key value from the user's input. This value is stored in the elementary data item WS-PR-EMPNO, which is subordinate to the group data item WS-PR-RECORD defined in WORKING-STORAGE. In the following paragraph, WS-PR-RECORD is MOVEd to I-PR-RECORD, thereby initialising the primary key. The next two paragraphs READ and DISPLAY the contents of the record accessed using the key.

At this point the program has successfully read and displayed the contents of the keyed record; the paragraph AB-040-READ-NEXT following does what its name suggests. This READ has an AT END, not an INVALID KEY, clause, because records after the keyed record are to be found sequentially. In this case, only one record is found using READ... NEXT but I could, as with earlier programs, have put this in a loop and read the file to the end.

If the key is invalid on the first READ – no matching record in the file – the program stops because of the GO TO statement subject to the

```
AB-PROCESS SECTION.
AB-000-GET-KEY.
    MOVE SPACES TO WS-PR-RECORD.
    DISPLAY "Enter number of employee to search for: "
        NO ADVANCING.
    ACCEPT WS-PR-EMPNO.

AB-010-MOVE-KEY.
    MOVE WS-PR-RECORD TO I-PR-RECORD.

AB-020-READ-RECORD.
    READ I-PAYROLL-MASTER INVALID KEY
        DISPLAY "Error " WS-PR-STATUS " reading employee "
            WS-PR-EMPNO " from payroll master file."
        GO TO A-999-EXIT
    END-READ.

AB-030-DISPLAY.
    MOVE I-PR-RECORD TO WS-PR-RECORD.
    DISPLAY WS-PR-NAME " " WS-PR-EMPNO " "
        WS-PR-PAY " " WS-PR-CAR.

AB-040-READ-NEXT.
    READ I-PAYROLL-MASTER NEXT RECORD AT END
        DISPLAY "Error " WS-PR-STATUS " reading employee "
            WS-PR-EMPNO " from payroll master file."
        GO TO A-999-EXIT
    END-READ.

AB-050-DISPLAY.
    MOVE I-PR-RECORD TO WS-PR-RECORD.
    DISPLAY WS-PR-NAME " " WS-PR-EMPNO " "
        WS-PR-PAY " " WS-PR-CAR.

AB-999-EXIT.
    EXIT.
```

Get start key from the user and move it to the record key.

READ ... AT END specifies records are to be read sequentially after indexed start.

INVALID KEY clause of READ. Even if that GO TO were not there, the READ... NEXT would not work properly after an invalid-key read on the file. In this way, the strategy of reading a file sequentially by means of a keyed READ followed by READ... NEXT is less flexible and requires more accuracy than its START/READ counterpart demonstrated in the program IDXSTART.CBL.

This concludes our look at the various ways in which you can read an indexed file sequentially. We move on now to the real purpose of indexed files, the ad-hoc enquiry implemented with 'random' access.

Indexed file enquiry

Ever wonder how, when you telephone your travel agent, the bank or the tax office (!), they are able to tell you about your account almost before you've finished speaking? Or how they are able to find your details using *either* an account number of some sort *or* you name? The answer in both cases lies probably in 'random' access of COBOL files. The ad-hoc enquiry application is extremely important to business. You wouldn't, these days, retain a travel agent if they took half-an-hour or longer searching paper records for your details. Come to think of it though, maybe random access should be outlawed in the case of the tax office!

In this section, I present just one program, IDXENQ.CBL. This program uses our familiar IDXPMAST.DAT file, performing ad-hoc enquiry with both primary and alternate keys. Here's the program:

IDXENQ.CBL

```
*******************************************************************
*                                                                 *
* Enquires directly on payroll master file with user-input keys. *
*                                                                 *
*******************************************************************
 IDENTIFICATION DIVISION.
 PROGRAM-ID. IDXENQ.

 ENVIRONMENT DIVISION.

 INPUT-OUTPUT SECTION.
 FILE-CONTROL.
     SELECT OPTIONAL I-PAYROLL-MASTER
         ASSIGN TO "IDXPMAST.DAT"
         ORGANIZATION IS INDEXED
         ACCESS MODE IS RANDOM
         RECORD KEY IS I-PR-EMPNO
         ALTERNATE RECORD KEY IS I-PR-NAME
         FILE STATUS IS WS-PR-STATUS.

 DATA DIVISION.
 FILE SECTION.
 FD  I-PAYROLL-MASTER
     BLOCK CONTAINS 20 RECORDS
     LABEL RECORDS ARE STANDARD
     RECORD CONTAINS 113 CHARACTERS.
```

INDEXED ... RANDOM! We're reading records non-sequentially by key.

Read by employee number by default, but access is also possible using the NAME secondary key.

```
01  I-PR-RECORD.
    02 I-PR-NAME          PIC X(20).
    02 I-PR-EMPNO         PIC X(8).
    02 FILLER             PIC X(85).

WORKING-STORAGE SECTION.
01  WS-PR-RECORD.
    02 WS-PR-NAME         PIC X(20).
    02 WS-PR-EMPNO        PIC X(8).
    02 WS-PR-EMPTYPE      PIC X.
    02 WS-PR-GRADE        PIC 99.
    02 WS-PR-AGE          PIC 999.
    02 WS-PR-GENDER       PIC X.
    02 WS-PR-REFNO        PIC 9999.
    02 WS-PR-ADDR         PIC X(30).
    02 WS-PR-EMPDATE.
       03 WS-PR-CCYY      PIC 9999.
       03 WS-PR-MM        PIC 99.
       03 WS-PR-DD        PIC 99.
    02 WS-PR-PAY          PIC 9(6)V99.
    02 WS-PR-BONUS        PIC 9(6)V99.
    02 WS-PR-CAR          PIC X(20).
01  WS-PR-STATUS          PIC XX.

PROCEDURE DIVISION.
A-MAIN-LINE SECTION.
A-000-MAIN.
    PERFORM AA-INITIALISE.
    PERFORM AB-PROCESS.
    PERFORM AC-TERMINATE.

A-999-EXIT.
    STOP RUN.

AA-INITIALISE SECTION.
AA-000-OPEN.
    OPEN INPUT I-PAYROLL-MASTER.
    IF WS-PR-STATUS NOT EQUAL ZERO THEN
        DISPLAY "Error " WS-PR-STATUS
            " opening payroll master file."
        GO TO A-999-EXIT
    END-IF.

AA-999-EXIT.
    EXIT.

AB-PROCESS SECTION.
AB-000-GET-PRIMARY-KEY.
    MOVE SPACES TO WS-PR-RECORD.
    DISPLAY "Enter number of employee to search for: "
        NO ADVANCING.
    ACCEPT WS-PR-EMPNO.
```

> Prompt for and accept from user the employee to be enquired on.

```
AB-010-MOVE-KEY.
    MOVE WS-PR-RECORD TO I-PR-RECORD.

AB-020-READ-RECORD.
    READ I-PAYROLL-MASTER INVALID KEY
        DISPLAY "Error " WS-PR-STATUS " reading employee "
            WS-PR-EMPNO " from payroll master file."
        GO TO A-999-EXIT
    END-READ.

AB-030-DISPLAY.
    MOVE I-PR-RECORD TO WS-PR-RECORD.
    DISPLAY WS-PR-NAME " " WS-PR-EMPNO " "
    WS-PR-PAY " " WS-PR-CAR.

AB-040-GET-ALTERNATE-KEY.
    MOVE SPACES TO WS-PR-RECORD.
        DISPLAY "Enter name of employee to search for: "
            NO ADVANCING.
    ACCEPT WS-PR-NAME.

AB-050-MOVE-KEY.
    MOVE WS-PR-RECORD TO I-PR-RECORD.

AB-060-READ-RECORD.
    READ I-PAYROLL-MASTER KEY IS I-PR-NAME INVALID KEY
        DISPLAY "Error " WS-PR-STATUS " reading employee "
            WS-PR-NAME " from payroll master file."
        GO TO A-999-EXIT
    END-READ.

AB-070-DISPLAY.
    MOVE I-PR-RECORD TO WS-PR-RECORD.
    DISPLAY WS-PR-NAME " " WS-PR-EMPNO " "
        WS-PR-PAY " " WS-PR-CAR.

AB-999-EXIT.
    EXIT.

AC-TERMINATE SECTION.
AC-000-CLOSE.
    CLOSE I-PAYROLL-MASTER.

AC-999-EXIT.
    EXIT.
```

> Get an employee record using the employee-number primary key.

> This time, use the secondary key.

Notice that the SELECT statement specifies ACCESS MODE IS RANDOM. This is the normal ACCESS MODE for ad-hoc enquiry on indexed files. You could use DYNAMIC and enable yourself to read the file sequentially also, but you should use the minimum power necessary for the purpose.

Otherwise, the file's logical definition in the `FD` and its record specifications are as before, the '`I`' prefix to the names suggesting what is in fact the case: the file is opened for `INPUT`. With this `OPEN` mode, we can only make enquiries on the file; we can't update records as we read them. I leave until the next section the program that demonstrates the indexed update capability.

`AA-INITIALISE` section `OPEN`s the file `idxpmast.dat` for `INPUT`. In paragraphs `AB-000-GET-PRIMARY-KEY` through `AB-020-READ-RECORD`, we accept the search key – an employee number – as input from the user, initialise the record key and `READ` the file record. If there's no matching record, the `INVALID KEY` option is taken. `AB-030-DISPLAY` does as its name suggests and displays on the screen some of the contents of the retrieved record.

In the next four paragraphs, we go again, as it were, this time using the alternate key `I-PR-NAME` to search the file for a name input by the user. The procedure used is exactly the same as that employed for the primary key: initialise the alternate key and `READ` the record, exiting with `INVALID KEY` if the record does not exist or is not found. Finally, the paragraph `AB-070-DISPLAY` displays the contents of the second retrieved record.

Here's the interaction that appeared on the screen when I ran it:

```
Enter number of employee to search for: 2456
Cash, Mike          2456      05000000 Ferrari Testarossa
Enter name of employee to search for: Cash, Mike
Cash, Mike          2456      05000000 Ferrari Testarossa
```

You'll notice that the record found on both `READ`s is the same one but that on the second access, I retrieved Mr. Cash's record by using his name as the alternate key.

Remember that alternate keys can be specified `WITH DUPLICATES`, unlike primary keys and that the primary key cannot be used as an alternate key. Also, and sometimes usefully, primary and alternate keys can overlap. You could, for example, specify an employee name and number, taken together in a group data item, to be the primary key, with just the number being the secondary key.

Indexed file update

Having enquired and found a file, it's really useful to be able to update the retrieved record on the spot. You wouldn't be very impressed if the travel agent said, no, we can't upgrade your holiday reservation from Blackpool to the Seychelles, because we can't change a booking once it is made. Indexed file update-in-place solves the problem. This variant of the employee-file program, `IDXUPD.CBL`, that does it:

IDXUPD.CBL

```
****************************************************************
*                                                              *
*  This program enquires directly on the payroll master file   *
*  with a user-input key, and updates the record if it is found.*
*                                                              *
****************************************************************
      IDENTIFICATION DIVISION.
      PROGRAM-ID. IDXUPD.

      ENVIRONMENT DIVISION.

      INPUT-OUTPUT SECTION.
      FILE-CONTROL.
          SELECT OPTIONAL IO-PAYROLL-MASTER
              ASSIGN TO "IDXPMAST.DAT"
              ORGANIZATION IS INDEXED
              ACCESS MODE IS RANDOM
              RECORD KEY IS IO-PR-EMPNO
              ALTERNATE RECORD KEY IS IO-PR-NAME
              FILE STATUS IS WS-PR-STATUS.

      DATA DIVISION.
      FILE SECTION.
      FD  IO-PAYROLL-MASTER
          BLOCK CONTAINS 20 RECORDS
          LABEL RECORDS ARE STANDARD
          RECORD CONTAINS 113 CHARACTERS.
      01  IO-PR-RECORD.
          02 IO-PR-NAME        PIC X(20).
          02 IO-PR-EMPNO       PIC X(8).
          02 FILLER            PIC X(85).

      WORKING-STORAGE SECTION.
      01  WS-PR-RECORD.
          02 WS-PR-NAME        PIC X(20).
          02 WS-PR-EMPNO       PIC X(8).
          02 WS-PR-EMPTYPE     PIC X.
          02 WS-PR-GRADE       PIC 99.
```

> I-O means input-output, or that the file will be OPENed for update.

```
        02 WS-PR-AGE          PIC 999.
        02 WS-PR-GENDER       PIC X.
        02 WS-PR-REFNO        PIC 9999.
        02 WS-PR-ADDR         PIC X(30).
        02 WS-PR-EMPDATE.
            03 WS-PR-CCYY     PIC 9999.
            03 WS-PR-MM       PIC 99.
            03 WS-PR-DD       PIC 99.
        02 WS-PR-PAY          PIC 9(6)V99.
        02 WS-PR-BONUS        PIC 9(6)V99.
        02 WS-PR-CAR          PIC X(20).
    01 WS-PR-STATUS           PIC XX.

    PROCEDURE DIVISION.
    A-MAIN-LINE SECTION.
    A-000-MAIN.
        PERFORM AA-INITIALISE.
        PERFORM AB-PROCESS.
        PERFORM AC-TERMINATE.

    A-999-EXIT.
        STOP RUN.

    AA-INITIALISE SECTION.
    AA-000-OPEN.
        OPEN I-O IO-PAYROLL-MASTER.                 Open for output.
        IF WS-PR-STATUS NOT EQUAL ZERO THEN
            DISPLAY "Error " WS-PR-STATUS
                " opening payroll master file."
            GO TO A-999-EXIT
        END-IF.

    AA-999-EXIT.
        EXIT.

    AB-PROCESS SECTION.
    AB-000-GET-KEY.
        MOVE SPACES TO WS-PR-RECORD.
        DISPLAY "Enter number of employee to search for: "
                NO ADVANCING.
        ACCEPT WS-PR-EMPNO.
                                            READ in a record which will
    AB-010-MOVE-KEY.                        then be updated and rewritten.
        MOVE WS-PR-RECORD TO IO-PR-RECORD.

    AB-020-READ-RECORD.
        READ IO-PAYROLL-MASTER INVALID KEY
            DISPLAY "Error " WS-PR-STATUS " reading employee "
                WS-PR-EMPNO " from payroll master file."
            GO TO A-999-EXIT
        END-READ.
```

```
AB-030-DISPLAY.
    MOVE IO-PR-RECORD TO WS-PR-RECORD.
    DISPLAY "Employee number: " WS-PR-EMPNO.
    DISPLAY "Old employee pay: " WS-PR-PAY.

AB-040-ACCEPT-NEW.
    DISPLAY "Enter new employee pay: " NO ADVANCING.
    ACCEPT WS-PR-PAY.

AB-050-REWRITE-RECORD.
    MOVE WS-PR-RECORD TO IO-PR-RECORD.
    REWRITE IO-PR-RECORD INVALID KEY
        DISPLAY "Error " WS-PR-STATUS " writing employee "
            WS-PR-EMPNO " to payroll master file."
        GO TO A-999-EXIT
    END-REWRITE.

AB-999-EXIT.
    EXIT.

AC-TERMINATE SECTION.
AC-000-CLOSE.
    CLOSE IO-PAYROLL-MASTER.

AC-999-EXIT.
    EXIT.
```

> Update the changed record in place.

The file IDXPMAST.DAT is OPENed with ACCESS MODE IS RANDOM and in I-O mode. This mode is necessary for a record retrieved by key to be updated in place. The use of input-output mode is reflected in the naming convention; the prefix for the names in the file record is 'IO'.

The initial READ of a record by key is much the same as in the program IDXUPD.CBL shown in the last section. Having retrieved the record, the program in paragraph AB-030-DISPLAY then shows on the screen some of its contents.

The next two paragraphs are the essence of IDXUPD.CBL. We decide to give our trusty employee a pay rise. In paragraph AB-040-ACCEPT-NEW, the new level of remuneration is accepted from input by the user. In AB-050-REWRITE-RECORD, the recently-retrieved employee record is updated in place in the file with the new pay amount. To see the effect of the initial READ followed by the update, you need to run the program twice. Here's the interaction as it happened when I did the update with two runs of the program.

```
Enter number of employee to search for: 3769
Employee number: 3769
Old employee pay: 02500000
Enter new employee pay: 27500

Enter number of employee to search for: 3769
Employee number: 3769
Old employee pay: 02750000
Enter new employee pay: 30000
```

On the first execution, the pay of employee 3769 is increased from £25,000 to £27,500. This can be seen from the output of second run, which goes on to raise the pay further to £30,000. Executing the program IDXSEQ.CBL (see *Sequential access to an indexed file*) shows the final state of the file and of the lucky Ms. Hammersley's record:

```
Sexton, Conor       1234   01000000  Bubble Car
Cash, Mike          2456   05000000  Ferrari Testarossa
Hammersley, Rebecca 3769   03000000  E-type Jag
Dixon, Peter        5000   09000000  Mercedes S600
```

IDXUPD.CBL is about as simple as indexed update programs come. You should note its characteristics, especially those concerning the use of REWRITE. You must use REWRITE to update in this way; WRITE won't do. To use REWRITE, you must OPEN the file in I-O mode. The REWRITE statement must immediately follow a successful READ – you must update the same record as you've retrieved. You can't have two REWRITEs following a single READ. If the REWRITE fails, it will invoke the INVALID KEY option, as do the other I/O verbs used with indexed files. It's up to you to ensure that the record used with REWRITE will fit in the record space available in the file (this is important if you use REWRITE… FROM a data item not defined as part of the file's FD). You can use a REWRITE to update an alternate key, but not a primary key.

And, with that, I've shown all the programs that I'm going to in this chapter illustrating the possibilities of COBOL indexed files. You may have noticed that, among other things, I haven't presented an example showing how to DELETE a record, or how to add records to an indexed file opened in EXTEND mode. With the information I've given in this chapter, you shouldn't find these hard to do yourself. Accordingly, I've included these aspects as exercises at the end of the chapter.

Relative files

A relative file in COBOL is similar in characteristics and operation to an indexed file. The fundamental difference is that, instead of accessing records within the file using a logical key, you do so by means of an unsigned integer value, the *relative key*. This value represents by position (*relative* to the start of the file) the actual 'slot' that the record occupies. If, using a relative file, the relative key value is what would be used for the primary key in an equivalent indexed file – in our examples, the employee number – the apparent difference in operation between the two file types is very small indeed.

The most appropriate use for a relative file is where the records naturally occupy a numeric sequence. Examples include records sequenced on cheque number or invoice number. The relative file is the least-important and least-used of the three COBOL file types. There's nothing you can achieve with relative files that you can't also do with indexed files. The latter are more generally useful and, in the real world, are predominant. Because of this, this section confines itself to a short summary of the characteristics of relative files.

The main differences between relative and indexed files are these:

● The primary key of a relative file is a number, stored outside the file's record definition, representing the record's position in the file. By contrast, an indexed file's key is stored in the record and provides a logical means of accessing the record.

● Depending on the environment, an indexed file may be stored as two files – the data file and the index file. There will in any case be data and an index. With a relative file, there is just one (data) file.

● The space occupied by a relative file is, at least logically, determined by the range of record numbers. You could, in an inefficient implementation, have a file of two records, 49 and 75, occupying a file physically of 75 records in size. An indexed file only ever occupies data space determined by the number of its records.

● Relative files don't give you the facility of alternate keys.

You create a relative file by sequentially writing records to the file in a manner similar to that shown for indexed files earlier in this chapter.

Let's assume that we've created such a relative file, `relpmast.dat`:

```
Sexton, Conor      1234      C10029M      Rathfarnham, Dublin, Ireland.
19951109010000000000000Bubble Car
Cash, Mike      2456      S25039M      Jordan Hill, Oxford, UK.
19871212050000000000500000Ferrari Testarossa
Hammersley, Rebecca 3769      S10023F      Summertown, Oxford, UK.
19960101025000000025000E-type Jag
Dixon, Peter      5000      S29045M      Blenheim, Oxford, UK.
198504010900000001000000Mercedes S600.
```

Here's a program, `RELUPD.CBL,` that effects a simple in-place update:

RELUPD.CBL

```
****************************************************************
*                                                              *
*   This program updates the relative payroll master file in   *
*   place using random access and I-O open mode.               *
*                                                              *
****************************************************************
     IDENTIFICATION DIVISION.
     PROGRAM-ID. RELUPD.

     ENVIRONMENT DIVISION.

     INPUT-OUTPUT SECTION.
     FILE-CONTROL.
         SELECT OPTIONAL IO-PAYROLL-MASTER
             ASSIGN TO "RELPMAST.DAT"
             ORGANIZATION IS RELATIVE
             ACCESS MODE IS RANDOM
             RELATIVE KEY IS WS-RELATIVE-KEY
             FILE STATUS IS WS-PR-STATUS.

     DATA DIVISION.
     FILE SECTION.
     FD  IO-PAYROLL-MASTER
         BLOCK CONTAINS 20 RECORDS
         LABEL RECORDS ARE STANDARD
         RECORD CONTAINS 113 CHARACTERS.
     01  IO-PR-RECORD.
         02 IO-PR-NAME          PIC X(20).
         02 IO-PR-EMPNO         PIC X(8).
         02 FILLER              PIC X(85).

     WORKING-STORAGE SECTION.
     01  WS-PR-RECORD.
         02 WS-PR-NAME          PIC X(20).
         02 WS-PR-EMPNO         PIC X(8).
```

```
        02 WS-PR-EMPTYPE      PIC X.
        02 WS-PR-GRADE        PIC 99.
        02 WS-PR-AGE          PIC 999.
        02 WS-PR-GENDER       PIC X.
        02 WS-PR-REFNO        PIC 9999.
        02 WS-PR-ADDR         PIC X(30).
        02 WS-PR-EMPDATE.
            03 WS-PR-CCYY     PIC 9999.
            03 WS-PR-MM       PIC 99.
            03 WS-PR-DD       PIC 99.
        02 WS-PR-PAY          PIC 9(6)V99.
        02 WS-PR-BONUS        PIC 9(6)V99.
        02 WS-PR-CAR          PIC X(20).
01  WS-PR-STATUS              PIC XX.
01  WS-RELATIVE-KEY           PIC 9999.
```

Relative key is **not** part of the file record.

```
PROCEDURE DIVISION.
A-MAIN-LINE SECTION.
A-000-MAIN.
    PERFORM AA-INITIALISE.
    PERFORM AB-PROCESS.
    PERFORM AC-TERMINATE.

A-999-EXIT.
    STOP RUN.

AA-INITIALISE SECTION.
AA-000-OPEN.
    OPEN I-O IO-PAYROLL-MASTER.
    IF WS-PR-STATUS NOT EQUAL ZERO THEN
        DISPLAY "Error " WS-PR-STATUS
            " opening payroll master file."
        GO TO A-999-EXIT
    END-IF.

AA-999-EXIT.
    EXIT.

AB-PROCESS SECTION.
AB-000-GET-KEY.
    DISPLAY "Enter the record number to be retrieved: "
        NO ADVANCING.
    ACCEPT WS-RELATIVE-KEY.

AB-010-READ-RECORD.
    READ IO-PAYROLL-MASTER INVALID KEY
        DISPLAY "Cannot retrieve record number " WS-RELATIVE-KEY
            GO TO A-999-EXIT
    NOT INVALID KEY
        MOVE IO-PR-RECORD TO WS-PR-RECORD
        DISPLAY WS-PR-NAME " " WS-PR-EMPNO " "
            WS-PR-PAY " " WS-PR-CAR
    END-READ.
```

OPEN relative file for update.

Read a record by relative key. If successful, move it to WORKING-STORAGE to be changed.

```
AB-020-UPDATE-RECORD.
    DISPLAY "Enter updated pay amount: " NO ADVANCING.
    ACCEPT WS-PR-PAY.
    MOVE WS-PR-RECORD TO IO-PR-RECORD.
    REWRITE IO-PR-RECORD INVALID KEY
        DISPLAY "Cannot update record number " WS-RELATIVE-KEY
        GO TO A-999-EXIT
    NOT INVALID KEY
        MOVE IO-PR-RECORD TO WS-PR-RECORD
        DISPLAY WS-PR-NAME " " WS-PR-EMPNO " "
            WS-PR-PAY " " WS-PR-CAR
    END-REWRITE.

AB-999-EXIT.
    EXIT.

AC-TERMINATE SECTION.
AC-000-CLOSE.
    CLOSE IO-PAYROLL-MASTER.

AC-999-EXIT.
    EXIT.
```

> Change the data, move it back to the file record and REWRITE it.

In the paragraph AB-000-GET-KEY, the user is prompted to input a relative key, i.e. the number by position of a record. Notice that the key, WS-RELATIVE-KEY, is *not* part of the file record; this is a major difference between relative and indexed files. The READ statement in paragraph AB-010-READ-RECORD retrieves the record denoted by the key. The next paragraph, AB-020-UPDATE-RECORD, changes the pay of the selected employee and REWRITEs the record. Both READ and REWRITE are written with the INVALID KEY and the NOT INVALID KEY options.

When I ran the program, the displayed output was this:

```
Enter the record number to be retrieved: 4
Dixon, Peter        5000     09000000 Mercedes S600
Enter updated pay amount: 80000
Dixon, Peter        5000     08000000 Mercedes S600
```

Notice that Mr. Dixon's key number is input as 4; this is the relative position of his record in the file. In the equivalent indexed file keyed on employee-number, you would use the employee number 5000 instead. On the second display, generated by the NOT INVALID KEY option of REWRITE, we can see that the unfortunate Mr. Dixon's remuneration has been reduced to £80,000, though his car is untouched.

Exercises

1   Write a program, `IDXDEL.CBL`, which `DELETE`s a record from the file `idxpmast.dat`. The record to `DELETE` should be identified by a primary-key value `ACCEPT`ed from user input.

2   Write a variant of `IDXSEQ.CBL` (see *Sequential access to an indexed file*) that will add records to an existing file `idxpmast.dat` by `OPEN`ing it in `EXTEND` mode.

3   Write a program, derived from `IDXSTART.CBL`, to `START` reading the indexed file from a point not at the beginning of the file. Instead of using the primary key to do so, use the alternate key, the employee's name.

7 The Year 2000 problem

The problem

If you are conversant with the COBOL topics covered in the first seven chapters, you have a solid grounding in the language. There are bits I've had to go lightly on, such as screen I/O and file sort/merge, but what you have seen is the core of COBOL. What will you use it for? It's possible that you'll write new COBOL programs, most likely in conjunction with a database product such as DB/2 or Oracle. It's possible that you'll be asked to maintain old (legacy) COBOL programs. But, in the closing years of the 20th century, the major applications of your new-found COBOL knowledge will be two:

● Modifying existing code to handle dates from 2000 onward.

● In Europe at least, modifying existing software to cope with EMU (Economic and Monetary Union) and its new currency, the Euro.

European Monetary Union

This isn't a book about financial applications of COBOL, so let me dispose of the EMU issue first. (By the way, the term is really *Economic and Monetary Union*, although *European Monetary Union* is often used). At the time of writing, it seems that 11 of the 15 European Union (EU) member-states will sign up to the implementation within their borders of the new currency, starting a three-year phase-in on 1 January , 1999. Their individual currencies will be 'locked in' to the Euro at an irrevocable exchange rate fixed in May, 1998. The old currencies, from the mighty Deutschmark to the Portuguese escudo and the Irish pound, are scheduled to have been replaced altogether from 2002.

As a consequence of this truly millenial change, major modifications will be needed to legacy COBOL (and other) software, to implement rates of exchange that will convert financial transactions expressed in the old currencies to the Euro and vice-versa. Even countries, such as the UK and Sweden, that plan initially not to join EMU, will be affected. Companies and organisations in those countries, to continue intra-EU and international trade, will have to modify their software to take account of their trading partners' use of the Euro.

The Year 2000 (Y2K)

The larger global challenge is the one that arises when the leading digit on our years changes from '1' to '2'. This requires an enormous amount of COBOL re-programming and, perhaps for the first time in all the history of computing, the deadline cannot and will not slip.

Frankly, a great deal of flannel and hyperbole has been and is being written and spoken about the Y2K problem. As it is a simple problem, Y2K offers a rich field of possibilities for the cynic and the opportunist. In this chapter, I try to present the summary minus the sensationalism, that will be meaningful to programmers and managers alike. The fix is almost as simple as the problem. The difficulty is that dates are everywhere in almost all COBOL programs (about 90 billion lines of it, remember!), so the simple fix must be done in millions of places.

The essence of Y2K is that, to save space and processing on legacy systems, years were represented as two digits – say, 75 for 1975 – on the assumption that the code would be replaced before the year 2000. Because of the sheer scale of investment in the commercial software of the 1960s, 1970s and 1980s, this hasn't happened. The danger is that the year 00 will be regarded by existing programs as 1900, not 2000. An associated problem is that 2000 is a leap year, while 1900 wasn't.

The fix? There are two broad lines of attack:

- Expand the date-representation used in COBOL programs from YYMMDD to CCYYMMDD (where CC is the century), expand file and other data accordingly, and alter program logic as needed.

- Use a 'window' scheme in which the century runs from, say 1961 to 2060. The two-digit 75 is then taken to mean 1975, while 25 becomes 2025. Program logic must be altered.

Later in this chapter, I give some detailed techniques, in COBOL, for applying these fixes. First, let's consider some of the general implications of the problem. You will notice that, although the problem and the fix are easy, the problem is everywhere and the fix isn't, at least yet. The fix requires extensive change to almost all existing COBOL programs. Although there are many software tools that can assist with discovering Y2K dependencies in COBOL code, none can reliably find and fix all of them. Sight-checking is still necessary.

To compound the difficulty, it's quite possible, for many older programs, that the source code – the actual COBOL code – has gone missing and is not available for Y2K analysis and recompilation. There are techniques (*disassembly* of executable code) for regenerating the source code, but these are not always available or reliable. Database and screen formats used by the programs must be modified too.

Y2K affects mainly commercial applications, mostly written in COBOL. Typical date-dependent commercial applications include mortgage, insurance, pension, tax, stock-control, personnel, age-calculation and futures – in short, almost the whole gamut of business software as it is currently known. Possible effects of date-dependencies include:

- Renewal notices: the computer won't send you a notice that your insurance is going to expire on a date after January 1, 2000.

- Invoices and invoice reminders might not be sent if their dates straddle 1999 and 2000; cash-flow will be hurt as a result.

- A consequent rush of catch-up invoice generation – the system thinks you haven't been sent any invoices for many years!

- Reports sequenced on year may be wrong: 2000 will precede 1999.

- Day-of-week calculations based on a 00-99 year range will be wrong.

- If '00' or '99' are used as error-indicators in date calculations, a program will fail.

- September, 9, 1999. There is a long-standing habit among COBOL programmers of using 'all-nines' to represent an impossible or error condition. If programs start failing on that day, think of this.

- The system date may be generated wrongly. Look at the program `DATEIO.CBL` in (page 60), and you'll see that in the statement `ACCEPT WS-DATE FROM DATE.`, a two-digit year is returned.

These are considerations affecting commercial software. Less familiar are such aspects as hard-coded dates in computers, VCRs, cars and any device that can be programmed with a date and time. More frightening, are security and defence applications: what will happen, on January 1, 2000, to the world's nuclear power stations and ballistic missiles? With luck, at worst, they will 'fail-safe' and just shut down.

Some trivia on dates

The Y2K dependency is caused by using two digits to represent a four-digit quantity such as the year 1975. The representation 19980128 for 28 January, 1998 refers to the *Gregorian* calendar, after the 16th century Pope Gregory XIII. Gregory's calendar is rooted in the fact that it takes the Earth 365 days, 5 hours, 48 minutes and 46 seconds to orbit the Sun, that period of time being the solar year.

This stuff is relevant, in particular when we consider leap years and so-called Julian dates used in commercial software. Also, because Gregory and Julius (Caesar) didn't assign a year zero, centuries run from 1 through 100. Therefore, the 21st century begins in the year 2001 and not 2000. Not that anyone will care about the distinction.

An aside: if I betray a certain delight in all this, it could be to do with the fact that I was a UNIX aficionado, and that operating system has remarkably extensive date- and time-calculation facilities. For example, UNIX calculates all its times in seconds from the start of January 1, 1970. It uses a long integer (32 bits) to do so and, as such, can increment from zero up to 2,147,483,647 seconds. There are 31,556,926 seconds in a solar year (refer to 365 days, 5 hours...). Thus, the UNIX timing scheme is good for slightly over 68 years – which means we run into the wall early in 2038. There's another possible date-dependency, although I'll probably by then be beyond caring and anyway, they might have implemented the number of seconds in 64 bits.

In 46 BC, Julius Caesar directed his court astronomer to fix the length of the year as an accurate number of days. The year was calculated to be 365ᵛ days – a close approximation. Each fourth year had an extra day appended at the end of February to compensate for a quarter-day being lost on the other three. This is the essence of the system we still use and the scheme is referred to as the *Julian* calendar.

Even with this improvement in accuracy, the actual year is 11 minutes and 14 seconds shorter than 365ᵛ days. Over a long period of years, the 'drift' began to show when relating the calendar date to the Sun's position. In 1582, Pope Gregory XIII instructed the learned scholar Aloysius Lilius to rectify the problem. This Lilius did by means of an added refinement. Henceforth, century-years – including 1700, 1800 and 1900 – would not be leap years but century-years divisible by 400 would. This reduced the 'drift' inaccuracy to around 25 seconds a year. We consider this acceptable and we still use the Gregorian system. It also means that 2000 is a leap year while that other 00 year, 1900, isn't. As part of your Y2K code analysis *you must therefore make sure to change tests that assume 00 years are not leap years.*

Gregory instituted a one-time 'catch-up' for the 1600 years of 'drift' that had preceded his changes. He simply eliminated the dates 5 October 1582 to 14 October 1582 (inclusive of both) to compensate. In Britain, they delayed 170 years before following suit. By this time, one more day needed to be deleted to get rid of the 'drift'. So the dates 3 September to 13 September (inclusive of both) disappeared from the calendar. Because of the pre-eminence of British power in the 18th and 19th centuries, the British system was adopted and these dates disappeared from the Gregorian calendar used by the Western world.

A side-effect of all this is the establishment of the *Lilian* date (after Lilius): in this system, dates are represented by counting from October 14th, 1582, which is treated as day zero. It may surprise you, but this form is often used commercially, especially by IBM.

Another landmark date is the confusingly-named *Julian date* (first form, and distinct from the Julian calendar referred to above), invented by a gentleman called Joseph Scaliger, whose father's name was Julius. This counts the days from midday on 1 January 4713 BC.

There is an ANSI/ISO date also, counting the days from 31 December, 1600, which is treated as day zero.

Finally, we come to the *Julian date* (second form, and also distinct from the Julian calendar!), which is very widely used in commercial software. With this, the date is represented either as a five-digit or as a seven-digit quantity. 28 January 1998 is stored either as 98028 or as 1998028. When you're looking for Y2K dependencies in COBOL code, you have to watch out for this as well as dates of the YYMMDD form; Julian dates (second form) are everywhere.

Expanding the date

The Y2K dates problem, as expressed in COBOL is this. A date quantity is represented in memory or on file according to one of the following data definitions:

```
01 OLD-GREG-DATE.
    02 OLD-GREG-YY      PIC 99.
    02 OLD-GREG-MM      PIC 99.
    02 OLD-GREG-DD      PIC 99.

01 OLD-JUL-DATE.
    02 OLD-JUL-YY       PIC 99.
    02 OLD-JUL-DDD      PIC 999.
```

These definitions assume the year to be in the range 00 to 99 and, implicitly, that we're dealing with the twentieth century.

Finding the problem code

There are two steps involved in analysing Y2K: finding the affected code and fixing it. Finding the code is by no means as easy as it sounds. For example, the data-item names may not be as intuitive and sensible as those above. A year number might be stored in a data item called WS-ODDSNENDS and might be quite difficult to identify. Hard-coded checks may be done in a program against numbers such as 75 or 99 but you may not be able to tell just from looking at them if they are processing dates or not. Not every division by 4 is a leap-year check. Not every test for a variable being in the range 1 to 12 is a test for a valid month number. How do you know whether or not a key of an indexed file contains a two-digit date specification? It's for reasons like these that no program has yet been devised that can find all Y2K dependencies. Inspection by COBOL programmers is essential.

That said, the range of available tools is extensive and useful. Your organisation may already be using some of these, or you may have to find Y2K tools yourself. There's no point in my trying to list or describe any here. The field is changing too fast for that to be useful. As ever these days, you'll get the best results by searching the Web. The quickest way to start is to enter your Web browser and your favourite search engine (the one I find best is Alta Vista). Search globally on the string: "**Year 2000 Tools**".

You'll get a list of over 300 entries of which the first 20 or so are most useful. There are elaborate contributions from IBM, Digital Equipment Corporation and Sun Microsystems, to name but a few. I have found two sites from this list quite informative. They are the *Year 2000 Tools and Services Catalog* maintained by Mitre Corp, at this Web site:

```
www.mitre.org/research/y2k
```

and IBM's *Software Mall*, which you can find at the site:

```
www.softmall.ibm.com
```

The Mitre site groups its tools and services in the following categories:

- Consulting
- Clock simulation
- Integrated toolsets
- Project management tools
- Tools
- Full conversion service
- Testing tools/support

But search for yourself, if you have access to the Web. If you don't have access, get it; it's amazing how much free information and software you can get on the Web.

Fixing the problem code

I summarise techniques for fixing Y2K-dependent code in this chapter. The remainder of this section looks, in as simple a manner as possible, at the process of converting files and code. The next two sections deal with two major subcategories of windowing.

The most obvious solution to the Y2K problem as it affects COBOL programs is to expand data files to 4-digit year representation and modify code accordingly. It sound easy and, it is easy, but it's always a major change to files and code. Major change implies errors and extensive testing for elimination of errors – a time-consuming process.

To illustrate the conversion process, I've adapted the employee/payroll program seen so extensively in Chapters 5 and 6. In particular, I use the sequential-file version from Chapter 5, but with one change. If you look, for example, at the program SEQWRITE.CBL in that chapter (*File-update application*), you'll see that, like a good forward-looking

COBOL programmer, I use the following group data item for dates in the file `seqpmast.dat`:

```
02 WS-PR-EMPDATE.
    03 WS-PR-CCYY        PIC 9999.
    03 WS-PR-MM          PIC 99.
    03 WS-PR-DD          PIC 99.
```

This is Y2K-clean code. It wouldn't be if instead I had used:

```
02 WS-PR-EMPDATE.
    03 WS-PR-YY          PIC 99.
    03 WS-PR-MM          PIC 99.
    03 WS-PR-DD          PIC 99.
```

For this chapter, I wrote a version of SEQWRITE.CBL 'crippled' to handle only two-digit years. The data file it creates has these contents:

```
Conor Sexton        1234    C10029M    Rathfarnham, Dublin, Ireland.
5110901000000000000000Bubble Car        Mike Cash           2345
S25039M    Jordan Hill, Oxford, UK.    87121205000000000500000Ferrari
Testarossa Rebecca Hammersley 5643    S10023F    Summertown, Oxford, UK.
960101025000000250000E-type Jag        Peter Dixon         0089
S29045M    Blenheim, Oxford, UK. 850401 0900000001000000Mercedes S600
```

Careful examination will show that the dates are stored in YYMMDD format, for example 951109 and 850401. Our job now is to write a COBOL program that will convert this file (actually convert while copying to a new file) to the four-digit-year format. The program is called DATECONV.CBL. and starts on the next page.

Most of this program should by now be very familiar to you. You'll notice that the record-length of the input file, at 111, is two less than the length of the output-file record. This is because the input file data, stored in SEQPMAST.DAT, has two-digit dates and it's the job of this program to create an output file, SEQPCONV.DAT which stores its date in the four-digit form. As before, holding areas for the input and output records are defined in WORKING-STORAGE. The group data item names of these areas are WS-PR-RECORD (input) and WS-CV-RECORD (output).

```
*******************************************************************
*                                                                 *
*   This program reads the payroll master file and converts date  *
*   information stored there. File organization is sequential.     *
*                                                                 *
*******************************************************************
    IDENTIFICATION DIVISION.
    PROGRAM-ID. DATECONV.

    ENVIRONMENT DIVISION.

    INPUT-OUTPUT SECTION.
    FILE-CONTROL.
        SELECT OPTIONAL I-PAYROLL-MASTER
            ASSIGN TO "SEQPMAST.DAT"
            ORGANIZATION IS SEQUENTIAL
            ACCESS MODE IS SEQUENTIAL
            FILE STATUS IS WS-I-PR-STATUS.

        SELECT OPTIONAL O-PAYROLL-CONV
            ASSIGN TO "SEQPCONV.DAT"
            ORGANIZATION IS SEQUENTIAL
            ACCESS MODE IS SEQUENTIAL
            FILE STATUS IS WS-O-CONV-STATUS.

    DATA DIVISION.
    FILE SECTION.
    FD  I-PAYROLL-MASTER
        BLOCK CONTAINS 20 RECORDS
        LABEL RECORDS ARE STANDARD
        RECORD CONTAINS 111 CHARACTERS.
    01  I-PR-RECORD.
        02 FILLER            PIC X(111).

    FD  O-PAYROLL-CONV
        BLOCK CONTAINS 20 RECORDS
        LABEL RECORDS ARE STANDARD
        RECORD CONTAINS 113 CHARACTERS.
    01  O-PR-RECORD.
        02 FILLER            PIC X(113).

    WORKING-STORAGE SECTION.
    01  WS-PR-RECORD.
        02 WS-PR-NAME        PIC X(20).
        02 WS-PR-EMPNO       PIC X(8).
        02 WS-PR-EMPTYPE     PIC X.
        02 WS-PR-GRADE       PIC 99.
        02 WS-PR-AGE         PIC 999.
        02 WS-PR-GENDER      PIC X.
        02 WS-PR-REFNO       PIC 9999.
        02 WS-PR-ADDR        PIC X(30).
```

Input file contents are converted to Y2K-clean form and written to output file.

No need to specify the file records fully as all manipulation is done in WORKING-STORAGE.

Y2K-suspect record input.

```
     02 WS-PR-EMPDATE.
          03 WS-PR-YY          PIC 99.
          03 WS-PR-MM          PIC 99.
          03 WS-PR-DD          PIC 99.
     02 WS-PR-PAY              PIC 9(6)V99.
     02 WS-PR-BONUS            PIC 9(6)V99.
     02 WS-PR-CAR              PIC X(20).

01  WS-CV-RECORD.
     02 WS-PR-NAME             PIC X(20).
     02 WS-PR-EMPNO            PIC X(8).
     02 WS-PR-EMPTYPE          PIC X.
     02 WS-PR-GRADE            PIC 99.
     02 WS-PR-AGE              PIC 999.
     02 WS-PR-GENDER           PIC X.
     02 WS-PR-REFNO            PIC 9999.
     02 WS-PR-ADDR             PIC X(30).
     02 WS-CV-EMPDATE.
          03 WS-CV-CC          PIC 99.
          03 WS-PR-YY          PIC 99.
          03 WS-PR-MM          PIC 99.
          03 WS-PR-DD          PIC 99.
     02 WS-PR-PAY              PIC 9(6)V99.
     02 WS-PR-BONUS            PIC 9(6)V99.
     02 WS-PR-CAR              PIC X(20).

01  WS-I-END-FILE             PIC X VALUE "N".
01  WS-I-PR-STATUS            PIC XX.
01  WS-O-CONV-STATUS          PIC XX.

PROCEDURE DIVISION.
A-MAIN-LINE SECTION.
A-000-MAIN.
     PERFORM AA-INITIALISE.
     READ I-PAYROLL-MASTER AT END
     MOVE "Y" TO WS-I-END-FILE.
     PERFORM AB-PROCESS UNTIL WS-I-END-FILE = "Y".
     PERFORM AC-TERMINATE.

A-999-EXIT.
     STOP RUN.

AA-INITIALISE SECTION.
AA-000-OPEN.
     OPEN INPUT I-PAYROLL-MASTER.
     IF WS-I-PR-STATUS NOT EQUAL ZERO THEN
          DISPLAY "Error " WS-I-PR-STATUS
               " opening employee master file."
          GO TO A-999-EXIT
     END-IF.
```

> Converted record for output.

> Does the Y2K conversion.

```
        OPEN OUTPUT O-PAYROLL-CONV.
        IF WS-O-CONV-STATUS NOT EQUAL ZERO THEN
            DISPLAY "Error " WS-O-CONV-STATUS
                 " opening converted-date file."
            GO TO A-999-EXIT
        END-IF.

    AA-999-EXIT.
        EXIT.

    AB-PROCESS SECTION.
    AB-000-CONVERT-DATA.
        MOVE I-PR-RECORD TO WS-PR-RECORD.
        MOVE ZEROS TO WS-PR-REFNO OF WS-PR-RECORD.
        MOVE CORRESPONDING WS-PR-RECORD TO WS-CV-RECORD.
        MOVE CORRESPONDING WS-PR-EMPDATE TO WS-CV-EMPDATE.
        MOVE 19 TO WS-CV-CC.

    AB-010-WRITE-CONVERTED.
        MOVE WS-CV-RECORD TO O-PR-RECORD.
        DISPLAY O-PR-RECORD.
        WRITE O-PR-RECORD.
        IF WS-O-CONV-STATUS NOT EQUAL ZERO THEN
            DISPLAY "Error " WS-O-CONV-STATUS
                 " writing converted-date file."
            GO TO A-999-EXIT
        END-IF.

    AB-020-READ-DATA.
        READ I-PAYROLL-MASTER AT END
            MOVE "Y" TO WS-I-END-FILE.

    AB-999-EXIT.
        EXIT.

    AC-TERMINATE SECTION.
    AC-000-CLOSE.
        CLOSE I-PAYROLL-MASTER.
        CLOSE O-PAYROLL-CONV.

    AC-999-EXIT.
        EXIT.
```

> MOVE fields from input to output record.

> Convert the date.

The program DATECONV.CBL reads all the records from the input file in sequence and writes them all in sequence to the output (converted) file. The critical code that effects the conversion is this:

```
AB-000-CONVERT-DATA.
    MOVE I-PR-RECORD TO WS-PR-RECORD.
```

```
MOVE ZEROS TO WS-PR-REFNO OF WS-PR-RECORD.
MOVE CORRESPONDING WS-PR-RECORD TO WS-CV-RECORD.
MOVE CORRESPONDING WS-PR-EMPDATE TO WS-CV-EMPDATE.
MOVE 19 TO WS-CV-CC.
```

The first statement in the paragraph moves the input record to its holding area. As in earlier versions of the employee/payroll program, only one field was not initialised by user input. In order to use MOVE CORRESPONDING, that field must be initialised with a number so, for that purpose, I assign ZEROS to WS-PR-REFNO. The first MOVE CORRESPONDING assigns the subordinate data items of WS-PR-RECORD to subordinate data items of the same names in WS-CV-RECORD. If, as in the case of WS-PR-EMPDATE and WS-CV-EMPDATE, the names do not match, the MOVE is not done. The two dates are subject of a separate MOVE CORRESPONDING, which assigns the three parts of the six-digit date from the input file to the date in the output holding area. The two digits '19' are then moved to the 'century' field in the output holding area. From this the output-file record is written, and we end up with a converted file.

The contents of the output file, SEQPCONV.DAT are these:

```
Conor Sexton          1234    C10029M0000Rathfarnham, Dublin, Ireland.
19951109010000000000000000Bubble Car        Mike Cash          2345
S25039M0000Jordan Hill, Oxford, UK.
19871212050000000000500000Ferrari Testarossa  Rebecca Hammersley  5643
S10023F0000Summertown, Oxford, UK.        1996010102500000000250000E-
type Jag          Peter Dixon        0089      S29045M0000Blenheim,
Oxford, UK.        19850401090000000001000000Mercedes S600
```

The dates have indeed been converted to four-digit years. I assign '19' on the assumption that all existing dates in the file would be from the 20th century. This might not be the case, e.g. the expiry date of a 20-year life-assurance policy, so, in converting files, you will have to know for the application in question whether to use '19' or '20'.

The conversion is straightforward, although on *huge* files, it would take time and lots of disk space. The difficulty is that all code that handles the converted file must change its logic to accommodate the newly-four-digit year. This is a task either for manual inspection or for your organisation's chosen Y2K-dependency search tool.

Windowing the date

One of the major difficulties of the file-conversion approach is that converting files is a major exercise, not just in terms of the immediate processing , but also in getting up-to-date copies of the data files for input and performing the 'cut-over' to the output converted files.

Date 'windowing', in one form or another, allows us to avoid the file-conversion altogether. In the most common form we set an arbitrary *pivot year*, say 90, representing 1990. Then we adopt the convention that all two-digit years greater than or equal to 90 are of the twentieth century – 1994, 1997 and so on – while all those less than 90 are of the 21st century, with the two-digit year being prefixed with '20'. Rather than permanently converting file data, conversion is done by the COBOL code 'on the fly', leaving the file data unchanged. In fact, 90, is an unlikely year to choose for a pivot. Something like 60 or 70 would be better but, for illustrative purposes, 90 suits the employee/payroll file as I've shown it up to now. Here's that program, modified again to do date windowing and, this time, called DATEPIVT.CBL:

DATEPIVT.CBL

```
***********************************************************
*   This program reads the payroll master file and filters date   *
*   information using a pivot. File organization is sequential.    *
***********************************************************
    IDENTIFICATION DIVISION.
    PROGRAM-ID. DATEPIVT.

    ENVIRONMENT DIVISION.

    INPUT-OUTPUT SECTION.
    FILE-CONTROL.
        SELECT OPTIONAL I-PAYROLL-MASTER
            ASSIGN TO "SEQPMAST.DAT"
            ORGANIZATION IS SEQUENTIAL
            ACCESS MODE IS SEQUENTIAL
            FILE STATUS IS WS-I-PR-STATUS.

    DATA DIVISION.
    FILE SECTION.
    FD  I-PAYROLL-MASTER
        BLOCK CONTAINS 20 RECORDS
        LABEL RECORDS ARE STANDARD
        RECORD CONTAINS 111 CHARACTERS.
```

```
01   I-PR-RECORD.
     02 FILLER               PIC X(111).

WORKING-STORAGE SECTION.
01   WS-PR-RECORD.
     02 WS-PR-NAME           PIC X(20).
     02 WS-PR-EMPNO          PIC X(8).
     02 WS-PR-EMPTYPE        PIC X.
     02 WS-PR-GRADE          PIC 99.
     02 WS-PR-AGE            PIC 999.
     02 WS-PR-GENDER         PIC X.
     02 WS-PR-REFNO          PIC 9999.
     02 WS-PR-ADDR           PIC X(30).
     02 WS-PR-EMPDATE.
        03 WS-PR-YY          PIC 99.
        03 WS-PR-MM          PIC 99.
        03 WS-PR-DD          PIC 99.
     02 WS-PR-PAY            PIC 9(6)V99.
     02 WS-PR-BONUS          PIC 9(6)V99.
     02 WS-PR-CAR            PIC X(20).

01   WS-CV-RECORD.
     02 WS-PR-NAME           PIC X(20).
     02 WS-PR-EMPNO          PIC X(8).
     02 WS-PR-EMPTYPE        PIC X.
     02 WS-PR-GRADE          PIC 99.
     02 WS-PR-AGE            PIC 999.
     02 WS-PR-GENDER         PIC X.
     02 WS-PR-REFNO          PIC 9999.
     02 WS-PR-ADDR           PIC X(30).
     02 WS-CV-EMPDATE.
        03 WS-CV-CC          PIC 99.
        03 WS-PR-YY          PIC 99.
        03 WS-PR-MM          PIC 99.
        03 WS-PR-DD          PIC 99.
     02 WS-PR-PAY            PIC 9(6)V99.
     02 WS-PR-BONUS          PIC 9(6)V99.
     02 WS-PR-CAR            PIC X(20).

01   WS-I-PIVOT              PIC 99 VALUE 90.
01   WS-I-END-FILE           PIC X VALUE "N".
01   WS-I-PR-STATUS          PIC XX.

PROCEDURE DIVISION.
A-MAIN-LINE SECTION.
A-000-MAIN.
     PERFORM AA-INITIALISE.
     READ I-PAYROLL-MASTER AT END
         MOVE "Y" TO WS-I-END-FILE.
     PERFORM AB-PROCESS UNTIL WS-I-END-FILE = "Y".
     PERFORM AC-TERMINATE.
```

Input record.

Converted record.

```
        A-999-EXIT.
            STOP RUN.

        AA-INITIALISE SECTION.
        AA-000-OPEN.
            OPEN INPUT I-PAYROLL-MASTER.
            IF WS-I-PR-STATUS NOT EQUAL ZERO THEN
                DISPLAY "Error " WS-I-PR-STATUS
                    " opening employee master file."
                GO TO A-999-EXIT
            END-IF.

        AA-999-EXIT.
            EXIT.

        AB-PROCESS SECTION.
        AB-000-MOVE-DATA.
            MOVE I-PR-RECORD TO WS-PR-RECORD.
            MOVE ZEROS TO WS-PR-REFNO OF WS-PR-RECORD.
            MOVE CORRESPONDING WS-PR-RECORD TO WS-CV-RECORD.
            MOVE CORRESPONDING WS-PR-EMPDATE TO WS-CV-EMPDATE.
            IF WS-PR-YY OF WS-PR-RECORD < WS-I-PIVOT
                MOVE 20 TO WS-CV-CC
            ELSE
                MOVE 19 TO WS-CV-CC
            END-IF.

        AB-010-DISPLAY-CONVERTED.
            DISPLAY WS-CV-RECORD.

        AB-020-READ-DATA.
            READ I-PAYROLL-MASTER AT END
                MOVE "Y" TO WS-I-END-FILE.

        AB-999-EXIT.
            EXIT.

        AC-TERMINATE SECTION.
        AC-000-CLOSE.
            CLOSE I-PAYROLL-MASTER.

        AC-999-EXIT.
            EXIT.
```

> Do the date conversion on the record in WORKING-STORAGE.

> Pivot here.

The program isn't all that different from DATECONV.CBL, except that, as there's no need for the file to be converted, there's no output file. Instead, we define a 'pivot' data item called WS-I-PIVOT and initialise it with the value 90. Once again, the 'business end' of the program is the bit that executes the MOVE CORRESPONDING statements:

```
AB-000-MOVE-DATA.
    MOVE I-PR-RECORD TO WS-PR-RECORD.
    MOVE ZEROS TO WS-PR-REFNO OF WS-PR-RECORD.
    MOVE CORRESPONDING WS-PR-RECORD TO WS-CV-RECORD.
    MOVE CORRESPONDING WS-PR-EMPDATE TO WS-CV-EMPDATE.
    IF WS-PR-YY OF WS-PR-RECORD < WS-I-PIVOT
        MOVE 20 TO WS-CV-CC
    ELSE
        MOVE 19 TO WS-CV-CC
    END-IF.
```

As in DATECONV.CBL, the subordinate data items of the input holding
area, WS-PR-RECORD are moved to subordinate data items of WS-CV-
RECORD with the same name. If a name doesn't match, the contents of
the data item are not moved. Having MOVEd CORRESPONDING the input
date, we then 'pivot'. If the input year is less than the pivot, it's treated
as being of the 21st century, otherwise of the 20th century. The
displayed output (note again, there's no output file) is this:

```
Conor Sexton          1234      C10029M0000Rathfarnham, Dublin, Ireland.
199511090100000000000000Bubble Car
Mike Cash             2345      S25039M0000Jordan Hill, Oxford, UK.
208712120500000000500000Ferrari Testarossa
Rebecca Hammersley    5643      S10023F0000Summertown, Oxford, UK.
199601010250000000250000E-type Jag
Peter Dixon           0089      S29045M0000Blenheim, Oxford, UK.
208504010900000001000000Mercedes S600
```

From this, it's apparent that the in-memory date-conversion has
worked. With the pivot of 90, the 1985 and 1987 employment dates of
Messrs. Dixon and Cash have been converted to the 21st century,
while the others remain in the 20th century.

This form of date windowing is very good *if you're sure that all the
dates dealt with by your application fall within the hundred-year
'window'*. In DATEPIVT.CBL, there is no way of handling 1989 or 2091.
But, the great bonus is that you don't have to convert data files. True,
you have to change the program logic to handle the 'window', but you
must change code for all Y2K fixes anyway, so this is no worse than the
other techniques in this respect. And yes, we're stacking up another
problem for the folks in the second half of the next century. But (and
this is where the Y2K problem started) that's a long way away, isn't it?

Encoding the date

There's a second version of date-windowing that doesn't require file-conversion and extends the window to cover the whole of the 20th and 21st centuries. This gain is offset by a relative lack of clarity of the technique. In a six-digit date, the month field is a value between 1 and 12, inclusive of both. That fact isn't likely to change. As a consequence, we can encode things such that dates with months in the range 1-12 are interpreted as being 20th century dates, while those with a fixed added factor, say 50, are regarded as being of the 21st century. For example, month 11 is November. By adding 50, a 21st century November would be stored as 61 and interpreted accordingly.

The program is very much the same as DATEPIVT.CBL, so I don't present it all here. Instead, the important latter part follows:

```
01  WS-I-SHIFT          PIC 99 VALUE 50.
01  WS-I-END-FILE       PIC X VALUE "N".
01  WS-I-PR-STATUS      PIC XX.

PROCEDURE DIVISION.
A-MAIN-LINE SECTION.
A-000-MAIN.
    PERFORM AA-INITIALISE.
    READ I-PAYROLL-MASTER AT END
        MOVE "Y" TO WS-I-END-FILE.
    PERFORM AB-PROCESS UNTIL WS-I-END-FILE = "Y".
    PERFORM AC-TERMINATE.

A-999-EXIT.
    STOP RUN.

AA-INITIALISE SECTION.
AA-000-OPEN.
    OPEN INPUT I-PAYROLL-MASTER.
    IF WS-I-PR-STATUS NOT EQUAL ZERO THEN
        DISPLAY "Error " WS-I-PR-STATUS
            " opening employee master file."
        GO TO A-999-EXIT
    END-IF.

AA-999-EXIT.
    EXIT.

AB-PROCESS SECTION.
AB-000-MOVE-DATA.
    MOVE I-PR-RECORD TO WS-PR-RECORD.
```

```
        MOVE ZEROS TO WS-PR-REFNO OF WS-PR-RECORD.
        MOVE CORRESPONDING WS-PR-RECORD TO WS-CV-RECORD.
        MOVE CORRESPONDING WS-PR-EMPDATE TO WS-CV-EMPDATE.
        IF WS-PR-MM OF WS-CV-RECORD > 12
             MOVE 20 TO WS-CV-CC
             SUBTRACT WS-I-SHIFT FROM WS-PR-MM OF WS-CV-RECORD
        ELSE
             MOVE 19 TO WS-CV-CC
        END-IF.


    AB-010-DISPLAY-CONVERTED.
    ******* as DATPIVT.CBL from this point *****
```

Now, if the input year is in the upper range (51-62), we treat the whole date as a 21st century one. We need not convert our data files now but we must remember, when we get around to writing records containing 21st century dates, to encode them by adding to the month value the amount stored in WS-I-SHIFT, in this case 50. Additionally, all code processing such data must be changed. In particular, date-validation routines are affected with this technique; you may find some real difficulties in this area.

Assuming that the input file, SEQPMAST.DAT, contains a month-encoded date, 956109, in its first record, the displayed output from this program appears as follows:

```
Conor Sexton         1234     C10029M0000Rathfarnham, Dublin, Ireland.
20951109010000000000000000Bubble Car
Mike Cash            2345     S25039M0000Jordan Hill, Oxford, UK.
19871212050000000000500000Ferrari Testarossa
Rebecca Hammersley  5643     S10023F0000Summertown, Oxford, UK.
19960101025000000000250000E-type Jag
Peter Dixon          0089     S29045M0000Blenheim, Oxford, UK.
19850401090000000001000000Mercedes S600
```

from which you can see that my record from the file has been changed in memory to contain the year 2095 in its date.

With this approach we, to some extent, kick the problem down the road. Nasty, encoded, dates will probably not start appearing in our files for a few years and file conversion is avoided. However, the approach is the least-intuitive of the three I present in this chapter, and you'll have to live with that counter-intuitiveness for the whole 21st century – if you're around that long.

Organisational considerations

The Y2K problem affects all kinds of business applications, in the ways that I list at the start of this chapter, and more. Regardless of the kind of application you're dealing with, the specific date operations that you'll need to watch out for include these:

⟨ Calculations and sorting based on dates retrieved from databases and files.

⟨ Generation of the system date – the COBOL-85 DATE call is clearly not Y2K-clean.

⟨ Date conversions: code that changes dates from the North American MM/DD/(CC)YY to the European DD/MM/(CC)YY and back; conversion between Gregorian and Julian dates; change from DD/MM/(CC)YY to (CC)YY/MM/DD for sorting purposes.

⟨ Dates to be sorted: year 2000 represented as 00 will precede all other years.

⟨ Dates to be subtracted for date-ageing: a pensioner born in 1904 could in 2000 receive a notice to start kindergarten school!

I've mentioned the practical difficulty for an organisation of taking its data files 'off-line', converting them to four-digit-year representation and then 'cutting over' to the converted files. This isn't easy, as the business must continue while the files are being converted. This organisational difficulty is one of the main reasons for considering date windowing as an alternative to straight conversion.

This isn't the end of the organisational difficulties, though. The Y2K problem, although simple, is so pervasive – affecting date operations of the kinds I've described in all applications – that a coordinated project-based approach is needed in any organisation to address it.

This is a book primarily about COBOL programming. It's not intended as a guide to Y2K project management. Other publications look at administrative and management aspects, usually, in my opinion, using 57 words in most cases where three will do. Also, it's difficult, if not impossible, for any book to give a detailed guide to the remedial action needed for *your* application, when there are so many possibilities. As I've repeatedly stated, the Y2K problem is simple. Accordingly, I set out below a short, generic, approach that you can take to addressing the Y2K problem in any organisation.

1 *Get the support of senior management.* Y2K has diverse effects, involves all functions in the organisation and needs money to fix. Management – business, technical and legal – must understand the need for investment to solve the problem and must support the project aimed at doing so.

2 *Set up a Y2K group, with a project manager.* This group should include not just programmers but also analysts who specialise in the business impact of software changes, and liaison with management and the user departments.

3 *Establish a budget, and be realistic about it.* Nothing gets done without money; the jobs that will need to be done include project planning and execution; overtime and weekend working; acquisition of software tools; outsourcing of software staff; and new equipment for development. Re-evaluate the budget frequently as the project progresses. The project management, and its budget must have the full support of senior management.

4 *Make an inventory of possible Y2K exposure.* List all the organisation's software. Assess how likely any given module is to fail on Y2K. Set priorities, analysing critical systems first.

5 *Assess your organisation's legal entitlement to change the software.* This may not be a problem if the code was all written by your people under your roof. However, there may be bought-in components for which the case is not so clear.

6 *Produce a solid project plan with a definite time limit.* That limit should allow for testing converted applications and files and should not be too close to the Great Day itself. The plan should encompass all aspects of the project including: identification and acquisition of software tools; budgets; outsourcing of people; assignment of priorities for fixing applications; finding, fixing and testing; the transition (cut-over) schedule.

7 *Find and fix Y2K dependencies.* The subject of this chapter, you should settle on your approach. What Y2K tools do you intend to use? Will you go for conversion or for one of the forms of date windowing? What documentation, if any, exists? Do we have the source code? If not, what's involved in disassembling or rewriting the code?

8 *Test the changed applications.* Change the (independent, off-line) test system's date to a day in the next century and run a normal day's processing. You may find login IDs expiring, to your surprise, before even getting into the application itself. Data being used should span the 20th and 21st centuries. Change the system date to 31 December, 1999 and the time to 11pm. Verify that processing continues normally. Allow the system date to move forward to 1 January, 2000 and do another day's processing. Set the system date to 28 February, 2000 and do a day's processing. Allow the system date to move forward to 29 February – which is valid in 2000 – and go again. Check the output of any sort operations using dates. Check reports ordered on date. Query databases by date, watching for two-digit index files. Such index files may need to be regenerated.

9 Cut-over to the changed applications for a planned period, running in parallel with the pre-Y2K-fix systems.

This list isn't a detailed how-to cookbook specific to your applications. It is, however, a viable general guide which should at least set you thinking in the right directions. Like most projects, the major challenges are not the technical ones – as we've seen, Y2K is easy technically – but those of getting all parties 'on-side' and controlling the transition.

Index